Mastering Elasticsearch

Second Edition

Further your knowledge of the Elasticsearch server by learning more about its internals, querying, and data handling

Rafał Kuć

Marek Rogoziński

[PACKT] open source *
PUBLISHING   community experience distilled

BIRMINGHAM - MUMBAI

Mastering Elasticsearch
Second Edition

First published: October 2013

Second edition: February 2015

Production reference: 1230215

Published by Packt Publishing Ltd.
Livery Place
35 Livery Street
Birmingham B3 2PB, UK.

ISBN 978-1-78355-379-2

www.packtpub.com

Credits

Authors
Rafał Kuć

Marek Rogoziński

Reviewers
Hüseyin Akdoğan

Julien Duponchelle

Marcelo Ochoa

Commissioning Editor
Akram Hussain

Acquisition Editor
Rebecca Youé

Content Development Editors
Madhuja Chaudhari

Anand Singh

Technical Editors
Saurabh Malhotra

Narsimha Pai

Copy Editors
Stuti Srivastava

Sameen Siddiqui

Project Coordinator
Akash Poojary

Proofreaders
Paul Hindle

Joanna McMahon

Indexer
Hemangini Bari

Graphics
Sheetal Aute

Valentina D'silva

Production Coordinator
Alwin Roy

Cover Work
Alwin Roy

About the Author

Rafał Kuć is a born team leader and software developer. Currently, he is working as a consultant and a software engineer at Sematext Group, Inc., where he concentrates on open source technologies, such as Apache Lucene, Solr, Elasticsearch, and the Hadoop stack. He has more than 13 years of experience in various software branches—from banking software to e-commerce products. He is mainly focused on Java but is open to every tool and programming language that will make the achievement of his goal easier and faster. Rafał is also one of the founders of the `solr.pl` website, where he tries to share his knowledge and help people with their problems related to Solr and Lucene. He is also a speaker at various conferences around the world, such as Lucene Eurocon, Berlin Buzzwords, ApacheCon, Lucene Revolution, and DevOps Days.

He began his journey with Lucene in 2002, but it wasn't love at first sight. When he came back to Lucene in late 2003, he revised his thoughts about the framework and saw the potential in search technologies. Then came Solr, and that was it. He started working with Elasticsearch in the middle of 2010. Currently, Lucene, Solr, Elasticsearch, and information retrieval are his main points of interest.

Rafał is the author of *Solr 3.1 Cookbook*, its update—*Solr 4.0 Cookbook*—and its third release—*Solr Cookbook, Third Edition*. He is also the author of *Elasticsearch Server* and its second edition, along with the first edition of *Mastering Elasticsearch*, all published by *Packt Publishing*.

Acknowledgments

With Marek, we were thinking about writing an update to *Mastering Elasticsearch*, *Packt Publishing*. It was not a book for everyone, but the first version didn't put enough emphasis on that — we were treating *Mastering Elasticsearch* as an update to *Elasticsearch Server*. The same goes with *Mastering Elasticsearch Second Edition*. The book you are holding in your hands was written as an extension to *Elasticsearch Server Second Edition*, *Packt Publishing*, and should be treated as a continuation to that book. Because of such an approach, we could concentrate on topics such as choosing the right queries, scaling Elasticsearch, extensive scoring descriptions with examples, internals of filtering, new aggregations, comparison to documents' relations handling, and so on. Hopefully, after reading this book, you'll be able to easily get all the details about Elasticsearch and the underlying Apache Lucene architecture; this will let you get the desired knowledge easier and faster.

I would like to thank my family for the support and patience during all those days and evenings when I was sitting in front of a screen instead of being with them.

I would also like to thank all the people I'm working with at Sematext, especially Otis, who took his time and convinced me that Sematext is the right company for me.

Finally, I would like to thank all the people involved in creating, developing, and maintaining Elasticsearch and Lucene projects for their work and passion. Without them, this book wouldn't have been written and open source search wouldn't have been the same as it is today.

Once again, thank you.

About the Author

Marek Rogoziński is a software architect and consultant with over 10 years of experience. He specializes in solutions based on open source search engines, such as Solr and Elasticsearch, and software stack for Big Data analytics, including Hadoop, Hbase, and Twitter Storm.

He is also a cofounder of the `solr.pl` website, which publishes information and tutorials about Solr and Lucene libraries. He is the coauthor of *Mastering ElasticSearch*, *ElasticSearch Server*, and *Elasticsearch Server Second Edition*, both published by *Packt Publishing*.

Currently, he holds the position of chief technology officer and lead architect at ZenCard, a company processing and analyzing large amounts of payment transactions in real time, allowing automatic and anonymous identification of retail customers on all retailer channels (m-commerce / e-commerce / brick and mortar) and giving retailers a customer retention and loyalty tool.

Acknowledgments

This is our fourth book about Elasticsearch and, again, I am fascinated by how quickly Elasticsearch is evolving. We always have to find the balance between describing features marked as experimental or work in progress, and we have to take the risk that the final code might behave differently or even ignore some of the interesting features. The second edition of this book has quite a large number of rewrites and covers some new features; however, this comes at the cost of the removal of some information that was less useful for readers. With this book, we've tried to introduce some additional topics connected to Elasticsearch. However, the whole ecosystem and the ELK stack (Elasticsearch, Logstash, and Kibana) or Hadoop integration deserves a dedicated book.

Now, it is time to say thank you.

Thanks to all the people who created Elasticsearch, Lucene, and all the libraries and modules published around these projects or used by these projects.

I would also like to thank the team that worked on this book. First of all, thanks to the ones who worked on the extermination of all my errors, typos, and ambiguities. Many thanks to all the people who sent us remarks or wrote constructive reviews. I was surprised and encouraged by the fact that someone found our work useful. Thank you.

Last but not least, thanks to all the friends who stood by me and understood my constant lack of time.

About the Reviewers

Hüseyin Akdoğan's software adventure began with the GwBasic programming language. He started learning the Visual Basic language after QuickBasic, and developed many applications with it until 2000 when he stepped into the world of Web with PHP. After that, his path crossed with Java! In addition to counseling and training activities since 2005, he developed enterprise applications with Java EE technologies. His areas of expertise are JavaServer Faces, Spring frameworks, and Big Data technologies such as NoSQL and Elasticsearch. In addition, he is trying to specialize in other Big Data technologies.

Julien Duponchelle is a French engineer. He is a graduate of Epitech. During his professional career, he contributed to several open source projects and focused on tools that make the work of IT teams easier.

After he led the educational field at ETNA, a French IT school, Julien accompanied several start-ups as a lead backend engineer and participated in many significant and successful fundraising events (Plizy and Youboox).

I want to thank Maëlig, my girlfriend, for her benevolence and great patience during so many evenings when I was working on this book or on open source projects in general.

Marcelo Ochoa works at the system laboratory of Facultad de Ciencias Exactas of the Universidad Nacional del Centro de la Provincia de Buenos Aires and is the CTO at Scotas.com, a company that specializes in near real-time search solutions using Apache Solr and Oracle. He divides his time between university jobs and external projects related to Oracle and big data technologies. He has worked on several Oracle-related projects, such as the translation of Oracle manuals and multimedia CBTs. His background is in database, network, web, and Java technologies. In the XML world, he is known as the developer of the DB Generator for the Apache Cocoon project. He has worked on the open source projects DBPrism and DBPrism CMS, the Lucene-Oracle integration using the Oracle JVM Directory implementation, and the Restlet.org project, where he worked on the Oracle XDB Restlet Adapter, which is an alternative to writing native REST web services inside a database resident JVM.

Since 2006, he has been part of an Oracle ACE program. Oracle ACEs are known for their strong credentials as Oracle community enthusiasts and advocates, with candidates nominated by ACEs in the Oracle technology and applications communities.

He has coauthored *Oracle Database Programming using Java and Web Services* by *Digital Press* and *Professional XML Databases* by *Wrox Press*, and has been the technical reviewer for several PacktPub books, such as "*Apache Solr 4 Cookbook*", "*ElasticSearch Server*", and others.

www.PacktPub.com

Support files, eBooks, discount offers, and more

For support files and downloads related to your book, please visit www.PacktPub.com.

Did you know that Packt offers eBook versions of every book published, with PDF and ePub files available? You can upgrade to the eBook version at www.PacktPub.com and as a print book customer, you are entitled to a discount on the eBook copy. Get in touch with us at service@packtpub.com for more details.

At www.PacktPub.com, you can also read a collection of free technical articles, sign up for a range of free newsletters and receive exclusive discounts and offers on Packt books and eBooks.

https://www2.packtpub.com/books/subscription/packtlib

Do you need instant solutions to your IT questions? PacktLib is Packt's online digital book library. Here, you can search, access, and read Packt's entire library of books.

Why subscribe?

- Fully searchable across every book published by Packt
- Copy and paste, print, and bookmark content
- On demand and accessible via a web browser

Free access for Packt account holders

If you have an account with Packt at www.PacktPub.com, you can use this to access PacktLib today and view 9 entirely free books. Simply use your login credentials for immediate access.

Table of Contents

Preface

Welcome to the world of Elasticsearch and *Mastering Elasticsearch Second Edition*. While reading the book, you'll be taken through different topics—all connected to Elasticsearch. Please remember though that this book is not meant for beginners and we really treat the book as a follow-up or second part of *Elasticsearch Server Second Edition*. There is a lot of new content in the book and, sometimes, you can refer to the content of *Elasticsearch Server Second Edition* within this book.

Throughout the book, we will discuss different topics related to Elasticsearch and Lucene. We start with an introduction to the world of Lucene and Elasticsearch to introduce you to the world of queries provided by Elasticsearch, where we discuss different topics related to queries, such as filtering and which query to choose in a particular situation. Of course, querying is not all and, because of that, the book you are holding in your hands provides information on newly introduced aggregations and features that will help you give meaning to the data you have indexed in Elasticsearch indices, and provide a better search experience for your users.

Even though, for most users, querying and data analysis are the most interesting parts of Elasticsearch, they are not all that we need to discuss. Because of this, the book tries to bring you additional information when it comes to index architecture such as choosing the right number of shards and replicas, adjusting the shard allocation behavior, and so on. We will also get into the places where Elasticsearch meets Lucene, and we will discuss topics such as different scoring algorithms, choosing the right store mechanism, what the differences between them are, and why choosing the proper one matters.

Last, but not least, we touch on the administration part of Elasticsearch by discussing discovery and recovery modules, and the human-friendly Cat API, which allows us to very quickly get relevant administrative information in a form that most humans should be able to read without parsing JSON responses. We also talk about and use tribe nodes, giving us possibilities of creating federated searches across many nodes.

Because of the title of the book, we couldn't omit performance-related topics, and we decided to dedicate a whole chapter to it. We talk about doc values and the improvements they bring, how garbage collector works, and what to do when it does not work as we expect. Finally, we talk about Elasticsearch scaling and how to prepare it for high indexing and querying use cases.

Just as with the first edition of the book, we decided to end the book with the development of Elasticsearch plugins, showing you how to set up the Apache Maven project and develop two types of plugins—custom REST action and custom analysis.

If you think that you are interested in these topics after reading about them, we think this is a book for you and, hopefully, you will like the book after reading the last words of the summary in *Chapter 9, Developing Elasticsearch Plugins.*

What this book covers

Chapter 1, Introduction to Elasticsearch, guides you through how Apache Lucene works and will reintroduce you to the world of Elasticsearch, describing the basic concepts and showing you how Elasticsearch works internally.

Chapter 2, Power User Query DSL, describes how the Apache Lucene scoring works, why Elasticsearch rewrites queries, what query templates are, and how we can use them. In addition to that, it explains the usage of filters and which query should be used in a particular use case.

Chapter 3, Not Only Full Text Search, describes queries rescoring, multimatching control, and different types of aggregations that will help you with data analysis—significant terms aggregation and top terms aggregation that allow us to group documents with a certain criteria. In addition to that, it discusses relationship handling in Elasticsearch and extends your knowledge about scripting in Elasticsearch.

Chapter 4, Improving the User Search Experience, covers user search experience improvements. It introduces you to the world of Suggesters, which allows you to correct user query spelling mistakes and build efficient autocomplete mechanisms. In addition to that, you'll see how to improve query relevance by using different queries and the Elasticsearch functionality with a real-life example.

Chapter 5, The Index Distribution Architecture, covers techniques for choosing the right amount of shards and replicas, how routing works, how shard allocation works, and how to alter its behavior. In addition to that, we discuss what query execution preference is and how it allows us to choose where the queries are going to be executed.

Chapter 6, Low-level Index Control, describes how to alter the Apache Lucene scoring and how to choose an alternative scoring algorithm. It also covers NRT searching and indexing and transaction log usage, and allows you to understand segment merging and tune it for your use case. At the end of the chapter, you will also find information about Elasticsearch caching and request breakers aiming to prevent out-of-memory situations.

Chapter 7, Elasticsearch Administration, describes what the discovery, gateway, and recovery modules are, how to configure them, and why you should bother. We also describe what the Cat API is, how to back up and restore your data to different cloud services (such as Amazon AWS or Microsoft Azure), and how to use tribe nodes — Elasticsearch federated search.

Chapter 8, Improving Performance, covers Elasticsearch performance-related topics ranging from using doc values to help with field data cache memory usage through the JVM garbage collector work, and queries benchmarking to scaling Elasticsearch and preparing it for high indexing and querying scenarios.

Chapter 9, Developing Elasticsearch Plugins, covers Elasticsearch plugins' development by showing and describing in depth how to write your own REST action and language analysis plugin.

What you need for this book

This book was written using Elasticsearch server 1.4.x, and all the examples and functions should work with it. In addition to that, you'll need a command that allows you to send HTTP requests such as curl, which is available for most operating systems. Please note that all examples in this book use the mentioned curl tool. If you want to use another tool, please remember to format the request in an appropriate way that is understood by the tool of your choice.

In addition to that, to run examples in *Chapter 9, Developing Elasticsearch Plugins*, you will need a Java Development Kit (JDK) installed and an editor that will allow you to develop your code (or Java IDE-like Eclipse). To build the code and manage dependencies in *Chapter 9, Developing Elasticsearch Plugins*, we are using Apache Maven.

Who this book is for

This book was written for Elasticsearch users and enthusiasts who are already familiar with the basic concepts of this great search server and want to extend their knowledge when it comes to Elasticsearch itself, as well as topics such as how Apache Lucene or the JVM garbage collector works. In addition to that, readers who want to see how to improve their query relevancy and learn how to extend Elasticsearch with their own plugin may find this book interesting and useful.

If you are new to Elasticsearch and you are not familiar with basic concepts such as querying and data indexing, you may find it difficult to use this book, as most of the chapters assume that you have this knowledge already. In such cases, we suggest that you look at our previous book about Elasticsearch— *Elasticsearch Server Second Edition, Packt Publishing.*

Conventions

In this book, you will find a number of styles of text that distinguish between different kinds of information. Here are some examples of these styles, and an explanation of their meaning.

Code words in text are shown as follows: "We can include other contexts through the use of the `include` directive."

A block of code is set as follows:

```
curl -XGET 'localhost:9200/clients/_search?pretty' -d '{
  "query" : {
   "prefix" : {
    "name" : {
     "prefix" : "j",
     "rewrite" : "constant_score_boolean"
    }
   }
  }
}'
```

When we wish to draw your attention to a particular part of a code block, the relevant lines or items are set in bold:

```
curl -XGET 'localhost:9200/clients/_search?pretty' -d '{
  "query" : {
   "prefix" : {
    "name" : {
```

```
      "prefix" : "j",
      "rewrite" : "constant_score_boolean"
    }
   }
  }
 }'
```

Any command-line input or output is written as follows:

```
curl -XPOST 'localhost:9200/scoring/doc/1' -d '{"name":"first document"}'
```

New terms and **important words** are shown in bold. Words that you see on the screen, in menus or dialog boxes for example, appear in the text like this: "clicking the **Next** button moves you to the next screen".

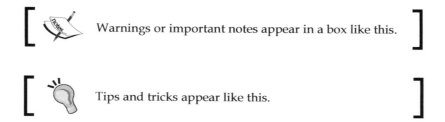

Warnings or important notes appear in a box like this.

Tips and tricks appear like this.

Reader feedback

Feedback from our readers is always welcome. Let us know what you think about this book—what you liked or may have disliked. Reader feedback is important for us to develop titles that you really get the most out of.

To send us general feedback, simply send an e-mail to feedback@packtpub.com, and mention the book title via the subject of your message.

If there is a topic that you have expertise in and you are interested in either writing or contributing to a book, see our author guide on www.packtpub.com/authors.

Customer support

Now that you are the proud owner of a Packt book, we have a number of things to help you to get the most from your purchase.

Downloading the example code

You can download the example code files for all Packt books you have purchased from your account at `http://www.packtpub.com`. If you purchased this book elsewhere, you can visit `http://www.packtpub.com/support` and register to have the files e-mailed directly to you.

Errata

Although we have taken every care to ensure the accuracy of our content, mistakes do happen. If you find a mistake in one of our books—maybe a mistake in the text or the code—we would be grateful if you would report this to us. By doing so, you can save other readers from frustration and help us improve subsequent versions of this book. If you find any errata, please report them by visiting `http://www.packtpub.com/submit-errata`, selecting your book, clicking on the **errata submission form** link, and entering the details of your errata. Once your errata are verified, your submission will be accepted and the errata will be uploaded on our website, or added to any list of existing errata, under the Errata section of that title. Any existing errata can be viewed by selecting your title from `http://www.packtpub.com/support`.

Piracy

Piracy of copyright material on the Internet is an ongoing problem across all media. At Packt, we take the protection of our copyright and licenses very seriously. If you come across any illegal copies of our works, in any form, on the Internet, please provide us with the location address or website name immediately so that we can pursue a remedy.

Please contact us at `copyright@packtpub.com` with a link to the suspected pirated material.

We appreciate your help in protecting our authors, and our ability to bring you valuable content.

Questions

You can contact us at `questions@packtpub.com` if you are having a problem with any aspect of the book, and we will do our best to address it.

Introduction to Elasticsearch

Before going further into the book, we would like to emphasize that we are treating this book as an extension to the *Elasticsearch Server Second Edition* book we've written, also published by Packt Publishing. Of course, we start with a brief introduction to both Apache Lucene and Elasticsearch, but this book is not for a person who doesn't know Elasticsearch at all. We treat *Mastering Elasticsearch* as a book that will systematize your knowledge about Elasticsearch and extend it by showing some examples of how to leverage your knowledge in certain situations. If you are looking for a book that will help you start your journey into the world of Elasticsearch, please take a look at *Elasticsearch Server Second Edition* mentioned previously.

That said, we hope that by reading this book, you want to extend and build on basic Elasticsearch knowledge. We assume that you already know how to index data to Elasticsearch using single requests as well as bulk indexing. You should also know how to send queries to get the documents you are interested in, how to narrow down the results of your queries by using filtering, and how to calculate statistics for your data with the use of the faceting/aggregation mechanism. However, before getting to the exciting functionality that Elasticsearch offers, we think we should start with a quick tour of Apache Lucene, which is a full text search library that Elasticsearch uses to build and search its indices, as well as the basic concepts on which Elasticsearch is built. In order to move forward and extend our learning, we need to ensure that we don't forget the basics. This is easy to do. We also need to make sure that we understand Lucene correctly as *Mastering Elasticsearch* requires this understanding. By the end of this chapter, we will have covered the following topics:

- What Apache Lucene is
- What overall Lucene architecture looks like
- How the analysis process is done
- What Apache Lucene query language is and how to use it
- What are the basic concepts of Elasticsearch
- How Elasticsearch communicates internally

Introducing Apache Lucene

In order to fully understand how Elasticsearch works, especially when it comes to indexing and query processing, it is crucial to understand how Apache Lucene library works. Under the hood, Elasticsearch uses Lucene to handle document indexing. The same library is also used to perform a search against the indexed documents. In the next few pages, we will try to show you the basics of Apache Lucene, just in case you've never used it.

Getting familiar with Lucene

You may wonder why Elasticsearch creators decided to use Apache Lucene instead of developing their own functionality. We don't know for sure since we were not the ones who made the decision, but we assume that it was because Lucene is mature, open-source, highly performing, scalable, light and, yet, very powerful. It also has a very strong community that supports it. Its core comes as a single file of Java library with no dependencies, and allows you to index documents and search them with its out-of-the-box full text search capabilities. Of course, there are extensions to Apache Lucene that allow different language handling, and enable spellchecking, highlighting, and much more, but if you don't need those features, you can download a single file and use it in your application.

Overall architecture

Although I would like to jump straight to Apache Lucene architecture, there are some things we need to know first in order to fully understand it, and those are as follows:

- **Document**: It is a main data carrier used during indexing and search, containing one or more fields, that contain the data we put and get from Lucene.
- **Field**: It is a section of the document which is built of two parts: the name and the value.
- **Term**: It is a unit of search representing a word from the text.
- **Token**: It is an occurrence of a term from the text of the field. It consists of term text, start and end offset, and a type.

Apache Lucene writes all the information to the structure called **inverted** index. It is a data structure that maps the terms in the index to the documents, not the other way round like the relational database does. You can think of an inverted index as a data structure, where data is term oriented rather than document oriented.

Let's see how a simple inverted index can look. For example, let's assume that we have the documents with only title field to be indexed and they look like the following:

- Elasticsearch Server (document 1)
- Mastering Elasticsearch (document 2)
- Apache Solr 4 Cookbook (document 3)

So, the index (in a very simple way) could be visualized as shown in the following figure:

Term	Count	Docs
4	1	<3>
Apache	1	<3>
Cooking	1	<3>
Elasticsearch	2	<1> <2>
Mastering	1	<1>
Server	1	<1>
Solr	1	<3>

As you can see, each term points to the number of documents it is present in. This allows for a very efficient and fast search such as the term-based queries. In addition to this, each term has a number connected to it: the count, telling Lucene how often it occurs.

Each index is divided into multiple write once and read many time segments. When indexing, after a single segment is written to disk, it can't be updated. For example, the information about deleted documents is stored in a separate file, but the segment itself is not updated.

However, multiple segments can be merged together in a process called **segments merge**. After forcing, segments are merged, or after Lucene decides it is time for merging to be performed, segments are merged together by Lucene to create larger ones. This can be I/O demanding; however, it is needed to clean up some information because during that time some information that is not needed anymore is deleted, for example the deleted documents. In addition to this, searching with the use of one larger segment is faster than searching against multiple smaller ones holding the same data. However, once again, remember that segments merging is an I/O demanding operation and you shouldn't force merging, just configure your merge policy carefully.

If you want to know what files are building the segments and what information is stored inside them, please take a look at Apache Lucene documentation available at `http://lucene.apache.org/core/4_10_3/core/org/apache/lucene/codecs/lucene410/package-summary.html`.

Getting deeper into Lucene index

Of course, the actual index created by Lucene is much more complicated and advanced, and consists of more than the terms their counts and documents in which they are present. We would like to tell you about a few of those additional index pieces because even though they are internal, it is usually good to know about them as they can be very handy.

Norms

A norm is a factor associated with each indexed document and stores normalization factors used to compute the score relative to the query. Norms are computed on the basis of index time boosts and are indexed along with the documents. With the use of norms, Lucene is able to provide an index time-boosting functionality at the cost of a certain amount of additional space needed for norms indexation and some amount of additional memory.

Term vectors

Term vectors are small inverted indices per document. They consist of pairs — a term and its frequency — and can optionally include information about term position. By default, Lucene and Elasticsearch don't enable term vectors indexing, but some functionality such as the fast vector highlighting requires them to be present.

Posting formats

With the release of Lucene 4.0, the library introduced the so-called codec architecture, giving developers control over how the index files are written onto the disk. One of the parts of the index is the posting format, which stores fields, terms, documents, terms positions and offsets, and, finally, the payloads (a byte array stored at an arbitrary position in Lucene index, which can contain any information we want). Lucene contains different posting formats for different purposes, for example one that is optimized for high cardinality fields like the unique identifier.

Doc values

As we already mentioned, Lucene index is the so-called inverted index. However, for certain features, such as faceting or aggregations, such architecture is not the best one. The mentioned functionality operates on the document level and not the term level and because Elasticsearch needs to uninvert the index before calculations can be done. Because of that, doc values were introduced and additional structure used for faceting, sorting and aggregations. The doc values store uninverted data for a field they are turned on for. Both Lucene and Elasticsearch allow us to configure the implementation used to store them, giving us the possibility of memory-based doc values, disk-based doc values, and a combination of the two.

Analyzing your data

Of course, the question arises of how the data passed in the documents is transformed into the inverted index and how the query text is changed into terms to allow searching. The process of transforming this data is called analysis.

Analysis is done by the analyzer, which is built of tokenizer and zero or more filters, and can also have zero or more character mappers.

A tokenizer in Lucene is used to divide the text into tokens, which are basically terms with additional information, such as its position in the original text and its length. The result of the tokenizer work is a so-called token stream, where the tokens are put one by one and are ready to be processed by filters.

Apart from tokenizer, Lucene analyzer is built of zero or more filters that are used to process tokens in the token stream. For example, it can remove tokens from the stream, change them or even produce new ones. There are numerous filters and you can easily create new ones. Some examples of filters are as follows:

- **Lowercase** filter: It makes all the tokens lowercase
- **ASCII folding** filter: It removes non ASCII parts from tokens
- **Synonyms** filter: It is responsible for changing one token to another on the basis of synonym rules
- **Multiple language stemming** filters: These are responsible for reducing tokens (actually the text part that they provide) into their root or base forms, the stem

Filters are processed one after another, so we have almost unlimited analysis possibilities with adding multiple filters one after another.

The last thing is the character mappings, which is used before tokenizer and is responsible for processing text before any analysis is done. One of the examples of character mapper is the HTML tags removal process.

Indexing and querying

We may wonder how that all affects indexing and querying when using Lucene and all the software that is built on top of it. During indexing, Lucene will use an analyzer of your choice to process the contents of your document; different analyzers can be used for different fields, so the `title` field of your document can be analyzed differently compared to the `description` field.

During query time, if you use one of the provided query parsers, your query will be analyzed. However, you can also choose the other path and not analyze your queries. This is crucial to remember because some of the Elasticsearch queries are being analyzed and some are not. For example, the prefix query is not analyzed and the match query is analyzed.

What you should remember about indexing and querying analysis is that the index should be matched by the query term. If they don't match, Lucene won't return the desired documents. For example, if you are using stemming and lowercasing during indexing, you need to be sure that the terms in the query are also lowercased and stemmed, or your queries will return no results at all.

Lucene query language

Some of the query types provided by Elasticsearch support Apache Lucene query parser syntax. Because of this, it is crucial to understand the Lucene query language.

Understanding the basics

A query is divided by Apache Lucene into terms and operators. A term, in Lucene, can be a single word or a phrase (group of words surrounded by double quote characters). If the query is set to be analyzed, the defined analyzer will be used on each of the terms that form the query.

A query can also contain Boolean operators that connect terms to each other forming clauses. The list of Boolean operators is as follows:

- **AND**: It means that the given two terms (left and right operand) need to match in order for the clause to be matched. For example, we would run a query, such as apache AND lucene, to match documents with both apache and lucene terms in a document field.

- **OR**: It means that any of the given terms may match in order for the clause to be matched. For example, we would run a query, such as apache OR lucene, to match documents with apache or lucene (or both) terms in a document field.

- **NOT**: It means that in order for the document to be considered a match, the term appearing after the NOT operator must not match. For example, we would run a query lucene NOT Elasticsearch to match documents that contain lucene term, but not the Elasticsearch term in the document field.

In addition to these, we may use the following operators:

- **+**: It means that the given term needs to be matched in order for the document to be considered as a match. For example, in order to find documents that match lucene term and may match apache term, we would run a query such as +lucene apache.

- **-**: It means that the given term can't be matched in order for the document to be considered a match. For example, in order to find a document with lucene term, but not Elasticsearch term, we would run a query such as +lucene -Elasticsearch.

When not specifying any of the previous operators, the default OR operator will be used.

In addition to all these, there is one more thing: you can use parenthesis to group clauses together for example, with something like the following query:

```
Elasticsearch AND (mastering OR book)
```

Querying fields

Of course, just like in Elasticsearch, in Lucene all your data is stored in fields that build the document. In order to run a query against a field, you need to provide the field name, add the colon character, and provide the clause that should be run against that field. For example, if you would like to match documents with the term Elasticsearch in the title field, you would run the following query:

```
title:Elasticsearch
```

You can also group multiple clauses. For example, if you would like your query to match all the documents having the Elasticsearch term and the mastering book phrase in the title field, you could run a query like the following code:

```
title:(+Elasticsearch +"mastering book")
```

The previous query can also be expressed in the following way:

```
+title:Elasticsearch +title:"mastering book"
```

Term modifiers

In addition to the standard field query with a simple term or clause, Lucene allows us to modify the terms we pass in the query with modifiers. The most common modifiers, which you will be familiar with, are wildcards. There are two wildcards supported by Lucene, the ? and * terms. The first one will match any character and the second one will match multiple characters.

 Please note that by default these wildcard characters can't be used as the first character in a term because of performance reasons.

In addition to this, Lucene supports fuzzy and proximity searches with the use of the ~ character and an integer following it. When used with a single word term, it means that we want to search for terms that are similar to the one we've modified (the so-called fuzzy search). The integer after the ~ character specifies the maximum number of edits that can be done to consider the term similar. For example, if we would run a query, such as `writer~2`, both the terms `writer` and `writers` would be considered a match.

When the ~ character is used on a phrase, the integer number we provide is telling Lucene how much distance between the words is acceptable. For example, let's take the following query:

```
title:"mastering Elasticsearch"
```

It would match the document with the `title` field containing `mastering Elasticsearch`, but not `mastering book Elasticsearch`. However, if we would run a query, such as `title:"mastering Elasticsearch"~2`, it would result in both example documents matched.

We can also use boosting to increase our term importance by using the ^ character and providing a float number. Boosts lower than one would result in decreasing the document importance. Boosts higher than one will result in increasing the importance. The default boost value is 1. Please refer to the *Default Apache Lucene scoring explained* section in *Chapter 2, Power User Query DSL*, for further information on what boosting is and how it is taken into consideration during document scoring.

In addition to all these, we can use square and curly brackets to allow range searching. For example, if we would like to run a range search on a numeric field, we could run the following query:

```
price:[10.00 TO 15.00]
```

The preceding query would result in all documents with the `price` field between `10.00` and `15.00` inclusive.

In case of string-based fields, we also can run a range query, for example name: [Adam TO Adria].

The preceding query would result in all documents containing all the terms between `Adam` and `Adria` in the `name` field including them.

If you would like your range bound or bounds to be exclusive, use curly brackets instead of the square ones. For example, in order to find documents with the `price` field between `10.00` inclusive and `15.00` exclusive, we would run the following query:

```
price:[10.00 TO 15.00}
```

If you would like your range bound from one side and not bound by the other, for example querying for documents with a price higher than `10.00`, we would run the following query:

```
price:[10.00 TO *]
```

Handling special characters

In case you want to search for one of the special characters (which are +, -, &&, ||, !, (,), { }, [ ], ^, ", ~, *, ?, :, \, /), you need to escape it with the use of the backslash (\) character. For example, to search for the `abc"efg` term you need to do something like `abc\"efg`.

Introducing Elasticsearch

Although we've said that we expect the reader to be familiar with Elasticsearch, we would really like you to fully understand Elasticsearch; therefore, we've decided to include a short introduction to the concepts of this great search engine.

As you probably know, Elasticsearch is production-ready software to build search and analysis-oriented applications. It was originally started by *Shay Banon* and published in February 2010. Since then, it has rapidly gained popularity just within a few years and has become an important alternative to other open source and commercial solutions. It is one of the most downloaded open source projects.

Basic concepts

There are a few concepts that come with Elasticsearch and their understanding is crucial to fully understand how Elasticsearch works and operates.

Index

Elasticsearch stores its data in one or more indices. Using analogies from the SQL world, index is something similar to a database. It is used to store the documents and read them from it. As already mentioned, under the hood, Elasticsearch uses Apache Lucene library to write and read the data from the index. What you should remember is that a single Elasticsearch index may be built of more than a single Apache Lucene index—by using shards.

Document

Document is the main entity in the Elasticsearch world (and also in the Lucene world). At the end, all use cases of using Elasticsearch can be brought at a point where it is all about searching for documents and analyzing them. Document consists of fields, and each field is identified by its name and can contain one or multiple values. Each document may have a different set of fields; there is no schema or imposed structure—this is because Elasticsearch documents are in fact Lucene ones. From the client point of view, Elasticsearch document is a JSON object (see more on the JSON format at http://en.wikipedia.org/wiki/JSON).

Type

Each document in Elasticsearch has its type defined. This allows us to store various document types in one index and have different mappings for different document types. If you would like to compare it to an SQL world, a type in Elasticsearch is something similar to a database table.

Mapping

As already mentioned in the *Introducing Apache Lucene* section, all documents are analyzed before being indexed. We can configure how the input text is divided into tokens, which tokens should be filtered out, or what additional processing, such as removing HTML tags, is needed. This is where mapping comes into play—it holds all the information about the analysis chain. Besides the fact that Elasticsearch can automatically discover field type by looking at its value, in most cases we will want to configure the mappings ourselves to avoid unpleasant surprises.

Node

The single instance of the Elasticsearch server is called a node. A single node in Elasticsearch deployment can be sufficient for many simple use cases, but when you have to think about fault tolerance or you have lots of data that cannot fit in a single server, you should think about multi-node Elasticsearch cluster.

Elasticsearch nodes can serve different purposes. Of course, Elasticsearch is designed to index and search our data, so the first type of node is the **data** node. Such nodes hold the data and search on them. The second type of node is the **master** node — a node that works as a supervisor of the cluster controlling other nodes' work. The third node type is the **tribe** node, which is new and was introduced in Elasticsearch 1.0. The tribe node can join multiple clusters and thus act as a bridge between them, allowing us to execute almost all Elasticsearch functionalities on multiple clusters just like we would be using a single cluster.

Cluster

Cluster is a set of Elasticsearch nodes that work together. The distributed nature of Elasticsearch allows us to easily handle data that is too large for a single node to handle (both in terms of handling queries and documents). By using multi-node clusters, we can also achieve uninterrupted work of our application, even if several machines (nodes) are not available due to outage or administration tasks such as upgrade. Elasticsearch provides clustering almost seamlessly. In our opinion, this is one of the major advantages over competition; setting up a cluster in the Elasticsearch world is really easy.

Shard

As we said previously, clustering allows us to store information volumes that exceed abilities of a single server (but it is not the only need for clustering). To achieve this requirement, Elasticsearch spreads data to several physical Lucene indices. Those Lucene indices are called shards, and the process of dividing the index is called sharding. Elasticsearch can do this automatically and all the parts of the index (shards) are visible to the user as one big index. Note that besides this automation, it is crucial to tune this mechanism for particular use cases because the number of shard index is built or configured during index creation and cannot be changed without creating a new index and re-indexing the whole data.

Replica

Sharding allows us to push more data into Elasticsearch that is possible for a single node to handle. Replicas can help us in situations where the load increases and a single node is not able to handle all the requests. The idea is simple—create an additional copy of a shard, which can be used for queries just as original, primary shard. Note that we get safety for free. If the server with the primary shard is gone, Elasticsearch will take one of the available replicas of that shard and promote it to the leader, so the service work is not interrupted. Replicas can be added and removed at any time, so you can adjust their numbers when needed. Of course, the content of the replica is updated in real time and is done automatically by Elasticsearch.

Key concepts behind Elasticsearch architecture

Elasticsearch was built with a few concepts in mind. The development team wanted to make it easy to use and highly scalable. These core features are visible in every corner of Elasticsearch. From the architectural perspective, the main features are as follows:

- Reasonable default values that allow users to start using Elasticsearch just after installing it, without any additional tuning. This includes built-in discovery (for example, field types) and auto-configuration.

- Working in distributed mode by default. Nodes assume that they are or will be a part of the cluster.

- Peer-to-peer architecture without **single point of failure** (SPOF). Nodes automatically connect to other machines in the cluster for data interchange and mutual monitoring. This covers automatic replication of shards.

- Easily scalable both in terms of capacity and the amount of data by adding new nodes to the cluster.

- Elasticsearch does not impose restrictions on data organization in the index. This allows users to adjust to the existing data model. As we noted in type description, Elasticsearch supports multiple data types in a single index, and adjustment to the business model includes handling relationships between documents (although, this functionality is rather limited).

- **Near Real Time** (NRT) searching and versioning. Because of the distributed nature of Elasticsearch, it is impossible to avoid delays and temporary differences between data located on the different nodes. Elasticsearch tries to reduce these issues and provide additional mechanisms as versioning.

Workings of Elasticsearch

The following section will include information on key Elasticsearch features, such as bootstrap, failure detection, data indexing, querying, and so on.

The startup process

When Elasticsearch node starts, it uses the discovery module to find the other nodes in the same cluster (the key here is the cluster name defined in the configuration) and connect to them. By default the multicast request is broadcast to the network to find other Elasticsearch nodes with the same cluster name. You can see the process illustrated in the following figure:

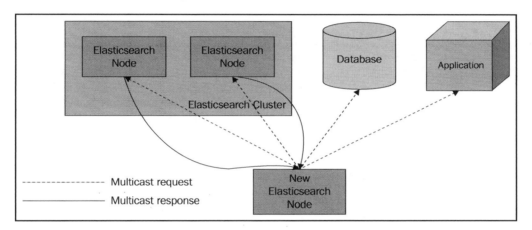

In the preceding figure, the cluster, one of the nodes that is master eligible is elected as master node (by default all nodes are master eligible). This node is responsible for managing the cluster state and the process of assigning shards to nodes in reaction to changes in cluster topology.

Note that a master node in Elasticsearch has no importance from the user perspective, which is different from other systems available (such as the databases). In practice, you do not need to know which node is a master node; all operations can be sent to any node, and internally Elasticsearch will do all the magic. If necessary, any node can send sub-queries in parallel to other nodes and merge responses to return the full response to the user. All of this is done without accessing the master node (nodes operates in peer-to-peer architecture).

The master node reads the cluster state and, if necessary, goes into the recovery process. During this state, it checks which shards are available and decides which shards will be the primary shards. After this, the whole cluster enters into a yellow state.

This means that a cluster is able to run queries, but full throughput and all possibilities are not achieved yet (it basically means that all primary shards are allocated, but not all replicas are). The next thing to do is to find duplicated shards and treat them as replicas. When a shard has too few replicas, the master node decides where to put missing shards and additional replicas are created based on a primary shard (if possible). If everything goes well, the cluster enters into a green state (which means that all primary shards and all their replicas are allocated).

Failure detection

During normal cluster work, the master node monitors all the available nodes and checks whether they are working. If any of them are not available for the configured amount of time, the node is treated as broken and the process of handling failure starts. For example, this may mean rebalancing of shards, choosing new leaders, and so on. As another example, for every primary shard that is present on the failed nodes, a new primary shard should be elected from the remaining replicas of this shard. The whole process of placing new shards and replicas can (and usually should) be configured to match our needs. More information about it can be found in *Chapter 7, Elasticsearch Administration*.

Just to illustrate how it works, let's take an example of a three nodes cluster. One of the nodes is the master node, and all of the nodes can hold data. The master node will send the ping requests to other nodes and wait for the response. If the response doesn't come (actually how many ping requests may fail depends on the configuration), such a node will be removed from the cluster. The same goes in the opposite way—each node will ping the master node to see whether it is working.

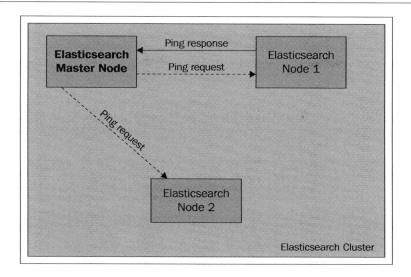

Communicating with Elasticsearch

We talked about how Elasticsearch is built, but, after all, the most important part for us is how to feed it with data and how to build queries. In order to do that, Elasticsearch exposes a sophisticated **Application Program Interface (API)**. In general, it wouldn't be a surprise if we would say that every feature of Elasticsearch has an API. The primary API is REST based (see `http://en.wikipedia.org/wiki/Representational_state_transfer`) and is easy to integrate with practically any system that can send HTTP requests.

Elasticsearch assumes that data is sent in the URL or in the request body as a JSON document (see `http://en.wikipedia.org/wiki/JSON`). If you use Java or language based on **Java Virtual Machine (JVM)**, you should look at the Java API, which, in addition to everything that is offered by the REST API, has built-in cluster discovery. It is worth mentioning that the Java API is also internally used by Elasticsearch itself to do all the node-to-node communication. Because of this, the Java API exposes all the features available through the REST API calls.

Indexing data

There are a few ways to send data to Elasticsearch. The easiest way is using the index API, which allows sending a single document to a particular index. For example, by using the curl tool (see http://curl.haxx.se/). An example command that would create a new document would look as follows:

```
curl -XPUT http://localhost:9200/blog/article/1 -d '{"title": "New
   version of Elastic Search released!", "tags": ["announce",
   "Elasticsearch", "release"] }'
```

The second way allows us to send many documents using the bulk API and the UDP bulk API. The difference between these methods is the connection type. Common bulk command sends documents by HTTP protocol and UDP bulk sends this using connection less datagram protocol. This is faster but not so reliable. The last method uses plugins, called rivers, but let's not discuss them as the rivers will be removed in future versions of Elasticsearch.

One very important thing to remember is that the indexing will always be first executed at the primary shard, not on the replica. If the indexing request is sent to a node that doesn't have the correct shard or contains a replica, it will be forwarded to the primary shard. Then, the leader will send the indexing request to all the replicas, wait for their acknowledgement (this can be controlled), and finalize the indexation if the requirements were met (like the replica quorum being updated).

The following illustration shows the process we just discussed:

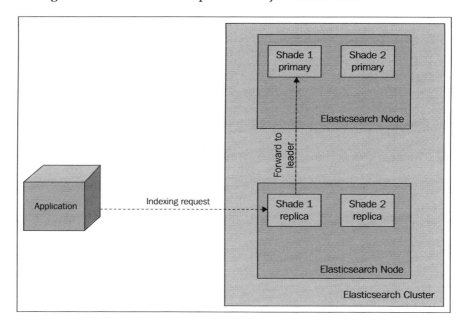

Querying data

The Query API is a big part of Elasticsearch API. Using the Query DSL (JSON-based language for building complex queries), we can do the following:

- Use various query types including simple term query, phrase, range, Boolean, fuzzy, span, wildcard, spatial, and function queries for human readable scoring control
- Build complex queries by combining the simple queries together
- Filter documents, throwing away ones that do not match selected criteria without influencing the scoring, which is very efficient when it comes to performance
- Find documents similar to a given document
- Find suggestions and corrections of a given phrase
- Build dynamic navigation and calculate statistics using aggregations
- Use prospective search and find queries matching a given document

When talking about querying, the important thing is that query is not a simple, single-stage process. In general, the process can be divided into two phases: the scatter phase and the gather phase. The scatter phase is about querying all the relevant shards of your index. The gather phase is about gathering the results from the relevant shards, combining them, sorting, processing, and returning to the client. The following illustration shows that process:

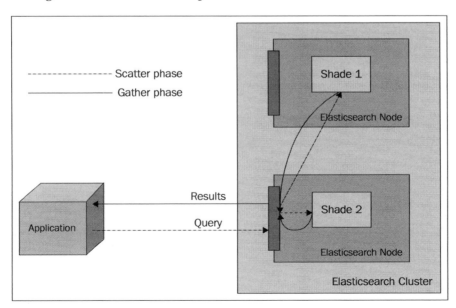

You can control the scatter and gather phases by specifying the search type to one of the six values currently exposed by Elasticsearch. We've talked about query scope in our previous book *Elasticsearch Server Second Edition* by *Packt Publishing*.

The story

As we said in the beginning of this chapter, we treat the book you are holding in your hands as a continuation of the *Elasticsearch Server Second Edition* book. Because of this, we would like to continue the story that we've used in that book. In general, we assume that we are implementing and running an online book store, as simple as that.

The mappings for our library index look like the following:

```
{
  "book" : {
    "_index" : {
      "enabled" : true
    },
    "_id" : {
      "index": "not_analyzed",
      "store" : "yes"
    },
    "properties" : {
      "author" : {
        "type" : "string"
      },
      "characters" : {
        "type" : "string"
      },
      "copies" : {
        "type" : "long",
        "ignore_malformed" : false
      },
      "otitle" : {
        "type" : "string"
      },
      "tags" : {
        "type" : "string",
        "index" : "not_analyzed"
      },
      "title" : {
        "type" : "string"
```

```
        },
        "year" : {
          "type" : "long",
          "ignore_malformed" : false
        },
        "available" : {
          "type" : "boolean"
        },
        "review" : {
          "type" : "nested",
          "properties" : {
            "nickname" : {
              "type" : "string"
            },
            "text" : {
              "type" : "string"
            },
            "stars" : {
              "type" : "integer"
            }
          }
        }
      }
    }
  }
}
```

The mappings can be found in the `library.json` file provided with the book.

The data that we will use is provided with the book in the `books.json` file. The example documents from that file look like the following:

```
{ "index": {"_index": "library", "_type": "book", "_id": "1"}}
{ "title": "All Quiet on the Western Front","otitle": "Im Westen
nichts
  Neues","author": "Erich Maria Remarque","year": 1929,"characters":
["Paul
  Bäumer", "Albert Kropp", "Haie Westhus", "Fredrich Müller",
"Stanislaus
  Katczinsky", "Tjaden"],"tags": ["novel"],"copies": 1, "available":
true,
  "section" : 3}
{ "index": {"_index": "library", "_type": "book", "_id": "2"}}
{ "title": "Catch-22","author": "Joseph Heller","year":
1961,"characters":
```

```
    ["John Yossarian", "Captain Aardvark", "Chaplain Tappman", "Colonel
    Cathcart", "Doctor Daneeka"],"tags": ["novel"],"copies": 6,
"available" :
    false, "section" : 1}
{ "index": {"_index": "library", "_type": "book", "_id": "3"}}
{ "title": "The Complete Sherlock Holmes","author": "Arthur Conan
    Doyle","year": 1936,"characters": ["Sherlock Holmes","Dr. Watson",
"G.
    Lestrade"],"tags": [],"copies": 0, "available" : false, "section" :
12}
{ "index": {"_index": "library", "_type": "book", "_id": "4"}}
{ "title": "Crime and Punishment","otitle": "Преступление и
наказание","author": "Fyodor Dostoevsky","year": 1886,"characters":
    ["Raskolnikov", "Sofia Semyonovna Marmeladova"],"tags": [],"copies":
0,
    "available" : true}
```

Downloading the example code

You can download the example code files for all Packt books you have purchased from your account at http://www.packtpub.com. If you purchased this book elsewhere, you can visit http://www.packtpub.com/support and register to have the files e-mailed directly to you.

To create the index using the provided mappings and to index the data, we would run the following commands:

```
curl -XPOST 'localhost:9200/library'
curl -XPUT 'localhost:9200/library/book/_mapping' -d @library.json
curl -s -XPOST 'localhost:9200/_bulk' --data-binary @books.json
```

Summary

In this chapter, we looked at the general architecture of Apache Lucene: how it works, how the analysis process is done, and how to use Apache Lucene query language. In addition to that, we discussed the basic concepts of Elasticsearch, its architecture, and internal communication.

In the next chapter, you'll learn about the default scoring formula Apache Lucene uses, what the query rewrite process is, and how it works. In addition to that, we'll discuss some of the Elasticsearch functionality, such as query templates, filters, and how they affect performance, what we can do with that, and how we can choose the right query to get the job done.

2
Power User Query DSL

In the previous chapter, we looked at what Apache Lucene is, how its architecture looks, and how the analysis process is handled. In addition to these, we saw what Lucene query language is and how to use it. We also discussed Elasticsearch, its architecture, and core concepts. In this chapter, we will dive deep into Elasticsearch focusing on the Query DSL. We will first go through how Lucene scoring formula works before turning to advanced queries. By the end of this chapter, we will have covered the following topics:

- How the default Apache Lucene scoring formula works
- What query rewrite is
- What query templates are and how to use them
- How to leverage complicated Boolean queries
- What are the performance implications of large Boolean queries
- Which query you should use for your particular use case

Default Apache Lucene scoring explained

A very important part of the querying process in Apache Lucene is scoring. Scoring is the process of calculating the score property of a document in a scope of a given query. What is a score? A score is a factor that describes how well the document matched the query. In this section, we'll look at the default Apache Lucene scoring mechanism: the **TF/IDF** (term frequency/inverse document frequency) algorithm and how it affects the returned document. Knowing how this works is valuable when designing complicated queries and choosing which queries parts should be more relevant than the others. Knowing the basics of how scoring works in Lucene allows us to tune queries more easily and the results retuned by them to match our use case.

When a document is matched

When a document is returned by Lucene, it means that it matched the query we've sent. In such a case, the document is given a score. Sometimes, the score is the same for all the documents (like for the `constant_score` query), but usually this won't be the case. The higher the score value, the more relevant the document is, at least at the Apache Lucene level and from the scoring formula point of view. Because the score is dependent on the matched documents, query, and the contents of the index, it is natural that the score calculated for the same document returned by two different queries will be different. Because of this, one should remember that not only should we avoid comparing the scores of individual documents returned by different queries, but we should also avoid comparing the maximum score calculated for different queries. This is because the score depends on multiple factors, not only on the boosts and query structure, but also on how many terms were matched, in which fields, the type of matching that was used on query normalization, and so on. In extreme cases, a similar query may result in totally different scores for a document, only because we've used a custom score query or the number of matched terms increased dramatically.

For now, let's get back to the scoring. In order to calculate the score property for a document, multiple factors are taken into account, which are as follows:

- **Document boost**: The boost value given for a document during indexing.

- **Field boost**: The boost value given for a field during querying.

- **Coord**: The coordination factor that is based on the number of terms the document has. It is responsible for giving more value to the documents that contain more search terms compared to other documents.

- **Inverse document frequency**: Term-based factor telling the scoring formula how rare the given term is. The higher the inverse document frequency, the rarer the term is. The scoring formula uses this factor to boost documents that contain rare terms.

- **Length norm**: A field-based factor for normalization based on the number of terms given field contains (calculated during indexing and stored in the index). The longer the field, the lesser boost this factor will give, which means that the Apache Lucene scoring formula will favor documents with fields containing lower terms.

- **Term frequency**: Term-based factor describing how many times a given term occurs in a document. The higher the term frequency, the higher the score of the document will be.

- **Query norm**: Query-based normalization factor that is calculated as a sum of a squared weight of each of the query terms. Query norm is used to allow score comparison between queries, which, as we said, is not always easy and possible.

TF/IDF scoring formula

Since the Lucene version 4.0, contains different scoring formulas and you are probably aware of them. However, we would like to discuss the default TF/IDF formula in greater detail. Please keep in mind that in order to adjust your query relevance, you don't need to understand the following equations, but it is very important to at least know how it works as it simplifies the relevancy tuning process.

Lucene conceptual scoring formula

The conceptual version of the TF/IDF formula looks as follows:

$$score(q,d) = coord(q,d) * queryBoost(q) * \frac{V(q) * V(d)}{|V(q)|} * lengthNorm(d) * docBoost(d)$$

The presented formula is a representation of a Boolean Model of Information Retrieval combined with a Vector Space Model of Information Retrieval. Let's not discuss this and let's just jump into the practical formula, which is implemented by Apache Lucene and is actually used.

 The information about the Boolean Model and Vector Space Model of Information Retrieval are far beyond the scope of this book. You can read more about it at http://en.wikipedia.org/wiki/Standard_Boolean_model and http://en.wikipedia.org/wiki/Vector_Space_Model.

Lucene practical scoring formula

Now, let's look at the following practical scoring formula used by the default Apache Lucene scoring mechanism:

$$score(q,d) = coord(q,d) * queryNorm(q) * \sum_{t\ in\ q} (tf(t\ in\ d) * idf(t)^2 * boost(t) * norm(t,d))$$

As you can see, the score factor for the document is a function of query q and document d, as we have already discussed. There are two factors that are not dependent directly on query terms, coord and queryNorm. These two elements of the formula are multiplied by the sum calculated for each term in the query.

The sum, on the other hand, is calculated by multiplying the term frequency for the given term, its inverse document frequency, term boost, and the norm, which is the length norm we've discussed previously.

Sounds a bit complicated, right? Don't worry, you don't need to remember all of that. What you should be aware of is what matters when it comes to document score. Basically, there are a few rules, as follows, which come from the previous equations:

- The rarer the matched term, the higher the score the document will have. Lucene treats documents with unique words as more important than the ones containing common words.

- The smaller the document fields (contain less terms), the higher the score the document will have. In general, Lucene emphasizes shorter documents because there is a greater possibility that those documents are exactly about the topic we are searching for.

- The higher the boost (both given during indexing and querying), the higher the score the document will have because higher boost means more importance of the particular data (document, term, phrase, and so on).

As we can see, Lucene will give the highest score for the documents that have many uncommon query terms matched in the document contents, have shorter fields (less terms indexed), and will also favor rarer terms instead of the common ones.

> If you want to read more about the Apache Lucene TF/IDF scoring formula, please visit Apache Lucene Javadocs for the TFIDFSimilarity class available at http://lucene.apache.org/core/4_9_0/core/org/apache/lucene/search/similarities/TFIDFSimilarity.html.

Elasticsearch point of view

On top of all this is Elasticsearch that leverages Apache Lucene and thankfully allows us to change the default scoring algorithm by specifying one of the available similarities or by implementing your own. But remember, Elasticsearch is more than just Lucene because we are not bound to rely only on Apache Lucene scoring.

We have different types of queries, where we can strictly control how the score of the documents is calculated, for example, by using the `function_score` query, we are allowed to use scripting to alter score of the documents; we can use the rescore functionality introduced in Elasticsearch 0.90 to recalculate the score of the returned documents, by another query run against top N documents, and so on.

> For more information about the queries from Apache Lucene point of view, please refer to Javadocs, for example, the one available at `http://lucene.apache.org/core/4_9_0/queries/org/apache/lucene/queries/package-summary.html`.

An example

Till now we've seen how scoring works. Now we would like to show you a simple example of how the scoring works in real life. To do this, we will create a new index called `scoring`. We do that by running the following command:

```
curl -XPUT 'localhost:9200/scoring' -d '{
  "settings" : {
  "index" : {
   "number_of_shards" : 1,
   "number_of_replicas" : 0
  }
 }
}'
```

We will use an index with a single physical shard and no replicas to keep it as simple as it can be (we don't need to bother about distributed document frequency in such a case). Let's start with indexing a very simple document that looks as follows:

```
curl -XPOST 'localhost:9200/scoring/doc/1' -d '{"name":"first
  document"}'
```

Let's run a simple `match` query that searches for the document term:

```
curl -XGET 'localhost:9200/scoring/_search?pretty' -d '{
  "query" : {
  "match" : { "name" : "document" }
 }
}'
```

The result returned by Elasticsearch would be as follows:

```
{
  "took" : 1,
  "timed_out" : false,
  "_shards" : {
    "total" : 1,
    "successful" : 1,
    "failed" : 0
  },
  "hits" : {
    "total" : 1,
    "max_score" : 0.19178301,
    "hits" : [ {
      "_index" : "scoring",
      "_type" : "doc",
      "_id" : "1",
      "_score" : 0.19178301,
      "_source":{"name":"first document"}
    } ]
  }
}
```

Of course, our document was matched and it was given a score. We can also check how the score was calculated by running the following command:

```
curl -XGET 'localhost:9200/scoring/doc/1/_explain?pretty' -d '{
 "query" : {
  "match" : { "name" : "document" }
 }
}'
```

The results returned by Elasticsearch would be as follows:

```
{
  "_index" : "scoring",
  "_type" : "doc",
  "_id" : "1",
  "matched" : true,
  "explanation" : {
    "value" : 0.19178301,
    "description" : "weight(name:document in 0)
    [PerFieldSimilarity], result of:",
    "details" : [ {
      "value" : 0.19178301,
```

```
            "description" : "fieldWeight in 0, product of:",
            "details" : [ {
              "value" : 1.0,
              "description" : "tf(freq=1.0), with freq of:",
              "details" : [ {
                "value" : 1.0,
                "description" : "termFreq=1.0"
              } ]
            }, {
              "value" : 0.30685282,
              "description" : "idf(docFreq=1, maxDocs=1)"
            }, {
              "value" : 0.625,
              "description" : "fieldNorm(doc=0)"
            } ]
          } ]
        }
      }
```

As we can see, we've got detailed information on how the score has been calculated for our query and the given document. We can see that the score is a product of the term frequency (which is 1 in this case), the inverse document frequency (0.30685282), and the field norm (0.625).

Now, let's add another document to our index:

```
curl -XPOST 'localhost:9200/scoring/doc/2' -d '{"name":"second
  example document"}'
```

If we run our initial query again, we will see the following response:

```
{
  "took" : 6,
  "timed_out" : false,
  "_shards" : {
    "total" : 1,
    "successful" : 1,
    "failed" : 0
  },
  "hits" : {
    "total" : 2,
    "max_score" : 0.37158427,
    "hits" : [ {
      "_index" : "scoring",
      "_type" : "doc",
      "_id" : "1",
```

```
            "_score" : 0.37158427,
            "_source":{"name":"first document"}
        }, {
            "_index" : "scoring",
            "_type" : "doc",
            "_id" : "2",
            "_score" : 0.2972674,
            "_source":{"name":"second example document"}
        } ]
    }
}
```

We can now compare how the TF/IDF scoring formula works in real life. After indexing the second document to the same shard (remember that we created our index with a single shard and no replicas), the score changed, even though the query is still the same. That's because different factors changed. For example, the inverse document frequency changed and thus the score is different. The other thing to notice is the scores of both the documents. We search for a single word (the document), and the query match was against the same term in the same field in case of both the documents. The reason why the second document has a lower score is that it has one more term in the name field compared to the first document. As you will remember, we already know that Lucene will give a higher score to the shorter documents.

Hopefully, this short introduction will give you better insight into how scoring works and will help you understand how your queries work when you are in need of relevancy tuning.

Query rewrite explained

We have already talked about scoring, which is valuable knowledge, especially when trying to improve the relevance of our queries. We also think that when debugging your queries, it is valuable to know how all the queries are executed; therefore, it is because of this we decided to include this section on how query rewrite works in Elasticsearch, why it is used, and how to control it.

If you have ever used queries, such as the prefix query and the wildcard query, basically any query that is said to be multiterm, you've probably heard about query rewriting. Elasticsearch does that because of performance reasons. The rewrite process is about changing the original, expensive query to a set of queries that are far less expensive from Lucene's point of view and thus speed up the query execution. The rewrite process is not visible to the client, but it is good to know that we can alter the rewrite process behavior. For example, let's look at what Elasticsearch does with a prefix query.

Prefix query as an example

The best way to illustrate how the rewrite process is done internally is to look at an example and see what terms are used instead of the original query term. Let's say we have the following data in our index:

```
curl -XPUT 'localhost:9200/clients/client/1' -d '{
  "id":"1", "name":"Joe"
}'
curl -XPUT 'localhost:9200/clients/client/2' -d '{
  "id":"2", "name":"Jane"
}'
curl -XPUT 'localhost:9200/clients/client/3' -d '{
  "id":"3", "name":"Jack"
}'
curl -XPUT 'localhost:9200/clients/client/4' -d '{
  "id":"4", "name":"Rob"
}'
```

We would like to find all the documents that start with the j letter. As simple as that, we run the following query against our clients index:

```
curl -XGET 'localhost:9200/clients/_search?pretty' -d '{
 "query" : {
  "prefix" : {
   "name" : {
    "prefix" : "j",
    "rewrite" : "constant_score_boolean"
   }
  }
 }
}'
```

We've used a simple prefix query; we've said that we would like to find all the documents with the j letter in the name field. We've also used the rewrite property to specify the query rewrite method, but let's skip it for now, as we will discuss the possible values of this parameter in the later part of this section.

As the response to the previous query, we've got the following:

```
{
  "took" : 2,
  "timed_out" : false,
  "_shards" : {
```

```
          "total" : 5,
          "successful" : 5,
          "failed" : 0
      },
      "hits" : {
          "total" : 3,
          "max_score" : 1.0,
          "hits" : [ {
            "_index" : "clients",
            "_type" : "client",
            "_id" : "3",
            "_score" : 1.0,
            "_source":{
      "id":"3", "name":"Jack"
}
        }, {
            "_index" : "clients",
            "_type" : "client",
            "_id" : "2",
            "_score" : 1.0,
            "_source":{
      "id":"2", "name":"Jane"
}
        }, {
            "_index" : "clients",
            "_type" : "client",
            "_id" : "1",
            "_score" : 1.0,
            "_source":{
      "id":"1", "name":"Joe"
}
        } ]
      }
}
```

As you can see, in response we've got the three documents that have the contents of the name field starting with the desired character. We didn't specify the mappings explicitly, so Elasticsearch has guessed the name field mapping and has set it to string-based and analyzed. You can check this by running the following command:

```
curl -XGET 'localhost:9200/clients/client/_mapping?pretty'
```

Elasticsearch response will be similar to the following code:

```
{
  "client" : {
    "properties" : {
      "id" : {
        "type" : "string"
      },
      "name" : {
        "type" : "string"
      }
    }
  }
}
```

Getting back to Apache Lucene

Now let's take a step back and look at Apache Lucene again. If you recall what Lucene inverted index is built of, you can tell that it contains a term, a count, and a document pointer (if you can't recall, please refer to the *Introduction to Apache Lucene* section in *Chapter 1, Introduction to Elasticsearch*). So, let's see how the simplified view of the index may look for the previous data we've put to the clients index, as shown in the following figure:

Term	Count	Docs
jack	1	<3>
jane	1	<2>
joe	1	<1>
rob	1	<4>

What you see in the column with the term text is quite important. If we look at Elasticsearch and Apache Lucene internals, you can see that our prefix query was rewritten to the following Lucene query:

```
ConstantScore(name:jack name:jane name:joe)
```

We can check the portions of the rewrite using the Elasticsearch API. First of all, we can use the Explain API by running the following command:

```
curl -XGET 'localhost:9200/clients/client/1/_explain?pretty' -d '{
  "query" : {
    "prefix" : {
      "name" : {
```

```
      "prefix" : "j",
      "rewrite" : "constant_score_boolean"
    }
  }
 }
}'
```

The result would be as follows:

```
{
   "_index" : "clients",
   "_type" : "client",
   "_id" : "1",
   "matched" : true,
   "explanation" : {
     "value" : 1.0,
     "description" : "ConstantScore(name:joe), product of:",
     "details" : [ {
       "value" : 1.0,
       "description" : "boost"
     }, {
       "value" : 1.0,
       "description" : "queryNorm"
     } ]
   }
}
```

We can see that Elasticsearch used a constant score query with the joe term against the name field. Of course, this is on Lucene level; Elasticsearch actually used a cache to get the terms. We can see this by using the Validate Query API with a command that looks as follows:

```
curl -XGET 'localhost:9200/clients/client/_validate/query?explain&pretty'
-d '{
 "query" : {
  "prefix" : {
   "name" : {
    "prefix" : "j",
    "rewrite" : "constant_score_boolean"
   }
  }
 }
}'
```

The result returned by Elasticsearch would look like the following:

```
{
  "valid" : true,
  "_shards" : {
    "total" : 1,
    "successful" : 1,
    "failed" : 0
  },
  "explanations" : [ {
    "index" : "clients",
    "valid" : true,
    "explanation" : "filtered(name:j*)->cache(_type:client)"
  } ]
}
```

Query rewrite properties

Of course, the `rewrite` property of multiterm queries can take more than a single `constant_score_boolean` value. We can control how the queries are rewritten internally. To do that, we place the `rewrite` parameter inside the JSON object responsible for the actual query, for example, like the following code:

```
{
  "query" : {
    "prefix" : {
      "name" : "j",
      "rewrite" : "constant_score_boolean"
    }
  }
}
```

The `rewrite` property can take the following values:

- `scoring_boolean`: This rewrite method translates each generated term into a Boolean should clause in a Boolean query. This rewrite method causes the score to be calculated for each document. Because of that, this method may be CPU demanding and for queries that many terms may exceed the Boolean query limit, which is set to `1024`. The default Boolean query limit can be changed by setting the `index.query.bool.max_clause_count` property in the `elasticsearch.yml` file. However, please remember that the more Boolean queries are produced, the lower the query performance may be.

- `constant_score_boolean`: This rewrite method is similar to the `scoring_boolean` rewrite method described previously, but is less CPU demanding because scoring is not computed, and instead of that, each term receives a score equal to the query boost (one by default and can be set using the boost property). Because this rewrite method also results in Boolean should clauses being created, similar to the `scoring_boolean` rewrite method, this method can also hit the maximum Boolean clauses limit.

- `constant_score_filter`: As Apache Lucene Javadocs state, this rewrite method rewrites the query by creating a private filter by visiting each term in a sequence and marking all documents for that term. Matching documents are given a constant score equal to the query boost. This method is faster than the `scoring_boolean` and `constant_score_boolean` methods, when the number of matching terms or documents is not small.

- `top_terms_N`: A rewrite method that translates each generated term into a Boolean should clause in a Boolean query and keeps the scores as computed by the query. However, unlike the `scoring_boolean` rewrite method, it only keeps the N number of top scoring terms to avoid hitting the maximum Boolean clauses limit and increase the final query performance.

- `top_terms_boost_N`: It is a rewrite method similar to the `top_terms_N` one, but the scores are not computed, but instead the documents are given the score equal to the value of the `boost` property (one by default).

> When the `rewrite` property is set to `constant_score_auto` value or not set at all, the value of `constant_score_filter` or `constant_score_boolean` will be used depending on the query and how it is constructed.

For example, if we would like our example query to use the `top_terms_N` with N equal to 2, our query would look like the following:

```
{
  "query" : {
    "prefix" : {
      "name" : {
        "prefix" :"j",
        "rewrite" : "top_terms_2"
      }
    }
  }
}
```

If you look at the results returned by Elasticsearch, you'll notice that unlike our initial query, the documents were given a score different than the default 1.0:

```
{
  "took" : 3,
  "timed_out" : false,
  "_shards" : {
    "total" : 5,
    "successful" : 5,
    "failed" : 0
  },
  "hits" : {
    "total" : 3,
    "max_score" : 0.30685282,
    "hits" : [ {
      "_index" : "clients",
      "_type" : "client",
      "_id" : "3",
      "_score" : 0.30685282,
      "_source":{
  "id":"3", "name":"Jack"
}
    }, {
      "_index" : "clients",
      "_type" : "client",
      "_id" : "2",
      "_score" : 0.30685282,
      "_source":{
  "id":"2", "name":"Jane"
}
    }, {
      "_index" : "clients",
      "_type" : "client",
      "_id" : "1",
      "_score" : 0.30685282,
      "_source":{
  "id":"1", "name":"Joe"
}
    } ]
  }
}
```

This is because the top_terms_N keeps the score for N top scoring terms.

Before we finish the query rewrite section of this chapter, we should ask ourselves one last question: when to use which rewrite types? The answer to this question greatly depends on your use case, but to summarize, if you can live with lower precision and relevancy (but higher performance), you can go for the top N rewrite method. If you need high precision and thus more relevant queries (but lower performance), choose the Boolean approach.

Query templates

When the application grows, it is very probable that the environment will start to be more and more complicated. In your organization, you probably have developers who specialize in particular layers of the application—for example, you have at least one frontend designer and an engineer responsible for the database layer. It is very convenient to have the development divided into several modules because you can work on different parts of the application in parallel without the need of constant synchronization between individuals and the whole team. Of course, the book you are currently reading is not a book about project management, but search, so let's stick to that topic. In general, it would be useful, at least sometimes, to be able to extract all queries generated by the application, give them to a search engineer, and let him/her optimize them, in terms of both performance and relevance. In such a case, the application developers would only have to pass the query itself to Elasticsearch and not care about the structure, query DSL, filtering, and so on.

Introducing query templates

With the release of Elasticsearch 1.1.0, we were given the possibility of defining a template. Let's get back to our example library e-commerce store that we started working on in the beginning of this book. Let's assume that we already know what type of queries should be sent to Elasticsearch, but the query structure is not final— we will still work on the queries and improve them. By using the query templates, we can quickly supply the basic version of the query, let application specify the parameters, and modify the query on the Elasticsearch side until the query parameters change.

Let's assume that one of our queries needs to return the most relevant books from our `library` index. We also allow users to choose whether they are interested in books that are available or the ones that are not available. In such a case, we will need to provide two parameters—the phrase itself and the Boolean that specifies the availability. The first, simplified example of our query could looks as follows:

```
{
  "query": {
    "filtered": {
```

```
  "query": {
   "match": {
    "_all": "QUERY"
   }
  },
  "filter": {
   "term": {
    "available": BOOLEAN
   }
  }
 }
}
}
```

The QUERY and BOOLEAN are placeholders for variables that will be passed to the query by the application. Of course, this query is too simple for our use case, but as we already said, this is only its first version—we will improve it in just a second.

Having our first query, we can now create our first template. Let's change our query a bit so that it looks as follows:

```
{
  "template": {
   "query": {
    "filtered": {
     "query": {
      "match": {
       "_all": "{{phrase}}"
      }
     },
     "filter": {
      "term": {
       "available": "{{avail}}"
      }
     }
    }
   }
  },
  "params": {
   "phrase": "front",
   "avail": true
  }
}
```

You can see that our placeholders were replaced by {{phrase}} and {{avail}}, and a new section params was introduced. When encountering a section like {{phrase}}, Elasticsearch will go to the params section and look for a parameter called phrase and use it. In general, we've moved the parameter values to the params section, and in the query itself we use references using the {{var}} notation, where var is the name of the parameter from the params section. In addition, the query itself is nested in the template element. This way we can parameterize our queries.

Let's now send the preceding query to the /library/_search/template REST endpoint (not the /library/_search as we usually do) using the GET HTTP method. To do this, we will use the following command:

```
curl -XGET 'localhost:9200/library/_search/template?pretty' -d '{
  "template": {
    "query": {
     "filtered": {
      "query": {
       "match": {
        "_all": "{{phrase}}"
       }
      },
      "filter": {
       "term": {
        "available": "{{avail}}"
       }
      }
     }
    }
  },
  "params": {
   "phrase": "front",
   "avail": true
  }
}'
```

Templates as strings

The template can also be provided as a string value. In such a case, our template will look like the following:

```
{
    "template": "{ \"query\": { \"filtered\": { \"query\": {
    \"match\": { \"_all\": \"{{phrase}}\" } }, \"filter\": {
    \"term\": { \"available\": \"{{avail}}\" } } } } }",
    "params": {
        "phrase": "front",
        "avail": true
    }
}
```

As you can see, this is not very readable or comfortable to write—every quotation needs to be escaped, and new line characters are also problematic and should be avoided. However, you'll be forced to use this notation (at least in Elasticsearch from 1.1.0 to 1.4.0 inclusive) when you want to use Mustache (a template engine we will talk about in the next section) features.

> There is a gotcha in the Elasticsearch version used during the writing of this book. If you prepare an incorrect template, the engine detects an error and writes info into the server logs, but from the API point of view, the query is silently ignored and all documents are returned, just like you would send the `match_all` query. You should remember to double-check your template queries until that is changed.

The Mustache template engine

Elasticsearch uses Mustache templates (see: `http://mustache.github.io/`) to generate resulting queries from templates. As you have already seen, every variable is surrounded by double curly brackets and this is specific to Mustache and is a method of dereferencing variables in this template engine. The full syntax of the Mustache template engine is beyond the scope of this book, but we would like to briefly introduce you to the most interesting parts of it: conditional expression, loops, and default values.

> The detailed information about Mustache syntax can be found at `http://mustache.github.io/mustache.5.html`.

Conditional expressions

The {{val}} expression results in inserting the value of the val variable. The {{#val}} and {{/val}} expressions inserts the values placed between them if the variable called val computes to true.

Let's take a look at the following example:

```
curl -XGET 'localhost:9200/library/_search/template?pretty' -d '{
  "template": "{ {{#limit}}\"size\": 2 {{/limit}}}",
  "params": {
   "limit": false
  }
}'
```

The preceding command returns all documents indexed in the library index. However, if we change the limit parameter to true and send the query once again, we would only get two documents. That's because the conditional would be true and the template would be activated.

> Unfortunately, it seems that versions of Elasticsearch available during the writing of this book have problems with conditional expressions inside templates. For example, one of the issues related to that is available at https://github.com/elasticsearch/elasticsearch/issues/8308. We decided to leave the section about conditional expressions with the hope that the issues will be resolved soon. The query templates can be a very handy functionality when used with conditional expressions.

Loops

Loops are defined between exactly the same as conditionals — between expression {{#val}} and {{/val}}. If the variable from the expression is an array, you can insert current values using the {{.}} expression.

For example, if we would like the template engine to iterate through an array of terms and create a terms query using them, we could run a query using the following command:

```
curl -XGET 'localhost:9200/library/_search/template?pretty' -d '{
  "template": {
   "query": {
    "terms": {
```

```
    "title": [
     "{{#title}}",
     "{{.}}",
     "{{/title}}"
    ]
   }
  }
 },
 "params": {
  "title": [ "front", "crime" ]
 }
}'
```

Default values

The default value tag allows us to define what value (or whole part of the template) should be used if the given parameter is not defined. The syntax for defining the default value for a variable called var is as follows:

```
{{var}}{{^var}}default value{{/var}}
```

For example, if we would like to have the default value of crime for the phrase parameter in our template query, we could send a query using the following command:

```
curl -XGET 'localhost:9200/library/_search/template?pretty' -d '{
  "template": {
   "query": {
    "term": {
     "title": "{{phrase}}{{^phrase}}crime{{/phrase}}"
    }
   }
  },
  "params": {
   "phrase": "front"
  }
}'
```

The preceding command will result in Elasticsearch finding all documents with term front in the title field. However, if the phrase parameter was not defined in the params section, the term crime will be used instead.

Storing templates in files

Regardless of the way we defined our templates previously, we were still a long way from decoupling them from the application. We still needed to store the whole query in the application, we were only able to parameterize the query. Fortunately, there is a simple way to change the query definition so it can be read dynamically by Elasticsearch from the config/scripts directory.

For example, let's create a file called bookList.mustache (in the config/scripts/ directory) with the following contents:

```
{
  "query": {
   "filtered": {
    "query": {
     "match": {
      "_all": "{{phrase}}"
     }
    },
    "filter": {
     "term": {
      "available": "{{avail}}"
     }
    }
   }
  }
}
```

We can now use the contents of that file in a query by specifying the template name (the name of the template is the name of the file without the .mustache extension). For example, if we would like to use our bookList template, we would send the following command:

```
curl -XGET 'localhost:9200/library/_search/template?pretty' -d '{
  "template": "bookList",
  "params": {
   "phrase": "front",
   "avail": true
  }
}'
```

The very convenient fact is that Elasticsearch can see the changes in the file without the need of a node restart. Of course, we still need to have the template file stored on all Elasticsearch nodes that are capable of handling the query execution. Starting from Elasticsearch 1.4.0, you can also store templates in a special index called .scripts. For more information please refer to the official Elasticsearch documentation available at http://www.elasticsearch.org/guide/en/elasticsearch/reference/current/search-template.html.

Handling filters and why it matters

Let's have a look at the filtering functionality provided by Elasticsearch. At first it may seem like a redundant functionality because almost all the filters have their query counterpart present in Elasticsearch Query DSL. But there must be something special about those filters because they are commonly used and they are advised when it comes to query performance. This section will discuss why filtering is important, how filters work, and what type of filtering is exposed by Elasticsearch.

Filters and query relevance

The first difference when comparing queries to filters is the influence on the document score. Let's compare queries and filters to see what to expect. We will start with the following query:

```
curl -XGET "http://127.0.0.1:9200/library/_search?pretty" -d'
{
    "query": {
        "term": {
            "title": {
                "value": "front"
            }
        }
    }
}'
```

The results for that query are as follows:

```
{
  "took" : 1,
  "timed_out" : false,
  "_shards" : {
```

```
      "total" : 5,
      "successful" : 5,
      "failed" : 0
    },
    "hits" : {
      "total" : 1,
      "max_score" : 0.11506981,
      "hits" : [ {
        "_index" : "library",
        "_type" : "book",
        "_id" : "1",
        "_score" : 0.11506981,
        "_source":{ "title": "All Quiet on the Western
        Front","otitle": "Im Westen nichts Neues","author": "Erich
        Maria Remarque","year": 1929,"characters": ["Paul Bäumer",
        "Albert Kropp", "Haie Westhus", "Fredrich Müller",
        "Stanislaus Katczinsky", "Tjaden"],"tags":
        ["novel"],"copies": 1,
        "available": true, "section" : 3}
      } ]
    }
  }
```

There is nothing special about the preceding query. Elasticsearch will return all the documents having the `front` value in the `title` field. What's more, each document matching the query will have its score calculated and the top scoring documents will be returned as the search results. In our case, the query returned one document with the score equal to `0.11506981`. This is normal behavior when it comes to querying.

Now let's compare a query and a filter. In case of both query and filter cases, we will add a fragment narrowing the documents to the ones having a single copy (the `copies` field equal to 1). The query that doesn't use filtering looks as follows:

```
curl -XGET "http://127.0.0.1:9200/library/_search?pretty" -d'
{
    "query": {
      "bool": {
        "must": [
            {
              "term": {
                "title": {
                    "value": "front"
                }
```

```
            }
        },
        {
            "term": {
                "copies": {
                    "value": "1"
                }
            }
        }
    ]
    }
  }
}'
```

The results returned by Elasticsearch are very similar and look as follows:

```
{
  "took" : 1,
  "timed_out" : false,
  "_shards" : {
    "total" : 5,
    "successful" : 5,
    "failed" : 0
  },
  "hits" : {
    "total" : 1,
    "max_score" : 0.98976034,
    "hits" : [ {
      "_index" : "library",
      "_type" : "book",
      "_id" : "1",
      "_score" : 0.98976034,
      "_source":{ "title": "All Quiet on the Western
      Front","otitle": "Im Westen nichts Neues","author": "Erich
      Maria Remarque","year": 1929,"characters": ["Paul Bäumer",
      "Albert Kropp", "Haie Westhus", "Fredrich Müller",
      "Stanislaus Katczinsky", "Tjaden"],"tags":
      ["novel"],"copies": 1,
      "available": true, "section" : 3}
    } ]
  }
}
```

The `bool` query in the preceding code is built of two `term` queries, which have to be matched in the document for it to be a match. In the response we again have the same document returned, but the score of the document is `0.98976034` now. This is exactly what we suspected after reading the *Default Apache Lucene scoring explained* section of this chapter—both terms influenced the score calculation.

Now let's look at the second case—the query for the value `front` in the `title` field and a filter for the `copies` field:

```
curl -XGET "http://127.0.0.1:9200/library/_search?pretty" -d'
{
    "query": {
        "term": {
            "title": {
                "value": "front"
            }
        }
    },
    "post_filter": {
        "term": {
            "copies": {
                "value": "1"
            }
        }
    }
}'
```

Now we have the simple `term` query, but in addition we are using the `term` filter. The results are the same when it comes to the documents returned, but the score is different now, as we can look in the following code:

```
{
  "took" : 1,
  "timed_out" : false,
  "_shards" : {
    "total" : 5,
    "successful" : 5,
    "failed" : 0
  },
  "hits" : {
    "total" : 1,
```

```
        "max_score" : 0.11506981,
        "hits" : [ {
          "_index" : "library",
          "_type" : "book",
          "_id" : "1",
          "_score" : 0.11506981,
          "_source":{ "title": "All Quiet on the Western
          Front","otitle": "Im Westen nichts Neues","author": "Erich
          Maria Remarque","year": 1929,"characters": ["Paul Bäumer",
          "Albert Kropp", "Haie Westhus", "Fredrich Müller",
          "Stanislaus Katczinsky", "Tjaden"],"tags":
          ["novel"],"copies": 1,
          "available": true, "section" : 3}
        } ]
      }
    }
```

Our single document has got a score of `0.11506981` now—exactly as the base query we started with. This leads to the main conclusion—filtering does not affect the score.

> Please note that previous Elasticsearch versions were using `filter` for the filters section instead of the `post_filter` used in the preceding query. In the 1.x versions of Elasticsearch, both versions can be used, but please remember that `filter` can be removed in the future.

In general, there is a single main difference between how queries and filters work. The only purpose of filters is to narrow down results with certain criteria. The queries not only narrow down the results, but also care about their score, which is very important when it comes to relevancy, but also has a cost—the CPU cycles required to calculate the document score. Of course, you should remember that this is not the only difference between them, and the rest of this section will focus on how filters work and what is the difference between different filtering methods available in Elasticsearch.

How filters work

We already mentioned that filters do not affect the score of the documents they match. This is very important because of two reasons. The first reason is performance. Applying a filter to a set of documents hold in the index is simple and can be very efficient. The only significant information filter holds about the document is whether the document matches the filter or not—a simple flag.

Filters provide this information by returning a structure called `DocIdSet` (org.

apache.lucene.search.DocIdSet). The purpose of this structure is to provide the view of the index segment with the filter applied on the data. It is possible by providing implementation of the Bits interface (org.apache.lucene.util.Bits), which is responsible for random access to information about documents in the filter (basically allows to check whether the document inside a segment matches the filter or not). The Bits structure is very effective because CPU can perform filtering using bitwise operations (and there is a dedicated CPU piece to handle such operations, you can read more about circular shifts at http://en.wikipedia.org/wiki/Circular_shift). We can also use the DocIdSetIterator on an ordered set of internal document identifiers, also provided by the DocIdSet.

The following figure shows how the classes using the Bits work:

doc	bits.get(doc)	Result
1	FALSE	
2	FALSE	
3	TRUE	3
4	TRUE	4

Lucene (and Elasticsearch) have various implementation of DocIdSet suitable for various cases. Each of the implementations differs when it comes to performance. However, choosing the correct implementation is the task of Lucene and Elasticsearch and we don't have to care about it, unless we extend the functionality of them.

Please remember that not all filters use the Bits structure. The filters that don't do that are numeric range filters, script ones, and the whole group of geographical filters. Instead, those filters put data into the field data cache and iterate over documents filtering as they operate on a document. This means that the next filter in the chain will only get documents allowed by the previous filters. Because of this, those filters allow optimizations, such as putting the heaviest filters on the end of the filters, execution chain.

Bool or and/or/not filters

We talked about filters in *Elasticsearch Server Second Edition*, but we wanted to remind you about one thing. You should remember that and, or, and not filters don't use Bits, while the bool filter does. Because of that you should use the bool filter when possible. The and, or, and not filters should be used for scripts, geographical filtering, and numeric range filters. Also, remember that if you nest any filter that is not using Bits inside the and, or, or not filter, Bits won't be used.

Basically, you should use the and, or, and not filters when you combine filters that are not using Bits with other filters. And if all your filters use Bits, then use the bool filter to combine them.

Performance considerations

In general, filters are fast. There are multiple reasons for this—first of all, the parts of the query handled by filters don't need to have a score calculated. As we have already said, scoring is strongly connected to a given query and the set of indexed documents.

 There is one thing when it comes to filtering. With the release of Elasticsearch 1.4.0, the bitsets used for nested queries execution are loaded eagerly by default. This is done to allow faster nested queries execution, but can lead to memory problems. To disable this behavior we can set the index.load_fixed_bitset_filters_eagerly to false. The size of memory used for fixed bitsets can be checked by using the curl -XGET 'localhost:9200/_cluster/stats?human&pretty' command and looking at the fixed_bit_set_memory_in_bytes property in the response.

When using a filter, the result of the filter does not depend on the query, so the result of the filter can be easily cached and used in the subsequent queries. What's more, the filter cache is stored as per Lucene segment, which means that the cache doesn't have to be rebuilt with every commit, but only on segment creation and segment merge.

 Of course, as with everything, there are also downsides of using filters. Not all filters can be cached. Think about filters that depend on the current time, caching them wouldn't make much sense. Sometimes caching is not worth it because of too many unique values that can be used and poor cache hit ratio, an example of this can be filters based on geographical location.

Post filtering and filtered query

If someone would say that the filter will be quicker comparing to the same query, it wouldn't be true. Filters have fewer things to care about and can be reused between queries, but Lucene is already highly optimized and the queries are very fast, even considering that scoring has to be performed. Of course, for a large number of results, filter will be faster, but there is always something we didn't tell you yet. Sometimes, when using `post_filter`, the query sent to Elasticsearch won't be as fast and efficient as we would want it to be. Let's assume that we have the following query:

```
curl -XGET 'http://127.0.0.1:9200/library/_search?pretty' -d '{
  "query": {
   "terms": {
    "title": [ "crime", "punishment", "complete", "front" ]
   }
  },
  "post_filter" : {
   "term": {
    "available": {
     "value": true,
     "_cache": true
    }
   }
  }
}'
```

The following figure shows what is going on during query execution:

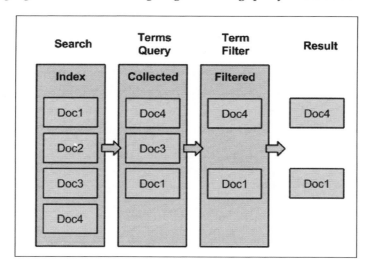

Of course, filtering matters for higher amounts of data, but for the purpose of this example, we've used our data. In the preceding figure, our index contains four documents. Our example `terms` query matches three documents: `Doc1`, `Doc3`, and `Doc4`. Each of them is scored and ordered on the basis of the calculated score. After that, our `post_filter` starts its work. From all of our documents in the whole index, it passes only two of them—`Doc1` and `Doc4`. As you can see from the three documents passed to the filter, only two of them were returned as the search result. So why are we bothering about calculating the score for the `Doc3`? In this case, we lost some CPU cycles for scoring a document that are not valid in terms of query. For a large number of documents returned, this can become a performance problem.

Please note that in the example we've used the `term` filter, which was cached by default until Elasticsearch 1.5. That behavior changed starting with Elasticsearch 1.5 (see `https://github.com/elasticsearch/elasticsearch/pull/7583`). Because of that, we decided to use the `term` filter in the example, but with forced caching.

Let's modify our query and let's filter the documents before the `Scorer` calculates the score for each document. The query that does that looks as follows:

```
curl -XGET 'http://127.0.0.1:9200/library/_search?pretty' -d '{
  "query": {
   "filtered": {
    "query": {
     "terms": {
      "title": [ "crime", "punishment", "complete", "front" ]
     }
    },
    "filter": {
     "term": {
      "available": {
       "value": true,
       "_cache": true
      }
     }
    }
   }
  }
}'
```

In the preceding example, we have used the `filtered` query. The results returned by the preceding query will be exactly the same, but the execution of the query will be a little bit different, especially when it comes to filtering. Let's look at the following figure showing the logical execution of the query:

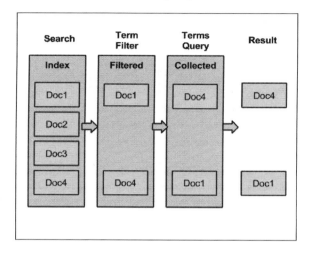

Now the initial work is done by the `term` filter. If it was already used, it will be loaded from the cache, and the whole document set will be narrowed down to only two documents. Finally, those documents are scored, but now the scoring mechanism has less work to do. Of course, in the example, our query matches the documents returned by the filter, but this is not always true.

Technically, our filter is wrapped by query, and internally Lucene library collects results only from documents that meet the enclosed filter criteria. And, of course, only the documents matching the filter are forwarded to the main query. Thanks to filter, the scoring process has fewer documents to look at.

Choosing the right filtering method

If you read the preceding explanations, you may think that you should always use the `filtered` query and run away from post filtering. Such statement will be true for most use cases, but there are exceptions to this rule. The rule of thumb says that the most expensive operations should be moved to the end of query processing. If the filter is fast, cheap, and easily cacheable, then the situation is simple—use `filtered` query. On the other hand, if the filter is slow, CPU-intensive, and hard to cache (i.e., because of too many distinct values), use post filtering or try to optimize the filter by simplifying it and making it more cache friendly, for example by reducing the resolution in case of time-based filters.

Choosing the right query for the job

In our *Elasticsearch Server Second Edition,* we described the full query language, the so-called **Query DSL** provided by Elasticsearch. A JSON structured query language that allows us to virtually build as complex queries as we can imagine. What we didn't talk about is when the queries can be used and when they should be used. For a person who doesn't have much prior experience with a full text search engine, the number of queries exposed by Elasticsearch can be overwhelming and very confusing. Because of that, we decided to extend what we wrote in the second edition of our first Elasticsearch book and show you, the reader, what you can do with Elasticsearch.

We decided to divide the following section into two distinct parts. The first part will try to categorize the queries and tell you what to expect from a query in that category. The second part will show you an example usage of queries from each group and will discuss the differences. Please take into consideration that the following section is not a full reference for the Elasticsearch Query DSL, for such reference please see *Elasticsearch Server Second Edition* from Packt Publishing or official Elasticsearch documentation available at `http://www.elasticsearch.org/ guide/en/elasticsearch/reference/current/query-dsl.html`.

Query categorization

Of course, categorizing queries is a hard task and we don't say that the following list of categories is the only correct one. We would even say that if you would ask other Elasticsearch users, they would provide their own categories or say that each query can be assigned to more than a single category. What's funny — they would be right. We also think that there is no single way of categorizing the queries; however, in our opinion, each Elasticsearch query can be assigned to one (or more) of the following categories:

- **Basic queries**: Category that groups queries allowing searching for a part of the index, either in an analyzed or a non-analysed manner. The key point in this category is that you can nest queries inside a basic query. An example of a basic query is the `term` query.

- **Compound queries**: Category grouping queries that allow us to combine multiple queries or filters inside them, for example a `bool` or `dismax` queries.

- **Not analyzed queries**: Category for queries that don't analyze the input and send it as is to Lucene index. An example of such query is the `term` query.

- **Full text search queries**: Quite a large group of queries supporting full text searching, analysing their content, and possibly providing Lucene query syntax. An example of such query is the `match` query.

- **Pattern queries**: Group of queries providing support for various wildcards in queries. For example, a `prefix` query can be assigned to this particular group.

- **Similarity supporting queries**: Group of queries sharing a common feature—support for match of similar words of documents. An example of such query is the `fuzzy_like_this` or the `more_like_this` query.

- **Score altering queries**: Very important group of queries, especially when combined with full text searching. This group includes queries that allow us to modify the score calculation during query execution. An example query that we can assign to this group is the `function_score` query, which we will talk about in detail in *Chapter 3, Not Only Full Text Search*.

- **Position aware queries**: Queries that allow us to use term position information stored in the index. A very good example of such queries is the `span_term` query.

- **Structure aware queries**: Group of queries that can work on structured data such as the parent–child documents. An example query from this group is the `nested one`.

Of course, we didn't talk about the filters at all, but you can use the same logic as for queries, so let's put the filters aside for now. Before going into examples for each type of query, let's briefly describe the purpose of each of the query category.

Basic queries

Queries that are not able to group any other queries, but instead they are used for searching the index only. Queries in this group are usually used as parts of the more complex queries or as single queries sent against Elasticsearch. You can think about those queries as bricks for building structures—more complex queries. For example, when you need to match a certain phrase in a document without any additional requirements, you should look at the basic queries—in such a case, the `match` query will be a good opportunity for this requirement and it doesn't need to be added by any other query.

Some examples of the queries from basic category are as follows:

- `Match`: A Query (actually multiple types of queries) used when you need a full text search query that will analyze the provided input. Usually, it is used when you need analysis of the provided text, but you don't need full Lucene syntax support. Because this query doesn't go through the query parsing process, it has a low chance of resulting in a parsing error, and because of this it is a good candidate for handling text entered by the user.

- `match_all`: A simple query matching all documents useful for situations when we need all the whole index contents returned for aggregations.

- `term`: A simple, not analyzed query that allows us to search for an exact word. An example use case for the `term` query is searching against non-analyzed fields, like ones storing `tags` in our example data. The `term` query is also used commonly combined with filtering, for example filtering on category field from our example data.

The queries from the complex category are: `match`, `multi_match`, `common`, `fuzzy_like_this`, `fuzzy_like_this_field`, `geoshape`, `ids`, `match_all`, `query_string`, `simple_query_string`, `range`, `prefix`, `regexp`, `span_term`, `term`, `terms`, `wildcard`.

Compound queries

Compound queries are the ones that we can use for grouping other queries together and this is their only purpose. If the simple queries were bricks for building houses, the complex queries are joints for those bricks. Because we can create a virtually indefinite level of nesting of the compound queries, we are able to produce very complex queries, and the only thing that limits us is performance.

Some examples of the compound queries and their usage are as follows:

- `bool`: One of the most common compound query that is able to group multiple queries with Boolean logical operator that allows us to control which part of the query must match, which can and which should not match. For example, if we would like to find and group together queries matching different criteria, then the `bool` query is a good candidate. The `bool` query should also be used when we want the score of the documents to be a sum of all the scores calculated by the partial queries.

- `dis_max`: A very useful query when we want the score of the document to be mostly associated with the highest boosting partial query, not the sum of all the partial queries (like in the `bool` query). The `dis_max` query generates the union of the documents returned by all the subqueries and scores the documents by the simple equation max (score of the matching clauses) + tie_breaker * (sum of scores of all the other clauses that are not max scoring ones). If you want the max scoring subquery to dominate the score of your documents, then the `dis_max` query is the way to go.

The queries from that category are: `bool`, `boosting`, `constant_score`, `dis_max`, `filtered`, `function_score`, `has_child`, `has_parent`, `indices`, `nested`, `span_first`, `span_multi`, `span_first`, `span_multi`, `span_near`, `span_not`, `span_or`, `span_term`, `top_children`.

Not analyzed queries

These are queries that are not analyzed and instead the text we provide to them is sent directly to Lucene index. This means that we either need to be aware exactly how the analysis process is done and provide a proper term, or we need to run the searches against the non-analyzed fields. If you plan to use Elasticsearch as NoSQL store this is probably the group of queries you'll be using, they search for the exact terms without analysing them, i.e., with language analyzers.

The following examples should help you understand the purpose of not analyzed queries:

- `term`: When talking about the not analyzed queries, the term query will be the one most commonly used. It provides us with the ability to match documents having a certain value in a field. For example, if we would like to match documents with a certain tag (tags field in our example data), we would use the term query.
- `Prefix`: Another type of query that is not analyzed. The prefix query is commonly used for autocomplete functionality, where the user provides a text and we need to find all the documents having terms that start with the given text. It is good to remember that even though the prefix query is not analyzed, it is rewritten by Elasticsearch so that its execution is fast.

The queries from that category are: `common`, `ids`, `prefix`, `span_term`, `term`, `terms`, `wildcard`.

Full text search queries

A group that can be used when you are building your Google-like search interface. Those queries analyze the provided input using the information from the mappings, support Lucene query syntax, support scoring capabilities, and so on. In general, if some part of the query you are sending comes from a user entering some text, you'll want to use one of the full text search queries such as the `query_string`, `match` or `simple_query_string` queries.

A Simple example of the full text search queries use case can be as follows:

- simple_query_string: A query built on top of Lucene SimpleQueryParser (`http://lucene.apache.org/core/4_9_0/queryparser/org/apache/lucene/queryparser/simple/SimpleQueryParser.html`) that was designed to parse human readable queries. In general, if you want your queries not to fail when a query parsing error occurs and instead figure out what the user wanted to achieve, this is a good query to consider.

The queries from that category are: `match`, `multi_match`, `query_string`, `simple_query_string`.

Pattern queries

Elasticsearch provides us with a few queries that can handle wildcards directly or indirectly, for example the `wildcard` query and the `prefix` query. In addition to that, we are allowed to use the `regexp` query that can find documents that have terms matching given patterns.

We've already discussed an example using the `prefix` query, so let's focus a bit on the `regexp` query. If you want a query that will find documents having terms matching a certain pattern, then the `regexp` query is probably the only solution for you. For example, if you store logs in your Elasticsearch indices and you would like to find all the logs that have terms starting with the `err` prefix, then having any number of characters and ending with `memory`, the `regexp` query will be the one to look for. However, remember that all the wildcard queries that have expressions matching large number of terms will be expensive when it comes to performance.

The queries from that category are: `prefix`, `regexp`, `wildcard`.

Similarity supporting queries

We like to think that the similarity supporting queries is a family of queries that allow us to search for similar terms or documents to the one we passed to the query. For example, if we would like to find documents that have terms similar to `crimea` term, we could run a `fuzzy` query. Another use case for this group of queries is providing us with "did you mean" like functionality. If we would like to find documents that have titles similar to the input we've provided, we would use the `more_like_this` query. In general, you would use a query from this group whenever you need to find documents having terms or fields similar to the provided input.

The queries from that category are: `fuzzy_like_this`, `fuzzy_like_this_field`, `fuzzy`, `more_like_this`, `more_like_this_field`.

Score altering queries

A group of queries used for improving search precision and relevance. They allow us to modify the score of the returned documents by providing not only a custom boost factor, but also some additional logic. A very good example of a query from this group is the `function_score` query that provides us with a possibility of using functions, which result in document score modification based on mathematical equations. For example, if you would like the documents that are closer to a given geographical point to be scored higher, then using the `function_score` query provides you with such a possibility.

The queries from that category are: `boosting`, `constant_score`, `function_score`, `indices`.

Position aware queries

These are a family of queries that allow us to match not only certain terms but also the information about the terms' positions. The most significant queries from this group are all the span queries in Elasticsearch. We can also say that the `match_phrase` query can be assigned to this group as it also looks at the position of the indexed terms, at least to some extent. If you want to find groups of words that are a certain distance in the index from other words, like "find me the documents that have `mastering` and `Elasticsearch` terms near each other and are followed by `second` and `edition` terms no further than three positions away," then span queries is the way to go. However, you should remember that span queries will be removed in future versions of Lucene library and thus from Elasticsearch as well. This is because those queries are resource-intensive and require vast amount of CPU to be properly handled.

The queries from that category are: `match_phrase`, `span_first`, `span_multi`, `span_near`, `span_not`, `span_or`, `span_term`.

Structure aware queries

The last group of queries is the structure aware queries. The queries that can be assigned to this group are as follows:

* `nested`
* `has_child`
* `has_parent`
* `top_children`

Basically, all the queries that allow us to search inside structured documents and don't require us to flatten the data can be classified as the structure aware queries. If you are looking for a query that will allow you to search inside the children document, nested documents, or for children having certain parents, then you need to use one of the queries that are mentioned in the preceding terms. If you want to handle relationships in the data, this is the group of queries you should look for; however, remember that although Elasticsearch can handle relations, it is still not a relational database.

The use cases

As we already know which groups of queries can be responsible for which tasks and what can we achieve using queries from each group, let's have a look at example use cases for each of the groups so that we can have a better view of what the queries are useful for. Please note that this is not a full and comprehensive guide to all the queries available in Elasticsearch, but instead a simple example of what can be achieved.

Example data

For the purpose of the examples in this section, we've indexed two additional documents to our `library` index.

First, we need to alter the index structure a bit so that it contains nested documents (we will need them for some queries). To do that, we will run the following command:

```
curl -XPUT 'http://localhost:9200/library/_mapping/book' -d '{
  "book" : {
   "properties" : {
    "review" : {
     "type" : "nested",
     "properties": {
      "nickname" : { "type" : "string" },
      "text" : { "type" : "string" },
      "stars" : { "type" : "integer" }
     }
    }
   }
  }
}'
```

The commands used for indexing two additional documents are as follows:

```
curl -XPOST 'localhost:9200/library/book/5' -d '{
  "title" : "The Sorrows of Young Werther",
   "author" : "Johann Wolfgang von Goethe",
    "available" : true,
     "characters" : ["Werther",
     "Lotte","Albert",
       " Fräulein von B"],
       "copies" : 1,
       "otitle" : "Die Leiden des jungen Werthers",
      "section" : 4,
     "tags" : ["novel", "classics"],
     "year" : 1774,
  "review" : [{"nickname" : "Anna","text" : "Could be good, but not
  my style","stars" : 3}]
}'
```

```
curl -XPOST 'localhost:9200/library/book/6' -d '{
 "title" : "The Peasants",
  "author" : "Władysław Reymont",
   "available" : true,
   "characters" : ["Maciej Boryna","Jankiel","Jagna Paczesiówna",
   "Antek Boryna"],
    "copies" : 4,
    "otitle" : "Chłopi",
     "section" : 4,
     "tags" : ["novel", "polish", "classics"],
    "year" : 1904,
  "review" : [{"nickname" : "anonymous","text" : "awsome
  book","stars" : 5},{"nickname" : "Jane","text" : "Great book, but
  too long","stars" : 4},{"nickname" : "Rick","text" : "Why bother,
  when you can find it on the internet","stars" : 3}]
}'
```

Basic queries use cases

Let's look at simple use cases for the basic queries group.

Searching for values in range

One of the simplest queries that can be run is a query matching documents in a given range of values. Usually, such queries are a part of a larger query or a filter. For example, a query that would return books with the number of copies from 1 to 3 inclusive would look as follows:

```
curl -XGET 'localhost:9200/library/_search?pretty' -d '{
  "query" : {
  "range" : {
   "copies" : {
    "gte" : 1,
    "lte" : 3
   }
  }
 }
}'
```

Simplified query for multiple terms

Imagine a situation where your users can show a number of tags the books returned by what the query should contain. The thing is that we require only 75 percent of the provided tags to be matched if the number of tags provided by the user is higher than three, and all the provided tags to be matched if the number of tags is three or less. We could run a `bool` query to allow that, but Elasticsearch provides us with the `terms` query that we can use to achieve the same requirement. The command that sends such query looks as follows:

```
curl -XGET 'localhost:9200/library/_search?pretty' -d '{
  "query" : {
   "terms" : {
    "tags" : [ "novel", "polish", "classics", "criminal", "new" ],
    "minimum_should_match" : "3<75%"
   }
  }
}'
```

Compound queries use cases

Let's now see how we can use compound queries to group other queries together.

Boosting some of the matched documents

One of the simplest examples is using the `bool` query to boost some documents by including not mandatory query part that is used for boosting. For example, if we would like to find all the books that have at least a single copy and boost the ones that are published after 1950, we could use the following query:

```
curl -XGET 'localhost:9200/library/_search?pretty' -d '{
  "query" : {
  "bool" : {
   "must" : [
    {
     "range" : {
      "copies" : {
       "gte" : 1
      }
     }
    }
```

```
    ],
    "should" : [
     {
       "range" : {
        "year" : {
         "gt" : 1950
        }
       }
      }
     ]
    }
  }
}'
```

Ignoring lower scoring partial queries

The dis_max query, as we have already covered, allows us to control how influential the lower scoring partial queries are. For example, if we only want to assign the score of the highest scoring partial query for the documents matching crime punishment in the title field or raskolnikov in the characters field, we would run the following query:

```
curl -XGET 'localhost:9200/library/_search?pretty' -d '{
 "fields" : [ "_id", "_score" ],
 "query" : {
  "dis_max" : {
   "tie_breaker" : 0.0,
   "queries" : [
    {
     "match" : {
      "title" : "crime punishment"
     }
    },
    {
     "match" : {
      "characters" : "raskolnikov"
     }
    }
```

```
      ]
    }
  }
}'
```

The result for the preceding query should look as follows:

```
{
  "took" : 3,
  "timed_out" : false,
  "_shards" : {
    "total" : 5,
    "successful" : 5,
    "failed" : 0
  },
  "hits" : {
    "total" : 1,
    "max_score" : 0.2169777,
    "hits" : [ {
      "_index" : "library",
      "_type" : "book",
      "_id" : "4",
      "_score" : 0.2169777,
      "fields" : {
        "_id" : "4"
      }
    } ]
  }
}
```

Now let's see the score of the partial queries alone. To do that we will run the partial queries using the following commands:

```
curl -XGET 'localhost:9200/library/_search?pretty' -d '{
 "fields" : [ "_id", "_score" ],
 "query" : {
  "match" : {
   "title" : "crime punishment"
  }
 }
}'
```

The response for the preceding query is as follows:

```json
{
    "took" : 2,
    "timed_out" : false,
    "_shards" : {
      "total" : 5,
      "successful" : 5,
      "failed" : 0
    },
    "hits" : {
      "total" : 1,
      "max_score" : 0.2169777,
      "hits" : [ {
        "_index" : "library",
        "_type" : "book",
        "_id" : "4",
        "_score" : 0.2169777,
        "fields" : {
          "_id" : "4"
        }
      } ]
    }
}
```

And the next command is as follows:

```
curl -XGET 'localhost:9200/library/_search?pretty' -d '{
 "fields" : [ "_id", "_score" ],
 "query" : {
  "match" : {
   "characters" : "raskolnikov"
  }
 }
}'
```

And the response is as follows:

```json
{
    "took" : 1,
    "timed_out" : false,
    "_shards" : {
      "total" : 5,
      "successful" : 5,
```

```
      "failed" : 0
    },
    "hits" : {
      "total" : 1,
      "max_score" : 0.15342641,
      "hits" : [ {
        "_index" : "library",
        "_type" : "book",
        "_id" : "4",
        "_score" : 0.15342641,
        "fields" : {
          "_id" : "4"
        }
      } ]
    }
  }
}
```

As you can see, the score of the document returned by our dis_max query is equal to the score of the highest scoring partial query (the first partial query). That is because we've set the tie_breaker property to 0.0.

Not analyzed queries use cases

Let's look at two example use cases for queries that are not processed by any of the defined analyzers.

Limiting results to given tags

One of the simplest examples of the not analyzed query is the term query provided by Elasticsearch. You'll probably very rarely use the term query alone; however, it may be commonly used in compound queries. For example, let's assume that we would like to search for all the books with the novel value in the tags field. To do that, we would run the following command:

```
curl -XGET 'localhost:9200/library/_search?pretty' -d '{
  "query" : {
   "term" : {
    "tags" : "novel"
  }
 }
}'
```

Efficient query time stopwords handling

Elasticsearch provides the common terms query, which allows us to handle query time stopwords in an efficient way. It divides the query terms into two groups—more important terms and less important terms. The more important terms are the ones that have a lower frequency; the less important terms are the opposite. Elasticsearch first executes the query with important terms and calculates the score for those documents. Then, a second query with the less important terms is executed, but the score is not calculated and thus the query is faster.

For example, the following two queries should be similar in terms of results, but not in terms of score computation. Please also note that to see the differences in scoring we would have to use a larger data sample and not use index time stopwords:

```
curl -XGET 'localhost:9200/library/_search?pretty' -d '{
  "query" : {
   "common" : {
    "title" : {
    "query" : "the western front",
    "cutoff_frequency" : 0.1,
    "low_freq_operator": "and"
    }
   }
  }
}'
```

And the second query would be as follows:

```
curl -XGET 'localhost:9200/library/_search?pretty' -d '{
  "query" : {
   "bool" : {
    "must" : [
     {
      "term" : { "title" : "western" }
     },
     {
      "term" : { "title" : "front" }
     }
    ],
    "should" : [
     {
      "term" : { "title" : "the" }
     }
    ]
   }
  }
}'
```

Full text search queries use cases

Full text search is a broad topic and so are the use cases for the full text queries.
However, let's look at two simple examples of queries from that group.

Using Lucene query syntax in queries

Sometimes, it is good to be able to use Lucene query syntax as it is. We talked
about this syntax in the *Lucene query language* section in *Chapter 1, Introduction to
Elasticsearch*. For example, if we would like to find books having sorrows and young
terms in their title, von goethe phrase in the author field and not having more than
five copies we could run the following query:

```
curl -XGET 'localhost:9200/library/_search?pretty' -d '{
 "query" : {
  "query_string" : {
   "query" : "+title:sorrows +title:young +author:\"von goethe\" -
   copies:{5 TO *]"
  }
 }
}'
```

As you can see, we've used the Lucene query syntax to pass all the matching
requirements and we've let query parser construct the appropriate query.

Handling user queries without errors

Sometimes, queries coming from users can contain errors. For example, let's look at
the following query:

```
curl -XGET 'localhost:9200/library/_search?pretty' -d '{
 "query" : {
  "query_string" : {
   "query" : "+sorrows +young \"",
   "default_field" : "title"
  }
 }
}'
```

The response would contain the following:

```
    "error" : "SearchPhaseExecutionException[Failed to execute phase
     [query]
```

This means that the query was not properly constructed and parse error happened. That's why the `simple_query_string` query was introduced. It uses a query parser that tries to handle user mistakes and tries to guess how the query should look. Our query using that parser would look as follows:

```
curl -XGET 'localhost:9200/library/_search?pretty' -d '{
 "query" : {
  "simple_query_string" : {
   "query" : "+sorrows +young \"",
   "fields" : [ "title" ]
  }
 }
}'
```

If you run the preceding query, you would see that the proper document has been returned by Elasticsearch, even though the query is not properly constructed.

Pattern queries use cases

There are multiple use cases for the wildcard queries; however, we wanted to show you the following two.

Autocomplete using prefixes

A very common use case provides autocomplete functionality on the indexed data. As we know, the prefix query is not analyzed and works on the basis of terms indexed in the field. So the actual functionality depends on what tokens are produced during indexing. For example, let's assume that we would like to provide autocomplete functionality on any token in the title field and the user provided wes prefix. A query that would match such a requirement looks as follows:

```
curl -XGET 'localhost:9200/library/_search?pretty' -d '{
 "query" : {
  "prefix" : {
   "title" : "wes"
  }
 }
}'
```

Pattern matching

If we need to match a certain pattern and our analysis chain is not producing tokens that allow us to do so, we can turn into the `regexp` query. One should remember, though, that this kind of query can be expensive during execution and thus should be avoided. Of course, this is not always possible. One thing to remember is that the performance of the `regexp` query depends on the chosen regular expression. If you choose a regular expression that will be rewritten into a high number of terms, then performance will suffer.

Let's now see the example usage of the `regexp` query. Let's assume that we would like to find documents that have a term starting with `wat`, then followed by two characters and ending with the n character, and those terms should be in the `characters` field. To match this requirement, we could use a `regexp` query like the one used in the following command:

```
curl -XGET 'localhost:9200/library/_search?pretty' -d '{
  "query" : {
   "regexp" : {
    "characters" : "wat..n"
   }
  }
}'
```

Similarity supporting queries use cases

Let's look at a couple of simple use cases about how we can find similar documents and terms.

Finding terms similar to a given one

A very simple example is using the fuzzy query to find documents having a term similar to a given one. For example, if we would like to find all the documents having a value similar to `crimea`, we could run the following query:

```
curl -XGET 'localhost:9200/library/_search?pretty' -d '{
  "query" : {
   "fuzzy" : {
    "title" : {
     "value" : "crimea",
     "fuzziness" : 3,
     "max_expansions" : 50
    }
```

```
  }
 }
}'
```

Finding documents with similar field values

Another example of similarity queries is a use case when we want to find all the documents having field values similar to what we provided in a query. For example, if we would like to find books having a title similar to the western front battles name, we could run the following query:

```
curl -XGET 'localhost:9200/library/_search?pretty' -d '{
  "query" : {
   "fuzzy_like_this_field" : {
    "title" : {
     "like_text" : "western front battles",
     "max_query_terms" : 5
    }
   }
  }
}'
```

The result of the preceding query would be as follows:

```
{
  "took" : 10,
  "timed_out" : false,
  "_shards" : {
    "total" : 5,
    "successful" : 5,
    "failed" : 0
  },
  "hits" : {
    "total" : 2,
    "max_score" : 1.0162667,
    "hits" : [ {
      "_index" : "library",
      "_type" : "book",
      "_id" : "1",
      "_score" : 1.0162667,
```

```
      "_source":{ "title": "All Quiet on the Western
      Front","otitle": "Im Westen nichts Neues","author": "Erich
      Maria Remarque","year": 1929,"characters": ["Paul B⊞umer",
      "Albert Kropp", "Haie Westhus", "Fredrich M⊣ller",
      "Stanislaus Katczinsky", "Tjaden"],"tags":
      ["novel"],"copies": 1,
      "available": true, "section" : 3}
  }, {
      "_index" : "library",
      "_type" : "book",
      "_id" : "5",
      "_score" : 0.4375,
      "_source":{"title" : "The Sorrows of Young Werther","author"
      : "Johann Wolfgang von Goethe","available" :
      true,"characters" : ["Werther","Lotte","Albert","Fraulein
      von B"],"copies" : 1, "otitle" : "Die Leiden des jungen
      Werthers","section" : 4,"tags" : ["novel",
      "classics"],"year" : 1774,"review" : [{"nickname" :
      "Anna","text" : "Could be good, but not my style","stars" :
      3}]}
  } ]
  }
}
```

As you can see, sometimes the results are not as obvious as we would expect (look at the second book title). This is because of what Elasticsearch thinks is similar to each other. In the case of the preceding query, Elasticsearch will take all the terms, run a fuzzy search on them, and choose a number of best differentiating terms for documents matching.

Score altering queries use cases

When it comes to relevancy, Elasticsearch provides us with a few queries that we can use to alter the score as per our need. Of course, in addition to this, most queries allow us to provide boost, which gives us even more control. Let's now look at two example use cases of score altering queries.

Favoring newer books

Let's assume that we would like to favor books that are newer, so that a book from the year 1986 is higher in the results list than a book from 1870. The query that would match that requirement looks as follows:

```
curl -XGET 'localhost:9200/library/_search?pretty' -d '{
  "query" : {
    "function_score" : {
```

```
    "query" : {
     "match_all" : {}
    },
    "score_mode" : "multiply",
    "functions" : [
     {
       "gauss" : {
        "year" : {
          "origin" : 2014,
          "scale" : 2014,
          "offset" : 0,
          "decay": 0.5
        }
       }
      }
     ]
   }
  }
}'
```

We will discuss the `function_score` query in *Chapter 3, Not Only Full Text Search*. For now, if you look at the results returned by the preceding query, you can see that the newer the book, the higher in the results it will be.

Decreasing importance of books with certain value

Sometimes, it is good to be able to decrease the importance of certain documents, while still showing them in the results list. For example, we may want to show all books, but put the ones that are not available on the bottom of the results list by lowering their score. We don't want sorting on availability because sometimes use may know what he or she is looking for and the score of a full text search query should be also important. However, if our use case is that we want the books that are not available on the bottom of the results list, we could use the following command to get them:

```
curl -XGET 'localhost:9200/library/_search?pretty' -d '{
  "query" : {
   "boosting" : {
    "positive" : {
```

```
  "match_all" : {}
 },
 "negative" : {
  "term" : {
   "available" : false
  }
 },
 "negative_boost" : 0.2
 }
 }
}'
```

Pattern queries use cases

Not very commonly used because of how resource hungry they are, pattern aware queries allow us to match documents having phrases and terms in the right order. Let's look at some examples.

Matching phrases

The simplest position aware query possible and the most performing one from the queries assigned in this group. For example, a query that would only match document leiden des jungen phrase in the otitle field would look as follows:

```
curl -XGET 'localhost:9200/library/_search?pretty' -d '{
 "query" : {
  "match_phrase" : {
   "otitle" : "leiden des jungen"
  }
 }
}'
```

Spans, spans everywhere

Of course, the phrase query is very simple when it comes to position handling. What if we would like to run a query to find documents that have des jungen phrase not more than two positions after the die term and just before the werthers term? This can be done with span queries, and the following command shows how such a query could look:

```
curl -XGET 'localhost:9200/library/_search?pretty' -d '{
 "query" : {
  "span_near" : {
```

```
    "clauses" : [
     {
      "span_near" : {
       "clauses" : [
         {
          "span_term" : {
           "otitle" : "die"
          }
         },
         {
          "span_near" : {
           "clauses" : [
             {
              "span_term" : {
               "otitle" : "des"
              }
             },
             {
              "span_term" : {
               "otitle" : "jungen"
              }
             }
           ],
           "slop" : 0,
           "in_order" : true
          }
         }
       ],
       "slop" : 2,
       "in_order" : false
      }
     },
     {
      "span_term" : {
       "otitle" : "werthers"
      }
     }
    ],
    "slop" : 0,
    "in_order" : true
```

```
    }
  }
}'
```

Please note that span queries are not analyzed. We can see that by looking at the response of the Explain API. To see that response, we should run the same request body (our query) to the `/library/book/5/_explain` REST endpoint. The interesting part of the output looks as follows:

```
"description" : "weight(spanNear([spanNear([otitle:die,
  spanNear([otitle:des, otitle:jungen], 0, true)], 2, false),
  otitle:werthers], 0, true) in 1) [PerFieldSimilarity], result
  of:",
```

Structure aware queries use cases

When it comes to the nested documents or the parent–child relationship, structure aware queries are the ones that will be needed sooner or later. Let's look at the following two examples of where the structure query can be used.

Returning parent documents having a certain nested document

The first example will be a very simple one. Let's return all the books that have at least a single review that was given four stars or more. The query that does that looks as follows:

```
curl -XGET 'localhost:9200/library/_search?pretty' -d '{
  "query" : {
  "nested" : {
    "path" : "review",
    "query" : {
     "range" : {
      "stars" : {
       "gte" : 4
      }
     }
    }
   }
  }
}'
```

Affecting parent document score with the score of nested documents

Let's assume that we want to find all the available books that have reviews and let's sort them on the maximum number of stars given in the review. The query that would fill such a requirement looks as follows:

```
curl -XGET 'localhost:9200/library/_search?pretty' -d '{
  "query" : {
    "nested" : {
      "path" : "review",
      "score_mode" : "max",
      "query" : {
       "function_score" : {
         "query" : { "match_all" : {} },
         "score_mode" : "max",
         "boost_mode" : "replace",
         "field_value_factor" : {
          "field" : "stars",
          "factor" : 1,
          "modifier" : "none"
        }
       }
      }
    }
  }
}'
```

Summary

In this chapter, we've looked at how the default Apache Lucene scoring works and we've discussed the query rewrite process — how it is done and why is it needed. We've discussed how query templates work and how they can simplify your queries. We've also looked at different query filtering methods, how they differ in comparison to each other, and when they can be used. Finally, we've assigned queries to different groups, we've learned when which query group can be used, and we've seen some example queries for each of the groups.

In the next chapter, we'll step away from full text search and focus on other search functionalities. We will start by extending our knowledge about the rescore functionality and the ability to recalculate the score for top documents in the results. After that we will look at how to load significant terms and add documents grouping using aggregations. We will also compare parent–child relationships to the nested documents, we will use function queries and, finally, we will learn how to efficiently page documents.

3
Not Only Full Text Search

In the previous chapter, we extensively talked about querying in Elasticsearch. We started by looking at how default Apache Lucene scoring works, through how filtering works, and we've finished with looking at which query to use in a particular situation. In this chapter, we will continue with discussions regarding some of the Elasticsearch functionalities connected to both querying and data analysis. By the end of this chapter, we will have covered the following areas:

- What query rescoring is and how you can use it to optimize your queries and recalculate the score for some documents

- Controlling multimatch queries

- Analyzing your data to get significant terms from it

- Grouping your documents in buckets using Elasticsearch

- Differences in relationship handling when using object, nested documents, and parent–child functionality

- Extended information regarding Elasticsearch scripting such as Groovy usage and Lucene expressions

Query rescoring

One of the great features provided by Elasticsearch is the ability to change the ordering of documents after they were returned by a query. Actually, Elasticsearch does a simple trick—it recalculates the score of top matching documents, so only part of the document in the response is reordered. The reasons why we want to do that can vary. One of the reasons may be performance—for example, calculating target ordering is very costly because scripts are used and we would like to do this on the subset of documents returned by the original query. You can imagine that rescore gives us many great opportunities for business use cases. Now, let's look at this functionality and how we can benefit from using it.

What is query rescoring?

Rescore in Elasticsearch is the process of recalculating the score for a defined number of documents returned by the query. This means that Elasticsearch first takes N documents for a given query (or the `post_filter` phase) and calculates their score using a provided rescore definition. For example, if we would take a `term` query and ask for all the documents that are available, we can use rescore to recalculate the score for 100 documents only, not for all documents returned by the query. Please note that the rescore phase will not be executed when using `search_type` of `scan` or `count`. This means that rescore won't be taken into consideration in such cases.

An example query

Let's start with a simple query that looks as follows:

```
{
 "fields" : ["title", "available"],
 "query" : {
 "match_all" : {}
 }
}
```

It returns all the documents from the index the query is run against. Every document returned by the query will have the score equal to `1.0` because of the `match_all` query. This is enough to show how rescore affects our result set.

Structure of the rescore query

Let's now modify our query so that it uses the rescore functionality. Basically, let's assume that we want the score of the document to be equal to the value of the `year` field. The query that does that would look as follows:

```
{
    "fields": ["title", "available"],
    "query": {
        "match_all": {}
    },
    "rescore": {
        "query": {
            "rescore_query": {
                "function_score": {
                    "query": {
                        "match_all": {}
                    },
```

```
        "script_score": {
            "script": "doc['year'].value"
        }
      }
    }
  }
}
```

> Please note that you need to specify the `lang` property with the `groovy` value in the preceding query if you are using Elasticsearch 1.4 or older. What's more, the preceding example uses dynamic scripting which was enabled in Elasticsearch until versions 1.3.8 and 1.4.3 for groovy and till 1.2 for MVEL. If you would like to use dynamic scripting with groovy you should add `script.groovy.sandbox.enabled` property and set it to `true` in your `elasticsearch.yml` file. However, please remember that this is a security risk.

Let's now look at the preceding query in more detail. The first thing you may have noticed is the `rescore` object. The mentioned object holds the query that will affect the scoring of the documents returned by the query. In our case, the logic is very simple—just assign the value of the `year` field as the score of the document. Please also note, that when using curl you need to escape the script value, so the `doc['year'].value` would look like `doc[\"year\"].value`

> In the preceding example, in the `rescore` object, you can see a `query` object. When this book was written, a `query` object was the only option, but in future versions, we may expect other ways to affect the resulting score.

If we save this query in the `query.json` file and send it using the following command:

```
curl localhost:9200/library/book/_search?pretty -d @query.json
```

The document that Elasticsearch should return should be as follows (please note that we've omitted the structure of the response so that it is as simple as it can be):

```
{
  "took" : 1,
  "timed_out" : false,
  "_shards" : {
    "total" : 5,
    "successful" : 5,
    "failed" : 0
  },
```

```
      "hits" : {
        "total" : 6,
        "max_score" : 1962.0,
        "hits" : [ {
          "_index" : "library",
          "_type" : "book",
          "_id" : "2",
          "_score" : 1962.0,
          "fields" : {
            "title" : [ "Catch-22" ],
            "available" : [ false ]
          }
        }, {
          "_index" : "library",
          "_type" : "book",
          "_id" : "3",
          "_score" : 1937.0,
          "fields" : {
            "title" : [ "The Complete Sherlock Holmes" ],
            "available" : [ false ]
          }
        }, {
          "_index" : "library",
          "_type" : "book",
          "_id" : "1",
          "_score" : 1930.0,
          "fields" : {
            "title" : [ "All Quiet on the Western Front" ],
            "available" : [ true ]
          }
        }, {
          "_index" : "library",
          "_type" : "book",
          "_id" : "6",
          "_score" : 1905.0,
          "fields" : {
            "title" : [ "The Peasants" ],
            "available" : [ true ]
          }
        }, {
          "_index" : "library",
          "_type" : "book",
          "_id" : "4",
          "_score" : 1887.0,
          "fields" : {
            "title" : [ "Crime and Punishment" ],
            "available" : [ true ]
          }
```

```
    }, {
      "_index" : "library",
      "_type" : "book",
      "_id" : "5",
      "_score" : 1775.0,
      "fields" : {
        "title" : [ "The Sorrows of Young Werther" ],
        "available" : [ true ]
      }
    } ]
  }
}
```

As we can see, Elasticsearch found all the documents from the original query. Now look at the score of the documents. Elasticsearch took the first N documents and applied the second query to them. In the result, the score of those documents is the sum of the score from the first and second queries.

As you know, scripts execution can be demanding when it comes to performance. That's why we've used it in the rescore phase of the query. If our initial match_all query would return thousands of results, calculating script-based scoring for all those can affect query performance. Rescore gave us the possibility to only calculate such scoring on the top N documents and thus reduce the performance impact.

> In our example, we have only seen a single rescore definition. Since Elasticsearch 1.1.0, there is a possibility of defining multiple rescore queries for a single result set. Thanks to this, you can build multilevel queries when the top N documents are reordered and this result is an input for the next reordering.

Now let's see how to tune rescore functionality behavior and what parameters are available.

Rescore parameters

In the query under the rescore object, we are allowed to use the following parameters:

- window_size (defaults to the sum of the from and size parameters): The number of documents used for rescoring on every shard

- `query_weight` (defaults to 1): The resulting score of the original query will be multiplied by this value before adding the score generated by rescore

- `rescore_query_weight` (defaults to 1): The resulting score of the rescore will be multiplied by this value before adding the score generated by the original query

To sum up, the target score for the document is equal to:

```
original_query_score * query_weight + rescore_query_score *
    rescore_query_weight
```

Choosing the scoring mode

By default, the score from the original query part and the score from the rescored part are added together. However, we can control that by specifying the `score_mode` parameter. The available values for it are as follows:

- `total`: Score values are added together (the default behavior)
- `multiply`: Values are multiplied by each other
- `avg`: The result score is an average of enclosed scores
- `max`: The result is equals of greater score value
- `min`: The result is equals of lower score value

To sum up

Sometimes, we want to show results, where the ordering of the first documents on the page is affected by some additional rules. Unfortunately, this cannot be achieved by the rescore functionality. The first idea points to the `window_size` parameter, but this parameter, in fact, is not connected with the first documents on the result list but with the number of results returned on every shard. In addition, the `window_size` value cannot be less than page size (Elasticsearch will set the `window_size` value to the value of the `size` property, when `window_size` is lower than `size`). Also, one very important thing, rescoring cannot be combined with sorting because sorting is done before the changes to the documents, score are done by rescoring, and thus sorting won't take the newly calculated score into consideration.

Controlling multimatching

Until Elasticsearch 1.1, we had limited control over the `multi_match` query. Of course, we had the possibility to specify the fields we want our query to be run against; we could use disjunction max queries (by setting the `use_dis_max` property to `true`). Finally, we could inform Elasticsearch about the importance of each field by using boosting. Our example query run against multiple fields could look as follows:

```
curl -XGET 'localhost:9200/library/_search?pretty' -d '{
  "query" : {
   "multi_match" : {
    "query" : "complete conan doyle",
    "fields" : [ "title^20", "author^10", "characters" ]
   }
  }
}'
```

A simple query that will match documents having given tokens in any of the mentioned fields. In addition to that required query, the `title` field is more important than the `author` field, and finally the `characters` field.

Of course, we could also use the disjunction max query:

```
curl -XGET 'localhost:9200/library/_search?pretty' -d '{
  "query" : {
   "multi_match" : {
    "query" : "complete conan doyle",
    "fields" : [ "title^20", "author^10", "characters" ],
    "use_dis_max" : true
   }
  }
}'
```

But apart from the score calculation for the resulting documents, using disjunction max didn't change much.

Multimatch types

With the release of Elasticsearch 1.1, the `use_dis_max` property was deprecated and Elasticsearch developers introduced a new property—the `type`. This property allows control over how the `multi_match` query is internally executed. Let's now look at the possibilities of controlling how Elasticsearch runs queries against multiple fields.

> Please note that the `tie_breaker` property was not deprecated and we can still use it without worrying about future compatibility.

Best fields matching

To use the best fields type matching, one should set the `type` property of the `multi_match` query to the `best_fields` query. This type of multimatching will generate a match query for each field specified in the `fields` property and it is best used for searching for multiple words in the same, best matching field. For example, let's look at the following query:

```
curl -XGET 'localhost:9200/library/_search?pretty' -d '{
  "query" : {
   "multi_match" : {
    "query" : "complete conan doyle",
    "fields" : [ "title", "author", "characters" ],
    "type" : "best_fields",
    "tie_breaker" : 0.8
   }
  }
}'
```

The preceding query would be translated into a query similar to the following one:

```
curl -XGET 'localhost:9200/library/_search?pretty' -d '{
  "query" : {
   "dis_max" : {
    "queries" : [
     {
      "match" : {
       "title" : "complete conan doyle"
      }
```

```
    },
    {
      "match" : {
        "author" : "complete conan doyle"
      }
    },
    {
      "match" : {
        "characters" : "complete conan doyle"
      }
    }
    ],
    "tie_breaker" : 0.8
  }
 }
}'
```

If you would look at the results for both of the preceding queries, you would notice the following:

```
{
  "took" : 1,
  "timed_out" : false,
  "_shards" : {
    "total" : 5,
    "successful" : 5,
    "failed" : 0
  },
  "hits" : {
    "total" : 1,
    "max_score" : 0.033352755,
    "hits" : [ {
      "_index" : "library",
      "_type" : "book",
      "_id" : "3",
      "_score" : 0.033352755,
      "_source":{ "title": "The Complete Sherlock
      Holmes","author": "Arthur Conan Doyle","year":
      1936,"characters": ["Sherlock Holmes","Dr. Watson", "G.
      Lestrade"],"tags": [],"copies": 0, "available" : false,
      "section" : 12}
```

```
      } ]
    }
  }
```

Both queries resulted in exactly the same results and the same scores calculated for the document. One thing to remember is how the score is calculated. If the `tie_breaker` value is present, the score for each document is the sum of the score for the best matching field and the score of the other matching fields multiplied by the `tie_breaker` value. If the `tie_breaker` value is not present, the document is assigned the score equal to the score of the best matching field.

There is one more question when it comes to the `best_fields` matching: what happens when we would like to use the AND operator or the `minimum_should_match` property? The answer is simple: the `best_fields` matching is translated into many `match` queries and both the `operator` property and the `minimum_should_match` property are applied to each of the generated match queries. Because of that, a query as follows wouldn't return any documents in our case:

```
curl -XGET 'localhost:9200/library/_search?pretty' -d '{
  "query" : {
   "multi_match" : {
    "query" : "complete conan doyle",
    "fields" : [ "title", "author", "characters" ],
    "type" : "best_fields",
    "operator" : "and"
   }
  }
}'
```

This is because the preceding query would be translated into:

```
curl -XGET 'localhost:9200/library/_search?pretty' -d '{
  "query" : {
   "dis_max" : {
    "queries" : [
     {
      "match" : {
       "title" : {
        "query" : "complete conan doyle",
        "operator" : "and"
       }
```

```
        }
      },
      {
        "match" : {
          "author" : {
            "query" : "complete conan doyle",
            "operator" : "and"
          }
        }
      },
      {
        "match" : {
          "characters" : {
            "query" : "complete conan doyle",
            "operator" : "and"
          }
        }
      }
    ]
  }
}
}'
```

And the preceding query looks as follows on the Lucene level:

```
(+title:complete +title:conan +title:doyle) | (+author:complete
  +author:conan +author:doyle) | (+characters:complete
  +characters:conan +characters:doyle)
```

We don't have any document in the index that has the `complete`, `conan`, and `doyle` terms in a single field. However, if we would like to match the terms in a different field, we can use the cross-field matching.

Cross fields matching

The `cross_fields` type matching is perfect when we want all the terms from the query to be found in the mentioned fields inside the same document. Let's recall our previous query, but this time instead of the `best_fields` matching, let's use the `cross_fields` matching type:

```
curl -XGET 'localhost:9200/library/_search?pretty' -d '{
```

```
  "query" : {
   "multi_match" : {
    "query" : "complete conan doyle",
    "fields" : [ "title", "author", "characters" ],
    "type" : "cross_fields",
    "operator" : "and"
   }
  }
 }'
```

This time, the results returned by Elasticsearch were as follows:

```
   {
     "took" : 1,
     "timed_out" : false,
     "_shards" : {
       "total" : 5,
       "successful" : 5,
       "failed" : 0
     },
     "hits" : {
       "total" : 1,
       "max_score" : 0.08154379,
       "hits" : [ {
         "_index" : "library",
         "_type" : "book",
         "_id" : "3",
         "_score" : 0.08154379,
         "_source":{ "title": "The Complete Sherlock
         Holmes","author": "Arthur Conan Doyle","year":
         1936,"characters": ["Sherlock Holmes","Dr. Watson", "G.
         Lestrade"],"tags": [],"copies": 0, "available" : false,
         "section" : 12}
       } ]
     }
   }
```

This is because our query was translated into the following Lucene query:

```
+(title:complete author:complete characters:complete)
   +(title:conan author:conan characters:conan) +(title:doyle
   author:doyle characters:doyle)
```

The results will only contain documents having all the terms in any of the mentioned fields. Of course, this is only the case when we use the AND Boolean operator. With the OR operator, we will get documents having at least a single match in any of the fields.

One more thing that is taken care of when using the cross_fields type is the problem of different term frequencies for each field. Elasticsearch handles that by blending the term frequencies for all the fields that are mentioned in a query. To put it simply, Elasticsearch gives almost the same weight to all the terms in the fields that are used in a query.

Most fields matching

Another type of multi_field configuration is the most_fields type. As the official documentation states, it was designed to help run queries against documents that contain the same text analyzed in different ways. One of the examples is having multiple languages in different fields. For example, if we would like to search for books that have die leiden terms in their title or original title, we could run the following query:

```
curl -XGET 'localhost:9200/library/_search?pretty' -d '{
  "query" : {
   "multi_match" : {
    "query" : "Die Leiden",
    "fields" : [ "title", "otitle" ],
    "type" : "most_fields"
   }
  }
}'
```

Internally, the preceding request would be translated to the following query:

```
curl -XGET 'localhost:9200/library/_search?pretty' -d '{
  "query" : {
  "bool" : {
   "should" : [
    {
     "match" : {
      "title" : "die leiden"
     }
    },
```

```
        {
          "match" : {
            "otitle" : "die leiden"
          }
        }
      ]
    }
  }
}'
```

The resulting documents are given a score equal to the sum of scores from each match query divided by the number of matching match clauses.

Phrase matching

The `phrase` matching is very similar to the `best_fields` matching we already discussed. However, instead of translating the query using match queries, it uses `match_phrase` queries. Let's take a look at the following query:

```
curl -XGET 'localhost:9200/library/_search?pretty' -d '{
  "query" : {
    "multi_match" : {
      "query" : "sherlock holmes",
      "fields" : [ "title", "author" ],
      "type" : "phrase"
    }
  }
}'
```

Because we use the `phrase` matching, it would be translated into the following:

```
curl -XGET 'localhost:9200/library/_search?pretty' -d '{
  "query" : {
    "dis_max" : {
      "queries" : [
        {
          "match_phrase" : {
            "title" : "sherlock holmes"
          }
```

```
    },
    {
      "match_phrase" : {
        "author" : "sherlock holmes"
      }
    }
  ]
  }
 }
}'
```

Phrase with prefixes matching

This is exactly the same as the phrase matching, but instead of using match_phrase query, the match_phrase_prefix query is used. Let's assume we run the following query:

```
curl -XGET 'localhost:9200/library/_search?pretty' -d '{
 "query" : {
  "multi_match" : {
   "query" : "sherlock hol",
   "fields" : [ "title", "author" ],
   "type" : "phrase_prefix"
  }
 }
}'
```

What Elasticsearch would do internally is run a query similar to the following one:

```
curl -XGET 'localhost:9200/library/_search?pretty' -d '{
 "query" : {
  "dis_max" : {
   "queries" : [
    {
     "match_phrase_prefix" : {
      "title" : "sherlock hol"
     }
    },
    {
```

```
      "match_phrase_prefix" : {
        "author" : "sherlock hol"
      }
    }
  ]
 }
}
}'
```

As you can see, by using the `type` property of the `multi_match` query, you can achieve different results without the need of writing complicated queries. What's more, Elasticsearch will also take care of the scoring and problems related to it.

Significant terms aggregation

One of the aggregations introduced after the release of Elasticsearch 1.0 is the `significant_terms` aggregation that we can use starting from release 1.1. It allows us to get the terms that are relevant and probably the most significant for a given query. The good thing is that it doesn't only show the top terms from the results of the given query, but also shows the one that seems to be the most important one.

The use cases for this aggregation type can vary from finding the most troublesome server working in your application environment to suggesting nicknames from the text. Whenever Elasticsearch can see a significant change in the popularity of a term, such a term is a candidate for being significant.

 Please remember that the `significant_terms` aggregation is marked as experimental and can change or even be removed in the future versions of Elasticsearch.

An example

The best way to describe the `significant_terms` aggregation type will be through an example. Let's start with indexing 12 simple documents, which represent reviews of work done by interns (commands are also provided in a `significant.sh` script for easier execution on Linux-based systems):

```
curl -XPOST 'localhost:9200/interns/review/1' -d '{"intern" :
  "Richard", "grade" : "bad", "type" : "grade"}'

curl -XPOST 'localhost:9200/interns/review/2' -d '{"intern" : "Ralf",
  "grade" : "perfect", "type" : "grade"}'
```

```
curl -XPOST 'localhost:9200/interns/review/3' -d '{"intern" :
    "Richard", "grade" : "bad", "type" : "grade"}'
curl -XPOST 'localhost:9200/interns/review/4' -d '{"intern" :
    "Richard", "grade" : "bad", "type" : "review"}'
curl -XPOST 'localhost:9200/interns/review/5' -d '{"intern" :
    "Richard", "grade" : "good", "type" : "grade"}'
curl -XPOST 'localhost:9200/interns/review/6' -d '{"intern" : "Ralf",
    "grade" : "good", "type" : "grade"}'
curl -XPOST 'localhost:9200/interns/review/7' -d '{"intern" : "Ralf",
    "grade" : "perfect", "type" : "review"}'
curl -XPOST 'localhost:9200/interns/review/8' -d '{"intern" :
    "Richard", "grade" : "medium", "type" : "review"}'
curl -XPOST 'localhost:9200/interns/review/9' -d '{"intern" :
    "Monica", "grade" : "medium", "type" : "grade"}'
curl -XPOST 'localhost:9200/interns/review/10' -d '{"intern" :
    "Monica", "grade" : "medium", "type" : "grade"}'
curl -XPOST 'localhost:9200/interns/review/11' -d '{"intern" :
    "Ralf", "grade" : "good", "type" : "grade"}'
curl -XPOST 'localhost:9200/interns/review/12' -d '{"intern" :
    "Ralf", "grade" : "good", "type" : "grade"}'
```

Of course, to show the real power of the significant_terms aggregation, we should use a way larger dataset. However, for the purpose of this book, we will concentrate on this example, so it is easier to illustrate how this aggregation works.

Now let's try finding the most significant grade for Richard. To do that we will use the following query:

```
curl -XGET 'localhost:9200/interns/_search?pretty' -d '{
  "query" : {
    "match" : {
      "intern" : "Richard"
    }
  },
  "aggregations" : {
    "description" : {
      "significant_terms" : {
        "field" : "grade"
      }
    }
  }
}'
```

The result of the preceding query looks as follows:

```
{
  "took" : 2,
  "timed_out" : false,
  "_shards" : {
    "total" : 5,
    "successful" : 5,
    "failed" : 0
  },
  "hits" : {
    "total" : 5,
    "max_score" : 1.4054651,
    "hits" : [ {
      "_index" : "interns",
      "_type" : "review",
      "_id" : "4",
      "_score" : 1.4054651,
      "_source":{"intern" : "Richard", "grade" : "bad"}
    }, {
      "_index" : "interns",
      "_type" : "review",
      "_id" : "3",
      "_score" : 1.0,
      "_source":{"intern" : "Richard", "grade" : "bad"}
    }, {
      "_index" : "interns",
      "_type" : "review",
      "_id" : "8",
      "_score" : 1.0,
      "_source":{"intern" : "Richard", "grade" : "medium"}
    }, {
      "_index" : "interns",
      "_type" : "review",
      "_id" : "1",
      "_score" : 1.0,
      "_source":{"intern" : "Richard", "grade" : "bad"}
    }, {
      "_index" : "interns",
      "_type" : "review",
      "_id" : "5",
      "_score" : 1.0,
      "_source":{"intern" : "Richard", "grade" : "good"}
    } ]
```

```
    },
    "aggregations" : {
      "description" : {
        "doc_count" : 5,
        "buckets" : [ {
          "key" : "bad",
          "doc_count" : 3,
          "score" : 0.84,
          "bg_count" : 3
        } ]
      }
    }
  }
}
```

As you can see, for our query, Elasticsearch informed us that the most significant grade for Richard is bad. Maybe it wasn't the best internship for him, who knows.

Choosing significant terms

To calculate significant terms, Elasticsearch looks for data that reports significant changes in their popularity between two sets of data: the **foreground** set and the **background** set. The foreground set is the data returned by our query, while the background set is the data in our index (or indices, depending on how we run our queries). If a term exists in 10 documents out of 1 million indexed documents, but appears in five documents from 10 returned, such a term is definitely significant and worth concentrating on.

Let's get back to our preceding example now to analyze it a bit. Richard got three grades from the reviewers: bad three times, medium one time, and good one time. From those three, the bad value appears in three out of five documents matching the query. In general, the bad grade appears in three documents (the bg_count property) out of the 12 documents in the index (this is our background set). This gives us 25 percent of the indexed documents. On the other hand, the bad grade appears in three out of five documents matching the query (this is our foreground set), which gives us 60 percent of the documents. As you can see, the change in popularity is significant for the bad grade and that's why Elasticsearch have chosen it to be returned in the significant_terms aggregation results.

Multiple values analysis

Of course, the `significant_terms` aggregation can be nested and provide us with nice data analysis capabilities that connect two multiple sets of data. For example, let's try to find a significant grade for each of the interns that we have information about. To do that, we will nest the `significant_terms` aggregation inside the `terms` aggregation and the query that does that looks as follows:

```
curl -XGET 'localhost:9200/interns/_search?size=0&pretty' -d '{
  "aggregations" : {
   "grades" : {
    "terms" : {
     "field" : "intern"
    },
    "aggregations" : {
     "significantGrades" : {
      "significant_terms" : {
       "field" : "grade"
      }
     }
    }
   }
  }
}'
```

The results returned by Elasticsearch for that query are as follows:

```
{
    "took" : 71,
    "timed_out" : false,
    "_shards" : {
      "total" : 5,
      "successful" : 5,
      "failed" : 0
    },
    "hits" : {
      "total" : 12,
      "max_score" : 0.0,
      "hits" : [ ]
    },
    "aggregations" : {
```

```
"grades" : {
  "doc_count_error_upper_bound" : 0,
  "sum_other_doc_count" : 0,
  "buckets" : [ {
    "key" : "ralf",
    "doc_count" : 5,
    "significantGrades" : {
      "doc_count" : 5,
      "buckets" : [ {
        "key" : "good",
        "doc_count" : 3,
        "score" : 0.21000000000000002,
        "bg_count" : 4
      } ]
    }
  }, {
    "key" : "richard",
    "doc_count" : 5,
    "significantGrades" : {
      "doc_count" : 5,
      "buckets" : [ {
        "key" : "bad",
        "doc_count" : 3,
        "score" : 0.6,
        "bg_count" : 3
      } ]
    }
  }, {
    "key" : "monica",
    "doc_count" : 2,
    "significantGrades" : {
      "doc_count" : 2,
      "buckets" : [ ]
    }
  } ]
}
```

As you can see, we got the results for interns Ralf (key property equals ralf) and Richard (key property equals richard). We didn't get information for Monica though. That's because there wasn't a significant change for the term in the grade field associated with the monica value in the intern field.

Significant terms aggregation and full text search fields

Of course, the `significant_terms` aggregation can also be used on full text search fields, practically useful for identifying text keywords. The thing is that, running this aggregation of analyzed fields may require a large amount of memory because Elasticsearch will attempt to load every term into the memory.

For example, we could run the `significant_terms` aggregation against the title field in our library index like the following:

```
curl -XGET 'localhost:9200/library/_search?size=0&pretty' -d '{
  "query" : {
   "term" : {
    "available" : true
   }
  },
  "aggregations" : {
   "description" : {
    "significant_terms" : {
     "field" : "title"
    }
   }
  }
}'
```

However, the results wouldn't bring us any useful insight in this case:

```
{
    "took" : 2,
    "timed_out" : false,
    "_shards" : {
      "total" : 5,
      "successful" : 5,
      "failed" : 0
    },
    "hits" : {
      "total" : 4,
      "max_score" : 0.0,
      "hits" : [ ]
    },
```

```
    "aggregations" : {
      "description" : {
        "doc_count" : 4,
        "buckets" : [ {
          "key" : "the",
          "doc_count" : 3,
          "score" : 1.125,
          "bg_count" : 3
        } ]
      }
    }
  }
}
```

The reason for this is that we don't have large enough data for the results to be meaningful. However, from a logical point of view, the the term is significant for the title field.

Additional configuration options

We could stop here and let you play with the significant_terms aggregation, but we will not. Instead, we will show you a few of the vast configuration options available for this aggregation type so that you can configure internal calculations and adjust it to your needs.

Controlling the number of returned buckets

Elasticsearch allows, how many buckets at maximum we want to have returned in the results. We can control it by using the size property. However, the final bucket list may contain more buckets than we set the size property to. This is the case when the number of unique terms is larger than the specified size property.

If you want to have even more control over the number of returned buckets, you can use the shard_size property. This property specifies how many candidates for significant terms will be returned by each shard. The thing to consider is that usually the low-frequency terms are the ones turning out to be the most interested ones, but Elasticsearch can't see that before merging the results on the aggregation node. Because of this, it is good to keep the shard_size property value higher than the value of the size property.

There is one more thing to remember: if you set the shard_size property lower than the size property, then Elasticsearch will replace the shard_size property with the value of the size property.

Please note that starting from Elasticsearch 1.2.0, if the `size` or `shard_size` property is set to `0`, Elasticsearch will change that and set it to `Integer.MAX_VALUE`.

Background set filtering

If you remember, we said that the background set of term frequencies used by the `significant_terms` aggregation is the whole index or indices. We can alter that behavior by using filter (using the `background_filter` property) to narrow down the background set. This is useful when we want to find significant terms in a given context.

For example, if we would like to narrow down the background set from our first example only to documents that are the real grades, not reviews, we would add the following `term` filter to our query:

```
curl -XGET 'localhost:9200/interns/_search?pretty&size=0' -d '{
  "query" : {
   "match" : {
    "intern" : "Richard"
   }
  },
  "aggregations" : {
   "description" : {
    "significant_terms" : {
     "field" : "grade",
     "background_filter" : {
      "term" : {
       "type" : "grade"
      }
     }
    }
   }
  }
}'
```

If you would look more closely at the results, you would notice that Elasticsearch calculated the significant terms for a smaller number of documents:

```
{
  "took" : 4,
  "timed_out" : false,
  "_shards" : {
    "total" : 5,
    "successful" : 5,
    "failed" : 0
  },
  "hits" : {
    "total" : 5,
    "max_score" : 0.0,
    "hits" : [ ]
  },
  "aggregations" : {
    "description" : {
      "doc_count" : 5,
      "buckets" : [ {
        "key" : "bad",
        "doc_count" : 3,
        "score" : 1.02,
        "bg_count" : 2
      } ]
    }
  }
}
```

Notice that bg_count is now 2 instead of 3 in the initial example. That's because there are only two documents having the bad value in the grade field and matching our filter specified in background_filter.

Minimum document count

A good thing about the significant_terms aggregation is that we can control the minimum number of documents a term needs to be present in to be included as a bucket. We do that by adding the min_doc_count property with the count of our choice.

For example, let's add this parameter to our query that resulted in significant grades for each of our interns. Let's lower the default value of 3 that the `min_doc_count` property is set to and let's set it to 2. Our modified query would look as follows:

```
curl -XGET 'localhost:9200/interns/_search?size=0&pretty' -d '{
  "aggregations" : {
   "grades" : {
    "terms" : {
     "field" : "intern"
    },
    "aggregations" : {
     "significantGrades" : {
      "significant_terms" : {
       "field" : "grade",
       "min_doc_count" : 2
      }
     }
    }
   }
  }
}'
```

The results of the preceding query would be as follows:

```
{
   "took" : 3,
   "timed_out" : false,
   "_shards" : {
     "total" : 5,
     "successful" : 5,
     "failed" : 0
   },
   "hits" : {
     "total" : 12,
     "max_score" : 0.0,
     "hits" : [ ]
   },
   "aggregations" : {
     "grades" : {
       "doc_count_error_upper_bound" : 0,
```

```
      "sum_other_doc_count" : 0,
      "buckets" : [ {
        "key" : "ralf",
        "doc_count" : 5,
        "significantGrades" : {
          "doc_count" : 5,
          "buckets" : [ {
            "key" : "perfect",
            "doc_count" : 2,
            "score" : 0.3200000000000001,
            "bg_count" : 2
          }, {
            "key" : "good",
            "doc_count" : 3,
            "score" : 0.21000000000000002,
            "bg_count" : 4
          } ]
        }
      }, {
        "key" : "richard",
        "doc_count" : 5,
        "significantGrades" : {
          "doc_count" : 5,
          "buckets" : [ {
            "key" : "bad",
            "doc_count" : 3,
            "score" : 0.6,
            "bg_count" : 3
          } ]
        }
      }, {
        "key" : "monica",
        "doc_count" : 2,
        "significantGrades" : {
          "doc_count" : 2,
          "buckets" : [ {
            "key" : "medium",
            "doc_count" : 2,
            "score" : 1.0,
            "bg_count" : 3
          } ]
        }
      } ]
    }
  }
}
```

As you can see, the results differ from the original example—this is because the constraints on the significant terms have been lowered. Of course, that also means that our results may be worse now. Setting this parameter to 1 may result in typos and strange words being included in the results and is generally not advised.

There is one thing to remember when it comes to using the min_doc_count property. During the first phase of aggregation calculation, Elasticsearch will collect the highest scoring terms on each shard included in the process. However, because shard doesn't have the information about the global term frequencies, the decision about term being a candidate to a significant terms list is based on shard term frequencies. The min_doc_count property is applied during the final stage of the query, once all the results are merged from the shards. Because of this, it may happen that high-frequency terms are missing in the significant terms list and the list is populated by high-scoring terms instead. To avoid this, you can increase the shard_size property and the cost of memory consumption and higher network usage.

Execution hint

Elasticsearch allows us to specify execution mode, which should be used to calculate the significant_terms aggregation. Depending on the situation, we can either set the execution_hint property to map or to ordinal. The first execution type tells Elasticsearch to aggregate the data per bucket using the values themselves. The second value tells Elasticsearch to use ordinals of the values instead of the values themselves. In most situations, setting the execution_hint property to ordinal should result in slightly faster execution, but the data we are working on must expose the ordinals. However, if the fields you calculate the significant_terms aggregation on is high cardinality one (if it contains a high number of unique terms), then using map is, in most cases, a better choice.

 Please note that Elasticsearch will ignore the execution_hint property if it can't be applied.

More options

Because Elasticsearch is constantly being developed and changed, we decided not to include all the options that are possible to set. We also omitted the options that we think are very rarely used by the users so that we are able to write in further detail about more commonly used features. See the full list of options at http://www. elasticsearch.org/guide/en/elasticsearch/reference/current/search-aggregations-bucket-significantterms-aggregation.html.

There are limits

While we were working on this book, there were a few limitations when it comes to the `significant_terms` aggregation. Of course, those are no showstoppers that will force you to totally forget about that aggregation, but it is useful to know about them.

Memory consumption

Because the `significant_terms` aggregation works on indexed values, it needs to load all the unique terms into the memory to be able to do its job. Because of this, you have to be careful when using this aggregation on large indices and on fields that are analyzed. In addition to this, we can't lower the memory consumption by using doc values fields because the `significant_terms` aggregation doesn't support them.

Shouldn't be used as top-level aggregation

The `significant_terms` aggregation shouldn't be used as a top-level aggregation whenever you are using the `match_all` query, its equivalent returning all the documents or no query at all. In such cases, the foreground and background sets will be the same, and Elasticsearch won't be able to calculate the differences in frequencies. This means that no significant terms will be found.

Counts are approximated

Elasticsearch approximates the counts of how many documents contain a term based on the information returned for each shard. You have to be aware of that because this means that those counts can be miscalculated in certain situations (for example, count can be approximated too low when shards didn't include data for a given term in the top samples returned). As the documentation states, this was a design decision to allow faster execution at the cost of potentially small inaccuracies.

Floating point fields are not allowed

Fields that are floating point type-based ones are not allowed as the subject of calculation of the `significant_terms` aggregation. You can use the `long` or `integer` based fields though.

Documents grouping

One of the most desired functionalities in Elasticsearch was always a feature called document folding or document grouping. This functionality was the most +1 marked issue for Elasticsearch. It is not surprising at all. It is sometimes very convenient to show a list of documents grouped by a particular value, especially when the number of results is very big. In this case, instead of showing all the documents one by one, we would return only one (or a few) documents from every group. For example, in our library, we could prepare a query returning all the documents about wildlife sorted by publishing date, but limit the list to two books from every year. The other useful use case, where grouping can become very handy, is counting and showing distinct values in a field. An example of such behavior is returning only a single book that had many editions.

Top hits aggregation

The `top_hits` aggregation was introduced in Elasticsearch 1.3 along with the changes to scripting about which we will talk in the *Scripting changes* section later in this chapter. What is interesting is that we can force Elasticsearch to provide grouping functionality with this aggregation. In fact, it seems that a document folding is more or less a side effect and only one of the possible usage examples of the `top_hits` aggregation. In this section, we will only focus on how this particular aggregation works, and we assumed that you already know the basic rules that rule the world of the Elasticsearch aggregation framework.

 If you don't have any experience with this Elasticsearch functionality, please considering looking at *Elasticsearch Server Second Edition* published by *Packt Publishing* or reading the Elasticsearch documentation page available at `http://www.elasticsearch.org/guide/en/elasticsearch/reference/current/search-aggregations.html`.

The idea behind the `top_hits` aggregation is simple. Every document that is assigned to a particular bucket can be also remembered. By default, only three documents per bucket are remembered. Let's see how it works using our example `library` index.

An example

To show you a potential use case that leverages the `top_hits` aggregation, we decided to use the following query:

```
curl -XGET "http://127.0.0.1:9200/library/_search?pretty" -d'
{
  "size": 0,
  "aggs": {
    "when": {
      "histogram": {
        "field": "year",
        "interval": 100
      },
      "aggs": {
        "book": {
          "top_hits": {
            "_source": {
              "include": [
                "title",
                "available"
              ]
            },
            "size": 1
          }
        }
      }
    }
  }
}'
```

In the preceding example, we did the `histogram` aggregation on year ranges. Every bucket is created for every 100 years. The nested `top_hits` aggregations will remember a single document with the greatest score from each bucket (because of the `size` property set to 1). We added the `include` option only for simplicity of the results, so that we only return the `title` and `available` fields for every aggregated document. The response returned by Elasticsearch should be similar to the following one:

```
{
    "took": 2,
    "timed_out": false,
```

```
  "_shards": {
    "total": 5,
    "successful": 5,
    "failed": 0
  },
  "hits": {
    "total": 4,
    "max_score": 0,
    "hits": []
  },
  "aggregations": {
    "when": {
      "buckets": [
        {
          "key_as_string": "1800",
          "key": 1800,
          "doc_count": 1,
          "book": {
            "hits": {
              "total": 1,
              "max_score": 1,
              "hits": [
                {
                  "_index": "library",
                  "_type": "book",
                  "_id": "4",
                  "_score": 1,
                  "_source": {
                    "title": "Crime and Punishment",
                    "available": true
                  }
                }
              ]
            }
          }
        },
        {
          "key_as_string": "1900",
          "key": 1900,
          "doc_count": 3,
          "book": {
            "hits": {
              "total": 3,
```

```
            "max_score": 1,
            "hits": [
                {
                    "_index": "library",
                    "_type": "book",
                    "_id": "3",
                    "_score": 1,
                    "_source": {
                        "title": "The Complete Sherlock
                        Holmes",
                        "available": false
                    }
                }
            ]
                    }
                }
            }
        ]
    }
}
}
```

The interesting parts of the response are highlighted. We can see that because of the top_hits aggregation, we have the most scoring document (from each bucket) included in the response. In our particular case, the query was the match_all one and all the documents have the same score, so the top scoring document for every bucket is more or less random. Elasticsearch used the match_all query because we didn't specify any query at all—this is the default behavior. If we want to have a custom sorting, this is not a problem for Elasticsearch. For example, we can return the first book from a given century. What we just need to do is add a proper sorting option, just like in the following query:

```
curl -XGET 'http://127.0.0.1:9200/library/_search?pretty' -d '{
  "size": 0,
  "aggs": {
    "when": {
      "histogram": {
        "field": "year",
        "interval": 100
      },
      "aggs": {
        "book": {
```

```
        "top_hits": {
          "sort": {
              "year": "asc"
          },
          "_source": {
            "include": [
              "title",
              "available"
            ]
          },
          "size": 1
        }
       }
      }
     }
    }
   }
}'
```

Please take a look at the highlighted fragment of the preceding query. We've added sorting to the `top_hits` aggregation, so the results are sorted on the basis of the `year` field. This means that the first document will be the one with the lowest value in that field and this is the document that is going to be returned for each bucket.

Additional parameters

However, sorting and field inclusion is not everything that we can we do inside the `top_hits` aggregation. Elasticsearch allows using several other functionalities related to documents retrieval. We don't want to discuss them all in detail because you should be familiar with most of them if you are familiar with the Elasticsearch aggregation module. However, for the purpose of this chapter, let's look at the following example:

```
curl -XGET 'http://127.0.0.1:9200/library/_search?pretty' -d '{
    "query": {
        "filtered": {
            "query": {
                "match": {
                    "_all": "quiet"
                }
```

```
        },
        "filter": {
            "term": {
                "copies": 1,
                "_name": "copies_filter"
            }
        }
    }
},
"size": 0,
"aggs": {
    "when": {
        "histogram": {
            "field": "year",
            "interval": 100
        },
        "aggs": {
            "book": {
                "top_hits": {
                    "highlight": {
                        "fields": {
                            "title": {}
                        }
                    },
                    "explain": true,
                    "version": true,
                    "_source": {
                        "include": [
                            "title",
                            "available"
                        ]
                    },
                    "fielddata_fields" : ["title"],
                    "script_fields": {
                        "century": {
```

```
                              "script": "(doc[\"year\"].value /
                              100).intValue()"
                     }
                },
                "size": 1
            }
          }
        }
      }
    }
}'
```

As you can see, our query contains the following functionalities:

- Named filters and queries (in our example the filter is named `copies_filter`)
- Document version inclusion
- Document source filtering (choosing fields that should be returned)
- Using field-data fields and script fields
- Inclusion of explained information that tells us why a given document was matched and included
- Highlighting usage

Relations between documents

While Elasticsearch is gaining more and more attention, it is no longer used as a search engine only. It is seen as a data analysis solution and sometimes as a primary data store. Having a single data store that enables fast and efficient full text searching often seems like a good idea. We not only can store documents, but we can also search them and analyze their contents bringing meaning to the data. This is usually more than we could expect from traditional SQL databases. However, if you have any experience with SQL databases, when dealing with Elasticsearch, you soon realize the necessity of modeling relationships between documents. Unfortunately, it is not easy and many of the habits and good practices from relation databases won't work in the world of the inverted index that Elasticsearch uses. You should already be familiar with how Elasticsearch handles relationships because we already mentioned nested objects and parent–child functionality in our *Elasticsearch Server Second Edition* book, but let's go through available possibilities and look closer at the traps connected with them.

The object type

Elasticsearch tries to interfere as little as possible when modeling your data and turning it into an inverted index. Unlike the relation databases, Elasticsearch can index structured objects and it is natural to it. It means that if you have any JSON document, you can index it without problems and Elasticsearch adapts to it. Let's look at the following document:

```
{
    "title": "Title",
    "quantity": 100,
    "edition": {
        "isbn": "1234567890",
        "circulation": 50000
    }
}
```

As you can see, the preceding document has two simple properties and a nested object inside it (the edition one) with additional properties. The mapping for our example is simple and looks as follows (it is also stored in the relations.json file provided with the book):

```
{
    "book" : {
        "properties" : {
            "title" : {"type": "string" },
            "quantity" : {"type": "integer" },
            "edition" : {
                "type" : "object",
                "properties" : {
                    "isbn" : {"type" : "string", "index" : "not_analyzed" },
                    "circulation" : {"type" : "integer" }
                }
            }
        }
    }
}
```

Unfortunately, everything will work only when the inner object is connected to its parent with a one-to-one relation. If you add the second object, for example, like the following:

```
{
    "title": "Title",
    "quantity": 100,
    "edition": [
        {
            "isbn": "1234567890",
            "circulation": 50000
        },
        {
            "isbn": "9876543210",
            "circulation": 2000
        }
    ]
}
```

Elasticsearch will flatten it. To Elasticsearch, the preceding document will look more or less like the following one (of course, the _source field will still look like the preceding document):

```
{
    "title": "Title",
    "quantity": 100,
    "edition": {
        "isbn": [ "1234567890", "9876543210" ],
        "circulation": [50000, 2000 ]
    }
}
```

This is not exactly what we want, and such representation will cause problems when you search for books containing editions with given ISBN numbers and given circulation. Simply, cross-matches will happen—Elasticsearch will return books containing editions with given ISBNs and any circulation.

We can test this by indexing our document by using the following command:

```
curl -XPOST 'localhost:9200/object/doc/1' -d '{
 "title": "Title",
 "quantity": 100,
 "edition": [
```

```
  {
    "isbn": "1234567890",
    "circulation": 50000
  },
  {
    "isbn": "9876543210",
    "circulation": 2000
  }
 ]
}'
```

Now, if we would run a simple query to return documents with the isbn field equal to 1234567890 and the circulation field equal to 2000, we shouldn't get any documents. Let's test that by running the following query:

```
curl -XGET 'localhost:9200/object/_search?pretty' -d '{
 "fields" : [ "_id", "title" ],
 "query" : {
  "bool" : {
   "must" : [
    {
     "term" : {
      "isbn" : "1234567890"
     }
    },
    {
     "term" : {
      "circulation" : 2000
     }
    }
   ]
  }
 }
}'
```

What we got as a result from Elasticsearch is as follows:

```
{
  "took" : 5,
  "timed_out" : false,
  "_shards" : {
    "total" : 5,
    "successful" : 5,
    "failed" : 0
  },
  "hits" : {
    "total" : 1,
    "max_score" : 1.0122644,
    "hits" : [ {
      "_index" : "object",
      "_type" : "doc",
      "_id" : "1",
      "_score" : 1.0122644,
      "fields" : {
        "title" : [ "Title" ]
      }
    } ]
  }
}
```

This cross-finding can be avoided by rearranging the mapping and document so that the source document looks like the following:

```
{
  "title": "Title",
  "quantity": 100,
  "edition": {
    "isbn": ["1234567890", "9876543210"],
    "circulation_1234567890": 50000,
    "circulation_9876543210": 2000
  }
}
```

Now, you can use the preceding mentioned query, which use the relationships between fields by the cost of greater complexity of query building. The important problem is that the mappings would have to contain information about all the possible values of the fields—this is not something that we would like to go for when having more than a couple of possible values. From the other side, this still does not allow us to create more complicated queries such as all books with a circulation of more than 10 000 and ISBN number starting with 23. In such cases, a better solution would be to use nested objects.

To summarize, the object type could be handy only for the simplest cases when problems with cross-field searching does not exist—for example, when you don't want to search inside nested objects or you only need to search on one of the fields without matching on the others.

The nested documents

From the mapping point of view, the definition of a nested document differs only in the use of nested type instead of object (which Elasticsearch will use by default when guessing types). For example, let's modify our previous example so that it uses nested documents:

```
{
  "book" : {
    "properties" : {
      "title" : {"type": "string" },
      "quantity" : {"type": "integer" },
      "edition" : {
        "type" : "nested",
        "properties" : {
          "isbn" : {"type" : "string", "index" : "not_analyzed" },
          "circulation" : {"type" : "integer" }
        }
      }
    }
  }
}
```

When we are using the nested documents, Elasticsearch, in fact, creates one document for the main object (we can call it a parent one, but that can bring confusion when talking about the parent–child functionality) and additional documents for inner objects. During normal queries, these additional documents are automatically filtered out and not searched or displayed. This is called a block join in Apache Lucene (you can read more about Apache Lucene block join queries at a blog post written by Lucene committer Mike McCandless, available at `http://blog.mikemccandless.com/2012/01/searching-relational-content-with.html`). For performance reasons, Lucene keeps these documents together with the main document, in the same segment block.

This is why the nested documents have to be indexed at the same time as the main document. Because both sides of the relation are prepared before storing them in the index and both sides are indexed at the same time. Some people refer to nested objects as an index-time join. This strong connection between documents is not a big problem when the documents are small and the data are easily available from the main data store. But what if documents are quite big, one of the relationship parts changes a lot, and reindexing the second part is not an option? The next problem is what if a nested document belongs to more than one main document? These problems do not exist in the parent–child functionality.

If we would get back to our example, and we would change our index to use the `nested` objects and we would change our query to use the `nested` query, no documents would be returned because there is no match for such a query in a single nested document.

Parent–child relationship

When talking about the parent–child functionality, we have to start with its main advantage—the true separation between documents—and each part of the relation can be indexed independently. The first cost of this advantage is more complicated queries and thus slower queries. Elasticsearch provides special query and filter types, which allow us to use this relation. This is why it is sometimes called a query-time join. The second disadvantage, which is more significant, is present in the bigger applications and multi-node Elasticsearch setups. Let's see how the parent–child relationship works in the Elasticsearch cluster that contains multiple nodes.

 Please note that unlike nested documents, the children documents can be queried without the context of the parent document, which is not possible with nested documents.

Parent–child relationship in the cluster

To better show the problem, let's create two indices: the `rel_pch_m` index holding documents being the parents and the `rel_pch_s` index with documents that are children:

```
curl -XPUT localhost:9200/rel_pch_m -d '{ "settings" : {
  "number_of_replicas" : 0  } }'
curl -XPUT localhost:9200/rel_pch_s -d '{ "settings" : {
  "number_of_replicas" : 0 } }'
```

Our mappings for the `rel_pch_m` index are simple and they can be sent to Elasticsearch by using the following command:

```
curl -XPOST localhost:9200/rel_pch_m/book/_mapping?pretty -d '{
  "book" : {
    "properties" : {
      "title" : { "type": "string" },
      "quantity" : { "type": "integer" }
    }
  }
}'
```

The mappings for the `rel_pch_s` index are simple as well, but we have to inform Elasticsearch what type of documents should be treated as parents. We can use the following command to send the mappings for the second index to Elasticsearch:

```
curl -XPOST localhost:9200/rel_pch_s/edition/_mapping?pretty -d '{
  "edition" : {
    "_parent" : {
      "type" : "book"
    },
    "properties" : {
      "isbn" : { "type" : "string", "index" : "not_analyzed" },
      "circulation" : { "type" : "integer" }
    }
  }
}'
```

The last step is to import data to these indices. We generated about `10000` records; an example document looks as follows:

```
{"index": {"_index": "rel_pch_m", "_type": "book", "_id": "1"}}
{"title" : "Doc no 1", "quantity" : 101}
{"index": {"_index": "rel_pch_s", "_type": "edition", "_id": "1",
 "_parent": "1"}}
{"isbn" : "no1", "circulation" : 501}
```

 If you are curious and want to experiment, you will find the simple bash script `create_relation_indices.sh` used to generate the example data.

The assumption is simple: we have `10000` documents of each type (`book` and `edition`). The key is the `_parent` field. In our example, it will always be set to `1`, so we have `10 000` books but our `10 000` edition belongs to that one particular book. This example is rather extreme, but it lets us point out an important thing.

 For visualization, we have used the ElasticHQ plugin available at `http://www.elastichq.org/`.

First let's look at the parent part of the relation and the index storing the parent documents, as shown in the following screenshot:

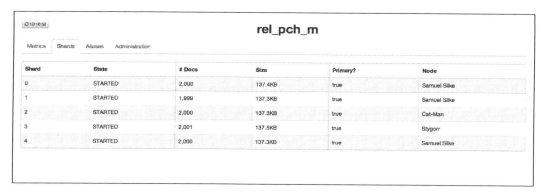

Shard	State	# Docs	Size	Primary?	Node
0	STARTED	2,000	137.4KB	true	Samuel Silke
1	STARTED	1,999	137.3KB	true	Samuel Silke
2	STARTED	2,000	137.3KB	true	Cat-Man
3	STARTED	2,001	137.5KB	true	Stygorr
4	STARTED	2,000	137.3KB	true	Samuel Silke

As we can see, the five shards of the index are located on three different nodes. Every shard has more or less the same number of documents. This is what we would expect—Elasticsearch used hashing to calculate the shard on which documents should be placed.

Now, let's look at the second index, which contains our children documents, as shown in the following screenshot:

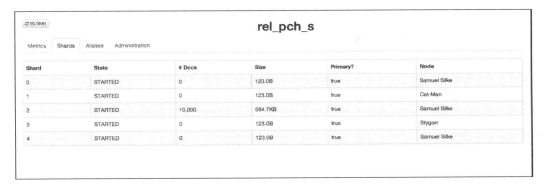

The situation is different. We still have five shards, but four of them are empty and the last one contains all the 10,000 documents! So something is not right—all the documents we indexed are located in one particular shard. This is because Elasticsearch will always put documents with the same parent in the same shard (in other words, the `routing` parameter value for children documents is always equal to the `parent` parameter value). Our example shows that in situations when some parent documents have substantially more children, we can end up with uneven shards, which may cause performance and storage issues—for example, some shards may be idling, while others will be constantly overloaded.

A few words about alternatives

As we have seen, the handling of relations between documents can cause different problems to Elasticsearch. Of course, this is not only the case with Elasticsearch because full text search solutions are extremely valuable for searching and data analysis, and not for modeling relationships between data. If it is a big problem for your application, and the full text capability is not a core part of it, you may consider using an SQL database that allows full text searching to some extent. Of course, these solutions won't be as flexible and fast as Elasticsearch, but we have to pay the price if we need full relationship support. However, in most other cases, the change of data architecture and the elimination of relations by de-normalization will be sufficient.

Scripting changes between Elasticsearch versions

One of the great things in Elasticsearch is its scripting capabilities. You can use script for calculating score, text-based scoring, data filtering, and data analysis. Although scripting can be slow in some cases, such as calculating the score for each document, we think that this part of Elasticsearch is important. Because of this, we decided that this section should bring you the information about the changes and will extend the information present in the *Elasticsearch Server Second Edition* book.

Scripting changes

Elasticsearch scripting has gone through a lot of refactoring in version 1.0 and in the versions that came after that. Because of those changes, some users were lost as to why their scripts stopped working when upgrading to version 1.2 of Elasticsearch and what is happening in general. This section will try to give you an insight on what to expect.

Security issues

During the lifetime of Elasticsearch 1.1, an exploit was published (see `http://bouk. co/blog/elasticsearch-rce/`): it showed that with the default configuration, Elasticsearch was not fully secure. Because of that, dynamic scripting was disabled by default in Elasticsearch 1.2. Although, disabling dynamic scripting was enough to make Elasticsearch secure, it made script usage far more complicated.

Groovy – the new default scripting language

With the release of Elasticsearch 1.3, we can use a new scripting language that will become default in the next version: Groovy (see `http://groovy.codehaus. org/`). The reason for this is that it can be closed in its own sandbox, preventing dynamic scripts from doing any harm to the cluster and the operating system. In addition to that, because Groovy can be sandboxed, Elasticsearch allows us to use dynamic scripting when using it. Generally speaking, starting from version 1.3, if a scripting language can be sandboxed, it can be used in dynamic scripts. However, Groovy is not everything: Elasticsearch 1.3 allows us to use Lucene expressions, which we will cover in this section. However, with the release of Elasticsearch 1.3.8 and 1.4.3 dynamic scripting was turned off even for Groovy. Because of that, if you still want to use dynamic scripting for Groovy you need to add `script.groovy. sandbox.enabled` property to `elasticsearch.yml` and set it to `true` or make your Elasticsearch a bit less dynamic with stored scripts. Please be aware that enabling dynamic scripting exposes security issues though and should be used with caution.

Removal of MVEL language

Because of the security issues and introduction of Groovy, starting from Elasticsearch 1.4, MVEL will no longer be available by default with Elasticsearch distribution. The default language will be Groovy, and MVEL will only be available as a plugin installed on demand. Remember that if you want to drop MVEL scripts, it is really easy to port them to Groovy. Of course, you will be able to install the MVEL plugin, but still dynamic scripting will be forbidden.

Short Groovy introduction

Groovy is a dynamic language for the Java Virtual Machine. It was built on top of Java, with some inspiration from languages such as Python, Ruby, or Smalltalk. Even though Groovy is out of the context of this book, we decided to describe it because, as you know, it is the default scripting language starting from Elasticsearch 1.4. If you already know Groovy and you know how to use it in Elasticsearch, you can easily skip this section and move to the *Scripting in full text context* section of this book.

The thing to remember is that Groovy is only sandboxed up to Elasticsearch 1.3.8 and 1.4.3. Starting from the mentioned versions it is not possible to run dynamic Groovy scripts unless Elasticsearch is configured to allow such. All the queries in the examples that we will show next require you to add `script.groovy.sandbox.enabled` property to `elasticsearch.yml` and set it to `true`.

Using Groovy as your scripting language

Before we go into an introduction to Groovy, let's learn how to use it in Elasticsearch scripts. To do this, check the version you are using. If you are using Elasticsearch older than 1.4, you will need to add the `lang` property with the value `groovy`. For example:

```
curl -XGET 'localhost:9200/library/_search?pretty' -d '{
 "fields" : [ "_id", "_score", "title" ],
 "query" : {
  "function_score" : {
   "query" : {
   "match_all" : {}
   },
   "script_score" : {
   "lang" : "groovy",
   "script" : "_index[\"title\"].docCount()"
   }
  }
 }
}'
```

If you are using Elasticsearch 1.4 or newer, you can easily skip the scripting language definition because Elasticsearch will use Groovy by default.

Variable definition in scripts

Groovy allows us to define variables in scripts used in Elasticsearch. To define a new variable, we use the `def` keyword followed by the variable name and its value. For example, to define a variable named `sum` and assign an initial value of `0`, to it we would use the following snippet of code:

```
def sum = 0
```

Of course, we are not only bound to simple variables definition. We can define lists, for example, a list of four values:

```
def listOfValues = [0, 1, 2, 3]
```

We can define a range of values, for example, from 0 to 9:

```
def rangeOfValues = 0..9
```

Finally, we can define maps:

```
def map = ['count':1, 'price':10, 'quantity': 12]
```

The preceding line of code will result in defining a map with three keys (`count`, `price`, and `quantity`) and three values corresponding to those keys (`1`, `10`, and `12`).

Conditionals

We are also allowed to use conditional statements in scripts. For example, we can use standard if - else if - else structures:

```
if (count > 1) {
  return count
} else if (count == 1) {
  return 1
} else {
  return 0
}
```

We can use the ternary operator:

```
def isHigherThanZero = (count > 0) ? true : false
```

The preceding code will assign a `true` value to the `isHigherThanZero` variable if the `count` variable is higher than 0. Otherwise, the value assigned to the `isHigherThanZero` variable will be `false`.

Of course, we are also allowed to use standard switch statements that allow us to use an elegant way of choosing the execution path based on the value of the statement:

```
def isEqualToTenOrEleven = false;
switch (count) {
  case 10:
    isEqualToTenOrEleven = true
    break
  case 11:
    isEqualToTenOrEleven = true
    break
  default:
    isEqualToTenOrEleven  = false
}
```

The preceding code will set the value of the `isEqualToTenOrEleven` variable to `true` if the `count` variable is equal to `10` or `11`. Otherwise, the value of the `isEqualToTenOrEleven` variable will be set to `false`.

Loops

Of course, we can also use loops when using Elasticsearch scripts and Groovy as the language in which scripts are written. Let's start with the `while` loop that is going to be executed until the statement in the parenthesis is true:

```
def i = 2
def sum = 0
while (i > 0) {
  sum = sum + i
  i--
}
```

The preceding loop will be executed twice and ended. In the first iteration, the `i` variable will have the value of `2`, which means that the `i > 0` statement is true. In the second iteration, the value of the `i` variable will be `1`, which again makes the `i > 0` statement true. In the third iteration, the `i` variable will be `0`, which will cause the `while` loop not to execute its body and exit.

We can also use the `for` loop, which you are probably familiar with if you've used programming languages before. For example, to iterate 10 times over the for loop body, we could use the following code:

```
def sum = 0
for ( i = 0; i < 10; i++) {
  sum += i
}
```

We can also iterate over a range of values:

```
def sum = 0
for ( i in 0..9 ) {
  sum += i
}
```

Or iterate over a list of values:

```
def sum = 0
for ( i in [0, 1, 2, 3, 4, 5, 6, 7, 8, 9] ) {
  sum += i
}
```

If we have a map, we can iterate over its entries:

```
def map = ['quantity':2, 'value':1, 'count':3]
def sum = 0
for ( entry in map ) {
  sum += entry.value
}
```

An example

Now after seeing some basics of Groovy, let's try to run an example script that will modify the score of our documents. We will implement the following algorithm for score calculation:

- if the year field holds the value lower than 1800, we will give the book a score of 1.0

- if the year field is between 1800 and 1900, we will give the book a score of 2.0

- the rest of the books should have the score equal to the value of the year field minus 1000

The query that does the preceding example looks as follows:

```
curl -XGET 'localhost:9200/library/_search?pretty' -d '{
 "fields" : [ "_id", "_score", "title", "year" ],
 "query" : {
  "function_score" : {
   "query" : {
   "match_all" : {}
   },
   "script_score" : {
   "lang" : "groovy",
   "script" : "def year = doc[\"year\"].value; if (year < 1800) {
   return 1.0 } else if (year < 1900) { return 2.0 } else { return
   year - 1000 }"
   }
  }
 }
}'
```

You may have noticed that we've separated the def year = doc[\"year\"].value statement in the script from the rest of it using the ; character. We did it because we have the script in a single line and we need to tell Groovy where our assign statement ends and where another statement starts.

The result returned by Elasticsearch for the preceding query is as follows:

```
{
   "took" : 4,
   "timed_out" : false,
   "_shards" : {
     "total" : 5,
     "successful" : 5,
     "failed" : 0
   },
   "hits" : {
     "total" : 6,
     "max_score" : 961.0,
     "hits" : [ {
       "_index" : "library",
       "_type" : "book",
```

```
       "_id" : "2",
       "_score" : 961.0,
       "fields" : {
         "title" : [ "Catch-22" ],
         "year" : [ 1961 ],
         "_id" : "2"
       }
     }, {
       "_index" : "library",
       "_type" : "book",
       "_id" : "3",
       "_score" : 936.0,
       "fields" : {
         "title" : [ "The Complete Sherlock Holmes" ],
         "year" : [ 1936 ],
         "_id" : "3"
       }
     }, {
       "_index" : "library",
       "_type" : "book",
       "_id" : "1",
       "_score" : 929.0,
       "fields" : {
         "title" : [ "All Quiet on the Western Front" ],
         "year" : [ 1929 ],
         "_id" : "1"
       }
     }, {
       "_index" : "library",
       "_type" : "book",
       "_id" : "6",
       "_score" : 904.0,
       "fields" : {
         "title" : [ "The Peasants" ],
         "year" : [ 1904 ],
         "_id" : "6"
       }
     }, {
       "_index" : "library",
       "_type" : "book",
       "_id" : "4",
       "_score" : 2.0,
       "fields" : {
         "title" : [ "Crime and Punishment" ],
```

```
        "year" : [ 1886 ],
        "_id" : "4"
      }
    }, {
      "_index" : "library",
      "_type" : "book",
      "_id" : "5",
      "_score" : 1.0,
      "fields" : {
        "title" : [ "The Sorrows of Young Werther" ],
        "year" : [ 1774 ],
        "_id" : "5"
      }
    } ]
  }
}
```

As you can see, our script worked as we wanted it to.

There is more

Of course, the information we just gave is not a comprehensive guide to Groovy and was never intended to be one. Groovy is out of the scope of this book and we wanted to give you a glimpse of what to expect from it. If you are interested in Groovy and you want to extend your knowledge beyond what you just read, we suggest going to the official Groovy web page and reading the documentation available at `http://groovy.codehaus.org/`.

Scripting in full text context

Of course, scripts are not only about modifying the score on the basis of data. In addition to this, we can use full text-specific statistics in our scripts, such as document frequency or term frequency. Let's look at these possibilities.

Field-related information

The first text-related information we can use in scripts we would like to talk about is field-related statistics. The field-related information Elasticsearch allows us to use is as follows:

* `_index['field_name'].docCount()`: Number of documents that contain a given field. This statistic doesn't take deleted documents into consideration.

- `_index['field_name'].sumttf()`: Sum of the number of times all terms appear in all documents in a given field.

- `_index['field_name'].sumdf()`: Sum of document frequencies. This shows the sum of the number of times all terms appear in a given field in all documents.

 Please remember that the preceding information is given for a single shard, not for the whole index, so they may differ between shards.

For example, if we would like to give our documents a score equal to the number of documents having the `title` field living in a given shard, we could run the following query:

```
curl -XGET 'localhost:9200/library/_search?pretty' -d '{
 "fields" : [ "_id", "_score", "title" ],
 "query" : {
  "function_score" : {
   "query" : {
   "match_all" : {}
   },
   "script_score" : {
    "lang" : "groovy",
    "script" : "_index[\"title\"].docCount()"
   }
  }
 }
}'
```

If we would look at the response, we would see the following:

```
{
   "took" : 3,
   "timed_out" : false,
   "_shards" : {
     "total" : 5,
     "successful" : 5,
     "failed" : 0
   },
   "hits" : {
```

```
"total" : 6,
"max_score" : 2.0,
"hits" : [ {
  "_index" : "library",
  "_type" : "book",
  "_id" : "1",
  "_score" : 2.0,
  "fields" : {
    "title" : [ "All Quiet on the Western Front" ],
    "_id" : "1"
  }
}, {
  "_index" : "library",
  "_type" : "book",
  "_id" : "6",
  "_score" : 2.0,
  "fields" : {
    "title" : [ "The Peasants" ],
    "_id" : "6"
  }
}, {
  "_index" : "library",
  "_type" : "book",
  "_id" : "4",
  "_score" : 1.0,
  "fields" : {
    "title" : [ "Crime and Punishment" ],
    "_id" : "4"
  }
}, {
  "_index" : "library",
  "_type" : "book",
  "_id" : "5",
  "_score" : 1.0,
  "fields" : {
    "title" : [ "The Sorrows of Young Werther" ],
    "_id" : "5"
  }
}, {
  "_index" : "library",
  "_type" : "book",
  "_id" : "2",
  "_score" : 1.0,
```

```
          "fields" : {
            "title" : [ "Catch-22" ],
            "_id" : "2"
          }
        }, {
          "_index" : "library",
          "_type" : "book",
          "_id" : "3",
          "_score" : 1.0,
          "fields" : {
            "title" : [ "The Complete Sherlock Holmes" ],
            "_id" : "3"
          }
        } ]
    }
}
```

As you can see, we have five documents that were queried to return the preceding results. The first two documents have a score of 2.0, which means that they are probably living in the same shard because the four remaining documents have a score of 1.0, which means that are alone in their shard.

Shard level information

The shard level information that we are allowed to use are as follows:

- `_index.numDocs()`: Number of documents in a shard
- `_index.maxDoc()`: Internal identifier of the maximum number of documents in a shard
- `_index.numDeletedDocs()`: Number of deleted documents in a given shard

 Please remember that the preceding information is given for a single shard, not for the whole index, so they may differ between shards.

For example, if we would like to sort documents on the basis of the highest internal identifier each shard has, we could send the following query:

```
curl -XGET 'localhost:9200/library/_search?pretty' -d '{
  "fields" : [ "_id", "_score", "title" ],
  "query" : {
    "function_score" : {
      "query" : {
```

```
    "match_all" : {}
  },
  "script_score" : {
   "lang" : "groovy",
   "script" : "_index.maxDoc()"
  }
 }
 }
}'
```

Of course, it doesn't make much sense to use those statistics alone, like we just did, but with addition to other text-related information, they can be very useful.

Term level information

The next type of information that we can use in scripts is term level information. Elasticsearch allows us to use the following:

- `_index['field_name']['term'].df()`: Returns the number of documents the term appears in a given field

- `_index['field_name']['term'].ttf()`: Returns the sum of the number of times a given term appears in all documents in a given field

- `_index['field_name']['term'].tf()`: Returns the information about the number of times a given term appears in a given field in a document

To give a good example of how we can use the preceding statistics, let's index two documents by using the following commands:

```
curl -XPOST 'localhost:9200/scripts/doc/1' -d '{"name":"This is a
  document"}'
curl -XPOST 'localhost:9200/scripts/doc/2' -d '{"name":"This is a
  second document after the first document"}'
```

Now, let's try filtering documents on the basis of how many times a given term appears in the name field. For example, let's match only those documents that have in the name field the document term appearing at least twice. To do this, we could run the following query:

```
curl -XGET 'localhost:9200/scripts/_search?pretty' -d '{
 "query" : {
  "filtered" : {
```

```
   "query" : {
    "match_all" : {}
   },
   "filter" : {
    "script" : {
     "lang" : "groovy",
     "script": "_index[\"name\"][\"document\"].tf() > 1"
    }
   }
  }
 }
}'
```

The result of the query would be as follows:

```
{
  "took" : 1,
  "timed_out" : false,
  "_shards" : {
    "total" : 5,
    "successful" : 5,
    "failed" : 0
  },
  "hits" : {
    "total" : 1,
    "max_score" : 1.0,
    "hits" : [ {
      "_index" : "scripts",
      "_type" : "doc",
      "_id" : "2",
      "_score" : 1.0,
      "_source":{"name":"This is a second document after the first
      document"}
    } ]
  }
}
```

As we can see, Elasticsearch did exactly what we wanted.

More advanced term information

In addition to already presented information, we can also use term positions, offsets, and payloads in our scripts. To get those, we can use one the `_index['field_name'].get('term', OPTION)` expression, where OPTION is one of the following:

- `_OFFSETS`: Term offsets
- `_PAYLOADS`: Term payloads
- `_POSITIONS`: Term positions

 Please remember that the field you want to get offsets or positions for needs to have this enabled during indexing.

In addition to this, we can also use the `_CACHE` option. It allows us to iterate multiple times over all the term positions. Options can also be combined using the | operator; for example, if you would like to get term offsets and positions for the document term in the `title` field, you could use the following expression in your script:

```
_index['title'].get('document', _OFFSETS | _POSITIONS).
```

One thing to remember is that all the preceding options return an object called that, depending on the options we have chosen, contains the following information:

- `startOffset`: Start offset for the term
- `endOffset`: End offset for the term
- `payload`: Payload for the term
- `payloadAsInt(value)`: Returns payload for the term converted to integer or the value in case the current position doesn't have a payload
- `payloadAsFloat(value)`: Returns payload for the term converted to float or the value in case the current position doesn't have a payload
- `payloadAsString(value)`: Returns payload for the term converted to string or the value in case the current position doesn't have a payload
- `position`: Position of a term

To illustrate an example, let's create a new index with the following mappings:

```
curl -XPOST 'localhost:9200/scripts2' -d '{
  "mappings" : {
   "doc" : {
    "properties" : {
```

```
      "name" : { "type" : "string", "index_options" : "offsets" }
    }
  }
 }
}'
```

After this, we index two documents using the following commands:

```
curl -XPOST 'localhost:9200/scripts2/doc/1' -d '{"name":"This is the
  first document"}'
```

```
curl -XPOST 'localhost:9200/scripts2/doc/2' -d '{"name":"This is a
  second simple document"}'
```

Now, let's set the score of our documents to the sum of all the start positions for the document term in the name field. To do this, we run the following query:

```
curl -XGET 'localhost:9200/scripts2/_search?pretty' -d '{
  "query" : {
   "function_score" : {
    "query" : {
     "match_all" : {}
    },
    "script_score" : {
     "lang" : "groovy",
"script": "def termInfo = _index[\"name\"].get(\"document\",_OFFSETS);
def sum = 0; for (offset in termInfo) { sum += offset.startOffset; };
return sum;"
    }
   }
  }
}'
```

The results returned by Elasticsearch would be as follows:

```
{
   "took" : 3,
   "timed_out" : false,
   "_shards" : {
     "total" : 5,
     "successful" : 5,
     "failed" : 0
   },
```

```
"hits" : {
  "total" : 2,
  "max_score" : 24.0,
  "hits" : [ {
    "_index" : "scripts2",
    "_type" : "doc",
    "_id" : "2",
    "_score" : 24.0,
    "_source":{"name":"This is a second simple document"}
  }, {
    "_index" : "scripts2",
    "_type" : "doc",
    "_id" : "1",
    "_score" : 18.0,
    "_source":{"name":"This is the first document"}
  } ]
}
}
```

As we can see, it works. If we look at the formatted script, we would see something like the following:

```
def termInfo = _index['name'].get('document',_OFFSETS);
def sum = 0;
for (offset in termInfo) {
  sum += offset.startOffset;
};
return sum;
```

As you can see, it is nothing sophisticated. First, we get the information about the offsets in an object; next, we create a variable to hold our offsets sum. Then, we have a loop for all the offsets information (we can have multiple instances of offsets for different occurrences of the same term in a field) and, finally, we return the sum that makes our score for the document to be set to the returned value.

In addition to all what we talked about in the preceding section, we are also able to get information about term vectors if we turned them on during indexing. To do that, we can use the _index.termVectors() expression, which will return Apache Lucene Fields object instance. You can find more about the Fields object in Lucene Javadocs available at https://lucene.apache.org/core/4_9_0/core/org/apache/lucene/index/Fields.html.

Lucene expressions explained

Although marked as experimental, we decided to talk about it because this is a new and very good feature. The reason that makes Lucene expressions very handy is using them is very fast—their execution is as fast as native scripts, but yet they are like dynamic scripts with some limitations. This section will show you what you can do with Lucene expressions.

The basics

Lucene provides functionality to compile a JavaScript expression to a Java bytecode. This is how Lucene expressions work and this is why they are as fast as native Elasticsearch scripts. Lucene expressions can be used in the following Elasticsearch functionalities:

- Scripts responsible for sorting
- Aggregations that work on numeric fields
- In the `function_score` query in the `script_score` query
- In queries using `script_fields`

In addition to this, you have to remember that:

- Lucene expressions can be only used on numeric fields
- Stored fields can't be accessed using Lucene expressions
- Missing values for a field will be given a value of 0
- You can use `_score` to access the document score and `doc['field_name'].value` to access the value of a single valued numeric field in the document
- No loops are possible, only single statements

An example

Knowing the preceding information, we can try using Lucene expressions to modify the score of our documents. Let's get back to our `library` index and try to increase the score of the given document by 10% of the year it was originally released. To do this, we could run the following query:

```
curl -XGET 'localhost:9200/library/_search?pretty' -d '{
 "fields" : [ "_id", "_score", "title" ],
 "query" : {
  "function_score" : {
```

```
      "query" : {
       "match_all" : {}
      },
      "script_score" : {
       "lang" : "expression",
       "script" : "_score + doc[\"year\"].value * percentage",
       "params" : {
        "percentage" : 0.1
       }
      }
     }
    }
   }
  }'
```

The query is very simple, but let's discuss its structure. First, we are using the `match_all` query wrapped in the `function_score` query because we want all documents to match and we want to use script for scoring. We are also setting the script language to `expression` (by setting the `lang` property to `expression`) to tell Elasticsearch that our script is a Lucene expressions script. Of course, we provide the script and we parameterize it, just like we would with any other script. The results of the preceding query look as follows:

```
{
  "took" : 4,
  "timed_out" : false,
  "_shards" : {
    "total" : 5,
    "successful" : 5,
    "failed" : 0
  },
  "hits" : {
    "total" : 6,
    "max_score" : 197.1,
    "hits" : [ {
      "_index" : "library",
      "_type" : "book",
      "_id" : "2",
      "_score" : 197.1,
      "fields" : {
        "title" : [ "Catch-22" ],
        "_id" : "2"
```

```
            }
    }, {
        "_index" : "library",
        "_type" : "book",
        "_id" : "3",
        "_score" : 194.6,
        "fields" : {
            "title" : [ "The Complete Sherlock Holmes" ],
            "_id" : "3"
        }
    }, {
        "_index" : "library",
        "_type" : "book",
        "_id" : "1",
        "_score" : 193.9,
        "fields" : {
            "title" : [ "All Quiet on the Western Front" ],
            "_id" : "1"
        }
    }, {
        "_index" : "library",
        "_type" : "book",
        "_id" : "6",
        "_score" : 191.4,
        "fields" : {
            "title" : [ "The Peasants" ],
            "_id" : "6"
        }
    }, {
        "_index" : "library",
        "_type" : "book",
        "_id" : "4",
        "_score" : 189.6,
        "fields" : {
            "title" : [ "Crime and Punishment" ],
            "_id" : "4"
        }
    }, {
        "_index" : "library",
        "_type" : "book",
        "_id" : "5",
        "_score" : 178.4,
        "fields" : {
```

```
        "title" : [ "The Sorrows of Young Werther" ],
        "_id" : "5"
      }
    } ]
  }
}
```

As we can see, Elasticsearch did what it was asked to do.

There is more

Of course, the provided example is a very simple one. If you are interested in what Lucene expressions provide, please visit the official Javadocs available at `http://lucene.apache.org/core/4_9_0/expressions/index.html?org/apache/lucene/expressions/js/package-summary.html`. The documents available at the given URL provide more information about what Lucene exposes in expressions module.

Summary

In this chapter, we extended our knowledge about query handling and data analysis. First of all, we discussed query rescore, which can help us when we need to recalculate the score of the top documents returned by a query. We also learned how to control multimatching queries. After that, we looked at two new aggregation types—one allowing us to get significant terms from a set of results and the other allowing documents grouping: a highly anticipated feature. We also discussed differences in relationship handling and approaches we can take when using Elasticsearch. Finally, we extended our knowledge about the Elasticsearch scripting module and we've learned what changes were introduced after Elasticsearch 1.0.

In the next chapter, we will try to improve our user query experience. We will start with user spelling mistakes and how Elasticsearch can help us by turning mistakes into good queries. We will also see what approaches we can take to handle user spelling mistake situations. After that, we will discuss improving query relevance on a given example. We will show you a query returning poor results and we will tune the query to match our needs.

4
Improving the User Search Experience

In the previous chapter, we extended our knowledge about query handling and data analysis. We started by looking at the query rescore that can help us when we need to recalculate the score of the top documents returned by a query. We controlled multi matching in Elasticsearch queries and looked at two new exciting aggregation types: significant terms aggregation and top hits aggregation. We discussed the differences in relationship handling and, finally, we extended our knowledge about the Elasticsearch scripting module and learned what the changes introduced were after the release of Elasticsearch 1.0. By the end of this chapter, we will have covered the following topics:

- Using the Elasticsearch Suggest API to correct user spelling mistakes
- Using the term suggester to suggest single words
- Using the phrase suggester to suggest whole phrases
- Configuring suggest capabilities to match your needs
- Using the completion suggester for the autocomplete functionality
- Improving query relevance by using different Elasticsearch functionalities

Correcting user spelling mistakes

One of the simplest ways to improve the user search experience is to correct their spelling mistakes either automatically or by just showing the correct query phrase and allowing the user to use it. For example, this is what **Google** shows us when we type in elasticsaerch instead of Elasticsearch:

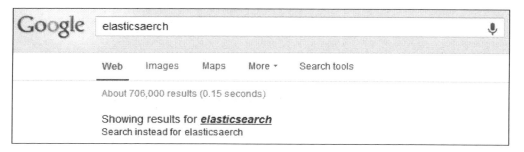

Starting from 0.90.0 Beta1, Elasticsearch allows us to use the Suggest API to correct the user spelling mistakes. With the newer versions of Elasticsearch, the API was changed, bringing new features and becoming more and more powerful. In this section, we will try to bring you a comprehensive guide on how to use the Suggest API provided by Elasticsearch, both in simple use cases and in ones that require more configuration.

Testing data

For the purpose of this section, we decided that we need a bit more data than a few documents. In order to get the data we need, we decided to use the *Wikipedia* river plugin (https://github.com/elasticsearch/elasticsearch-river-wikipedia) to index some public documents from *Wikipedia*. First, we need to install the plugin by running the following command:

```
bin/plugin -install elasticsearch/elasticsearch-river-wikipedia/2.4.1
```

After that, we run the following command:

```
curl -XPUT 'localhost:9200/_river/wikipedia_river/_meta' -d '{
  "type" : "wikipedia",
  "index" : {
   "index" : "wikipedia"
  }
}'
```

After that, Elasticsearch will start indexing the latest English dump from Wikipedia. If you look at the logs, you should see something like this:

```
[2014-08-28 22:35:01,566][INFO ][river.wikipedia         ] [Thing]
   [wikipedia][Wikipedia_river] creating wikipedia stream river for
   [http://download.wikimedia.org/enwiki/latest/enwiki-latest-pages-
   articles.xml.bz2]
[2014-08-28 22:35:01,568][INFO ][river.wikipedia         ] [Thing]
   [wikipedia][Wikipedia_river] starting wikipedia stream
```

As you can see, the river has started its work. After some time, you will have the data indexed in the index called wikipedia. If you want all data from the latest English Wikipedia dump to be indexed, you have to be patient, and we are not. The number of documents when we decided to cancel the indexation was 7080049. The index had about 19 GB in total size (without replicas).

Getting into technical details

Introduced in Version 0.90.3, the Suggest API is not the simplest one available in Elasticsearch. In order to get the desired suggest, we can either add a new suggest section to the query, or we can use a specialized REST endpoint that Elasticsearch exposes. In addition to this, we have multiple suggest implementations that allow us to correct user spelling mistakes, create the autocomplete functionality, and so on. All this gives us a powerful and flexible mechanism that we can use in order to make our search better.

Of course, the suggest functionality works on our data, so if we have a small set of documents in the index, the proper suggestion may not be found. When dealing with a smaller data set, Elasticsearch has fewer words in the index and, because of that, it has fewer candidates for suggestions. On the other hand, the more data, the bigger the possibility that we will have data that has some mistakes; however, we can configure Elasticsearch internals to handle such situations.

Please note that the layout of this chapter is a bit different. We start by showing you a simple example on how to query for suggestions and how to interpret the Suggest API response without getting too much into all the configuration options. We do this because we don't want to overwhelm you with technical details, but we want to show you what you can achieve. The nifty configuration parameters come later.

Suggesters

Before we continue with querying and analyzing the responses, we would like to write a few words about the available suggester types—the functionality responsible for finding suggestions when using the Elasticsearch Suggest API. Elasticsearch allows us to use three suggesters currently: the `term` one, the `phrase` one, and the `completion` one. The first two allow us to correct spelling mistakes, while the third one allows us to develop a very fast autocomplete functionality. However, for now, let's not focus on any particular suggester type, but let's look on the query possibilities and the responses returned by Elasticsearch. We will try to show you the general principles, and then we will get into more details about each of the available suggesters.

Using the _suggest REST endpoint

There is a possibility that we can get suggestions for a given text by using a dedicated _suggest REST endpoint. What we need to provide is the text to analyze and the type of used suggester (term or phrase). So if we would like to get suggestions for the words graphics desiganer (note that we've misspelled the word on purpose), we would run the following query:

```
curl -XPOST 'localhost:9200/wikipedia/_suggest?pretty' -d '{
  "first_suggestion" : {
   "text" : "wordl war ii",
   "term" : {
    "field" : "_all"
   }
  }
}'
```

As you can see, each suggestion request is send to Elasticsearch in its own object with the name we chose (in the preceding case, it is `first_suggestion`). Next, we specify the text for which we want the suggestion to be returned using the `text` parameter. Finally, we add the `suggester` object, which is either `term` or `phrase` currently. The `suggester` object contains its configuration, which for the `term` suggester used in the preceding command, is the field we want to use for suggestions (the `field` property).

We can also send more than one suggestion at a time by adding multiple suggestion names. For example, if in addition to the preceding suggestion, we would also include a suggestion for the word `raceing`, we would use the following command:

```
curl -XPOST 'localhost:9200/wikipedia/_suggest?pretty' -d '{
  "first_suggestion" : {
```

```
  "text" : "wordl war ii",
  "term" : {
   "field" : "_all"
  }
 },
 "second_suggestion" : {
  "text" : "raceing",
  "term" : {
   "field" : "text"
  }
 }
}'
```

Understanding the REST endpoint suggester response

Let's now look at the example response we can expect from the _suggest REST endpoint call. Although the response will differ for each suggester type, let's look at the response returned by Elasticsearch for the first command we've sent in the preceding code that used the term suggester:

```
{
  "_shards" : {
    "total" : 5,
    "successful" : 5,
    "failed" : 0
  },
  "first_suggestion" : [ {
    "text" : "wordl",
    "offset" : 0,
    "length" : 5,
    "options" : [ {
      "text" : "world",
      "score" : 0.8,
      "freq" : 130828
    }, {
      "text" : "words",
      "score" : 0.8,
      "freq" : 20854
    }, {
```

```
              "text" : "wordy",
              "score" : 0.8,
              "freq" : 210
          }, {
              "text" : "woudl",
              "score" : 0.8,
              "freq" : 29
          }, {
              "text" : "worde",
              "score" : 0.8,
              "freq" : 20
          } ]
      }, {
        "text" : "war",
        "offset" : 6,
        "length" : 3,
        "options" : [ ]
      }, {
        "text" : "ii",
        "offset" : 10,
        "length" : 2,
        "options" : [ ]
      } ]
  }
```

As you can see in the preceding response, the term suggester returns a list of possible suggestions for each term that was present in the text parameter of our first_suggestion section. For each term, the term suggester will return an array of possible suggestions with additional information. Looking at the data returned for the wordl term, we can see the original word (the text parameter), its offset in the original text parameter (the offset parameter), and its length (the length parameter).

The options array contains suggestions for the given word and will be empty if Elasticsearch doesn't find any suggestions. Each entry in this array is a suggestion and is characterized by the following properties:

- text: This is the text of the suggestion.
- score: This is the suggestion score; the higher the score, the better the suggestion will be.
- freq: This is the frequency of the suggestion. The frequency represents how many times the word appears in documents in the index we are running the suggestion query against. The higher the frequency, the more documents will have the suggested word in its fields and the higher the chance that the suggestion is the one we are looking for.

Please remember that the phrase suggester response will differ from the one returned by the terms suggester, and we will discuss the response of the phrase suggester later in this section.

Including suggestion requests in query

In addition to using the _suggest REST endpoint, we can include the suggest section in addition to the query section in the normal query sent to Elasticsearch. For example, if we would like to get the same suggestion we've got in the first example but during query execution, we could send the following query:

```
curl -XGET 'localhost:9200/wikipedia/_search?pretty' -d '{
  "query" : {
   "match_all" : {}
  },
  "suggest" : {
   "first_suggestion" : {
    "text" : "wordl war ii",
    "term" : {
     "field" : "_all"
    }
   }
  }
}'
```

As you would expect, the response for the preceding query would be the query results and the suggestions as follows:

```
{
   "took" : 5,
   "timed_out" : false,
   "_shards" : {
     "total" : 5,
     "successful" : 5,
     "failed" : 0
   },
   "hits" : {
     "total" : 7080049,
     "max_score" : 1.0,
     "hits" : [
```

```
        ...
    ]
  },
  "suggest" : {
    "first_suggestion" : [ {
      "text" : "wordl",
      "offset" : 0,
      "length" : 5,
      "options" : [ {
        "text" : "world",
        "score" : 0.8,
        "freq" : 130828
      }, {
        "text" : "words",
        "score" : 0.8,
        "freq" : 20854
      }, {
        "text" : "wordy",
        "score" : 0.8,
        "freq" : 210
      }, {
        "text" : "woudl",
        "score" : 0.8,
        "freq" : 29
      }, {
        "text" : "worde",
        "score" : 0.8,
        "freq" : 20
      } ]
    }, {
      "text" : "war",
      "offset" : 6,
      "length" : 3,
      "options" : [ ]
    }, {
      "text" : "ii",
      "offset" : 10,
      "length" : 2,
      "options" : [ ]
    } ]
  }
}
```

As we can see, we've got both search results and the suggestions whose structure we've already discussed earlier in this section.

There is one more possibility—if we have the same suggestion text, but we want multiple suggestion types, we can embed our suggestions in the suggest object and place the text property as the suggest object option. For example, if we would like to get suggestions for the wordl war ii text for the text field and for the _all field, we could run the following command:

```
curl -XGET 'localhost:9200/wikipedia/_search?pretty' -d '{
 "query" : {
  "match_all" : {}
 },
 "suggest" : {
  "text" : "wordl war ii",
  "first_suggestion" : {
   "term" : {
    "field" : "_all"
   }
  },
  "second_suggestion" : {
   "term" : {
    "field" : "text"
   }
  }
 }
}'
```

We now know how to make a query with suggestions returned or how to use the _suggest REST endpoint. Let's now get into more details of each of the available suggester types.

The term suggester

The `term` suggester works on the basis of the edit distance, which means that the suggestion with fewer characters that needs to be changed or removed to make the suggestion look like the original word is the best one. For example, let's take the words `worl` and `work`. In order to change the `worl` term to `work`, we need to change the `l` letter to `k`, so it means a distance of one. Of course, the text provided to the suggester is analyzed and then terms are chosen to be suggested. Let's now look at how we can configure the Elasticsearch `term` suggester.

Configuration

The Elasticsearch term suggester supports multiple configuration properties that allow us to tune its behavior to match our needs and to work with our data. Of course, we've already seen how it works and what it can give us, so we will concentrate on configuration now.

Common term suggester options

The common term suggester options can be used for all the suggester implementations that are based on the term suggester. Currently, these are the `phrase` suggester and, of course, the base `term` suggester. The available options are:

- `text`: This is the text we want to get the suggestions for. This parameter is required in order for the suggester to work.

- `field`: This is another required parameter. The field parameter allows us to set which field the suggestions should be generated for. For example, if we only want to consider title field terms in suggestions, we should set this parameter value to the title.

- `analyzer`: This is the name of the analyzer that should be used to analyze the text provided in the text parameter. If not set, Elasticsearch will use the analyzer used for the field provided by the field parameter.

- `size`: This is the maximum number of suggestions that are allowed to be returned by each term provided in the text parameter. It defaults to 5.

- `sort`: This allows us to specify how suggestions are sorted in the result returned by Elasticsearch. By default, this is set to a score, which tells Elasticsearch that the suggestions should be sorted by the suggestion score first, suggestion document frequency next, and finally, by the term. The second possible value is the frequency, which means that the results are first sorted by the document frequency, then by score, and finally, by the term.

- `suggest_mode`: This is another suggestion parameter that allows us to control which suggestions will be included in the Elasticsearch response. Currently, there are three values that can be passed to this parameter: `missing`, `popular`, and `always`. The default `missing` value will tell Elasticsearch to generate suggestions to only those words that are provided in the `text` parameter that doesn't exist in the index. If this property will be set to `popular`, then the term suggester will only suggest terms that are more popular (exist in more documents) than the original term for which the suggestion is generated. The last value, which is `always`, will result in a suggestion generated for each of the words in the `text` parameter.

Additional term suggester options

In addition to the common term suggester options, Elasticsearch allows us to use additional ones that will only make sense for the term suggester itself. These options are as follows:

- `lowercase_terms`: When set to `true`, this will tell Elasticsearch to make all terms that are produced from the `text` field after analysis, lowercase.

- `max_edits`: This defaults to `2` and specifies the maximum edit distance that the suggestion can have for it to be returned as a term suggestion. Elasticsearch allows us to set this value to `1` or `2`. Setting this value to `1` can result in fewer suggestions or no suggestions at all for words with many spelling mistakes. In general, if you see many suggestions that are not correct, because of errors, you can try setting `max_edits` to `1`.

- `prefix_length`: Because spelling mistakes usually don't appear at the beginning of the word, Elasticsearch allows us to set how much of the suggestion's initial characters must match with the initial characters of the original term. By default, this property is set to `1`. If we are struggling with the suggester performance increasing, this value will improve the overall performance, because less suggestions will be needed to be processed by Elasticsearch.

- `min_word_length`: This defaults to `4` and specifies the minimum number of characters a suggestion must have in order to be returned on the suggestions list.

- `shard_size`: This defaults to the value specified by the `size` parameter and allows us to set the maximum number of suggestions that should be read from each shard. Setting this property to values higher than the `size` parameter can result in more accurate document frequency (this is because of the fact that terms are held in different shards for our indices unless we have a single shard index created) being calculated but will also result in degradation of the spellchecker's performance.

- `max_inspections`: This defaults to 5 and specifies how many candidates Elasticsearch will look at in order to find the words that can be used as suggestions. Elasticsearch will inspect a maximum of `shard_size` multiplied by the `max_inspections` candidates for suggestions. Setting this property to values higher than the default 5 may improve the suggester accuracy but can also decrease the performance.

- `min_doc_freq`: This defaults to 0, which means not enabled. It allows us to limit the returned suggestions to only those that appear in the number of documents higher than the value of this parameter (this is a per-shard value and not a globally counted one). For example, setting this parameter to 2 will result in suggestions that appear in at least two documents in a given shard. Setting this property to values higher than 0 can improve the quality of returned suggestions; however, it can also result in some suggestion not being returned because it has a low shard document frequency. This property can help us with removing suggestions that come from a low number of documents and may be erroneous. This parameter can be specified as a percentage; if we want to do this, its value must be less than 1. For example, 0.01 means 1 percent, which again means that the minimum frequency of the given suggestion needs to be higher than 1 percent of the total term frequency (of course, per shard).

- `max_term_freq`: This defaults to 0.01 and specifies the maximum number of documents the term from the `text` field can exist for it to be considered a candidate for spellchecking. Similar to the `min_doc_freq` parameter, it can be either provided as an absolute number (such as 4 or 100), or it can be a percentage value if it is beyond 1 (for example, 0.01 means 1 percent). Please remember that this is also a per-shard frequency. The higher the value of this property, the better the overall performance of the spellchecker will be. In general, this property is very useful when we want to exclude terms that appear in many documents from spellchecking, because they are usually correct terms.

- `accuracy`: This defaults to 0.5 and can be a number from 0 to 1. It specifies how similar the term should be when compared to the original one. The higher the value, the more similar the terms need to be. This value is used in comparison during string distance calculation for each of the terms from the original input.

- `string_distance`: This specifies which algorithm should be used to compare how similar terms are when comparing them to each other. This is an expert setting. These options are available: `internal`, which is the default comparison algorithm based on an optimized implementation of the Damerau Levenshtein similarity algorithm; damerau_levenshtein, which is the implementation of the Damerau Levenshtein string distance algorithm (`http://en.wikipedia.org/wiki/Damerau%E2%80%93Levenshtein_distance`); levenstein, which is the implementation of the Levenshtein distance (`http://en.wikipedia.org/wiki/Levenshtein_distance`), jarowinkler, which is an implementation of the Jaro-Winkler distance algorithm (`http://en.wikipedia.org/wiki/Jaro%E2%80%93Winkler_distance`), and finally, ngram, which is an N-gram based distance algorithm.

Because of the fact that we've used the `terms` suggester during the initial examples, we decided to skip showing you how to query term suggesters and how the response looks. If you want to see how to query this suggester and what the response looks like, please refer to the beginning of the *Suggesters* section in this chapter.

The phrase suggester

The `term` suggester provides a great way to correct user spelling mistakes on a per-term basis. However, if we would like to get back phrases, it is not possible to do that when using this suggester. This is why the `phrase` suggester was introduced. It is built on top of the `term` suggester and adds additional phrase calculation logic to it so that whole phrases can be returned instead of individual terms. It uses N-gram based language models to calculate how good the suggestion is and will probably be a better choice to suggest whole phrases instead of the `term` suggester. The N-gram approach divides terms in the index into grams—word fragments built of one or more letters. For example, if we would like to divide the word `mastering` into bi-grams (a two letter N-gram), it would look like this: `ma as st te er ri in ng`.

If you want to read more about N-gram language models, refer to the Wikipedia article available at `http://en.wikipedia.org/wiki/Language_model#N-gram_models` and continue from there.

Usage example

Before we continue with all the possibilities, we have to configure the phrase
suggester; let's start with showing you an example of how to use it. This time, we
will run a simple query to the _search endpoint with only the suggests section in
it. We do this by running the following command:

```
curl -XGET 'localhost:9200/wikipedia/_search?pretty' -d '{
  "suggest" : {
   "text" : "wordl war ii",
   "our_suggestion" : {
    "phrase" : {
     "field" : "_all"
    }
   }
  }
}'
```

As you can see in the preceding command, it is almost the same as we sent
when using the term suggester, but instead of specifying the term suggester
type, we've specified the phrase type. The response to the preceding command
will be as follows:

```
{
   "took" : 58,
   "timed_out" : false,
   "_shards" : {
     "total" : 5,
     "successful" : 5,
     "failed" : 0
   },
   "hits" : {
     "total" : 7080049,
     "max_score" : 1.0,
     "hits" : [
     ...
     ]
   },
   "suggest" : {
     "our_suggestion" : [ {
       "text" : "wordl war ii",
       "offset" : 0,
```

```
      "length" : 12,
      "options" : [ {
        "text" : "world war ii",
        "score" : 7.055394E-5
      }, {
        "text" : "words war ii",
        "score" : 2.3738032E-5
      }, {
        "text" : "wordy war ii",
        "score" : 3.575829E-6
      }, {
        "text" : "worde war ii",
        "score" : 1.1586584E-6
      }, {
        "text" : "woudl war ii",
        "score" : 1.0753317E-6
      } ]
    } ]
  }
}
```

As you can see, the response is very similar to the one returned by the `term` suggester, but instead of a single word being returned as the suggestion for each term from the `text` field, it is already combined and Elasticsearch returns whole phrases. Of course, we can configure additional parameters in the `phrase` section and, now, we will look at what parameters are available for usage. Of course, the returned suggestions are sorted by their score by default.

Configuration

The `phrase` suggester configuration parameter can be divided into three groups: basic parameters that define the general behavior, the smoothing models configuration to balance N-grams' weights, and candidate generators that are responsible for producing the list of terms suggestions that will be used to return final suggestions.

Because the `phrase` suggester is based on the `term` suggester, it can also use some of the configuration options provided by it. These options are `text`, `size`, `analyzer`, and `shard_size`. Refer to the `term` suggester description earlier in this chapter to find out what they mean.

Basic configuration

In addition to properties mentioned in the preceding phrase, the suggester exposes the following basic options:

- `highlight`: This allows us to use suggestions highlighting. With the use of the `pre_tag` and `post_tag` properties, we can configure what prefix and postfix should be used to highlight suggestions. For example, if we would like to surround suggestions with the `<b>` and `</b>` tags, we should set `pre_tag` to `<b>` and `post_tag` to `</b>`.

- `gram_size`: This is the maximum size of the N-gram that is stored in the field and is specified by the `field` property. If the given field doesn't contain N-grams, this property should be set to `1` or not passed with the suggestion request at all. If not set, Elasticsearch will try to detect the proper value of this parameter by itself. For example, for fields using a `shingle` filter (http://www.elasticsearch.org/guide/en/elasticsearch/reference/current/analysis-shingle-tokenfilter.html), the value of this parameter will be set to the `max_shingle_size` property (of course, if not set explicitly).

- `confidence`: This is the parameter that allows us to limit the suggestion based on its score. The value of this parameter is applied to the score of the input phrase (the score is multiplied by the value of this parameter), and this score is used as a threshold for generated suggestions. If the suggestion score is higher than the calculated threshold, it will be included in the returned results; if not, then it will be dropped. For example, setting this parameter to `1.0` (which is the default value of it) will result in suggestions that are scored higher than the original phrase. On the other hand, setting it to `0.0` will result in the suggester returning all the suggestions (limited by the `size` parameter) no matter what their score is.

- `max_errors`: This is the property that allows us to specify the maximum number (or the percentage) of terms that can be erroneous (not correctly spelled) in order to create a correction using it. The value of this property can be either an integer number such as `1` or `5`, or it can be a float between 0 and 1, which will be treated as a percentage value. If we will set it as a float, it will specify the percentage of terms that can be erroneous. For example, a value of `0.5` will mean `50` percent. If we specify an integer number, such as `1` or `5`, Elasticsearch will treat it as a maximum number of erroneous terms. By default, it is set to `1`, which means that at most, a single term can be misspelled in a given correction.

- `separator`: This defaults to a whitespace character and specifies the separator that will be used to divide terms in the resulting bigram field.

- `force_unigrams`: This defaults to `true` and specifies whether the spellchecker should be forced to use a gram size of 1 (**unigram**).

- `token_limit`: This defaults to `10` and specifies the maximum number of tokens the corrections list can have in order for it to be returned. Setting this property to a value higher than the default one may improve the suggester accuracy at the cost of performance.

- `collate`: This allows us to check each suggestion against a specified query (using the `query` property inside the `collate` object) or filter (using the `filter` property inside the `collate` object). The provided query or filter is run as a template query and exposes the `{{suggestion}}` variable that represents the currently processed suggestion. By including an additional parameter called `prune` (in the `collate` object) and setting it to `true`, Elasticsearch will include the information if the suggestion matches the query or filter (this information will be included in the `collate_match` property in the results). In addition to this, the query preference can be included by using the `preference` property (which can take the same values as the ones used during the normal query processing).

- `real_word_error_likehood`: This is a percentage value, which defaults to `0.95` and specifies how likely it is that a term is misspelled even though it exists in the dictionary (built of the index). The default value of `0.95` tells Elasticsearch that `5%` of all terms that exist in its dictionary are misspelled. Lowering the value of this parameter will result in more terms being taken as misspelled ones even though they may be correct.

Let's now look at an example of using some of the preceding mentioned parameters, for example, suggestions highlighting. If we modify our initial phrase suggestion query and add highlighting, the command would look as follows:

```
curl -XGET 'localhost:9200/wikipedia/_search?pretty' -d '{
  "suggest" : {
   "text" : "wordl war ii",
   "our_suggestion" : {
    "phrase" : {
     "field" : "_all",
     "highlight" : {
      "pre_tag" : "<b>",
      "post_tag" : "</b>"
     },
     "collate" : {
```

```
      "prune" : true,
      "query" : {
       "match" : {
        "title" : "{{suggestion}}"
       }
      }
     }
    }
   }
  }
}'
```

The result returned by Elasticsearch for the preceding query would be as follows:

```
{
   "took" : 3,
   "timed_out" : false,
   "_shards" : {
     "total" : 5,
     "successful" : 5,
     "failed" : 0
   },
   "hits" : {
     "total" : 7080049,
     "max_score" : 1.0,
     "hits" : [
     ...
     ]
   },
     "suggest" : {
     "our_suggestion" : [ {
       "text" : "wordl war ii",
       "offset" : 0,
       "length" : 12,
       "options" : [ {
         "text" : "world war ii",
         "highlighted" : "<b>world</b> war ii",
         "score" : 7.055394E-5,
         "collate_match" : true
       }, {
         "text" : "words war ii",
```

```
          "highlighted" : "<b>words</b> war ii",
          "score" : 2.3738032E-5,
          "collate_match" : true
       }, {
          "text" : "wordy war ii",
          "highlighted" : "<b>wordy</b> war ii",
          "score" : 3.575829E-6,
          "collate_match" : true
       }, {
          "text" : "worde war ii",
          "highlighted" : "<b>worde</b> war ii",
          "score" : 1.1586584E-6,
          "collate_match" : true
       }, {
          "text" : "woudl war ii",
          "highlighted" : "<b>woudl</b> war ii",
          "score" : 1.0753317E-6,
          "collate_match" : true
       } ]
     } ]
  }
}
```

As you can see, the suggestions were highlighted.

Configuring smoothing models

A **Smoothing model** is a functionality of the phrase suggester whose responsibility is to measure the balance between the weight of infrequent N-grams that don't exist in the index and the frequent ones that exist in the index. It is rather an expert option and if you want to modify these N-grams, you should check suggester responses for your queries in order to see whether your suggestions are proper for your case. Smoothing is used in language models to avoid situations where the probability of a given term is equal to zero. The Elasticsearch phrase suggester supports multiple smoothing models.

 You can find out more about language models at http://en.wikipedia.org/wiki/Language_model.

In order to set which smoothing model we want to use, we need to add an object called smoothing and include a smoothing model name we want to use inside of it. Of course, we can include the properties we need or want to set for the given smoothing model. For example, we could run the following command:

```
curl -XGET 'localhost:9200/wikipedia/_search?pretty&size=0' -d '{
 "suggest" : {
  "text" : "wordl war ii",
  "generators_example_suggestion" : {
   "phrase" : {
    "analyzer" : "standard",
    "field" : "_all",
    "smoothing" : {
     "linear" : {
      "trigram_lambda" : 0.1,
      "bigram_lambda" : 0.6,
      "unigram_lambda" : 0.3
     }
    }
   }
  }
 }
}'
```

There are three smoothing models available in Elasticsearch. Let's now look at them.

Stupid backoff is the default smoothing model used by the Elasticsearch phrase suggester. In order to alter it or force its usage, we need to use the stupid_backoff name. The stupid backoff smoothing model is an implementation that will use a lower ordered N-gram (and will give it a discount equal to the value of the discount property) if the higher order N-gram count is equal to 0. To illustrate the example, let's assume that we use the ab bigram and the c unigram, which are common and exist in our index used by the suggester. However, we don't have the abc trigram present. What the stupid backoff model will do is that it will use the ab bigram model, because abc doesn't exist and, of course, the ab bigram model will be given a discount equal to the value of the discount property.

The stupid backoff model provides a single property that we can alter: discount. By default, it is set to 0.4, and it is used as a discount factor for the lower ordered N-gram model.

You can read more about N-gram smoothing models by looking at `http://en.wikipedia.org/wiki/N-gram#Smoothing_techniques` and `http://en.wikipedia.org/wiki/Katz's_back-off_model` (which is similar to the `stupid backoff` model described).

The **Laplace** smoothing model is also called additive smoothing. When used (to use it, we need to use the `laplace` value as its name), a constant value equal to the value of the `alpha` parameter (which is by `0.5` default) will be added to counts to balance weights of frequent and infrequent N-grams. As mentioned, the Laplace smoothing model can be configured using the `alpha` property, which is set to `0.5` by default. The usual values for this parameter are typically equal or below `1.0`.

You can read more about additive smoothing at `http://en.wikipedia.org/wiki/Additive_smoothing`.

Linear interpolation, the last smoothing model, takes the values of the lambdas provided in the configuration and uses them to calculate weights of trigrams, bigrams, and unigrams. In order to use the linear interpolation smoothing model, we need to provide the name of `linear` in the `smoothing` object in the suggester query and provide three parameters: `trigram_lambda`, `bigram_lambda`, and `unigram_lambda`. The sum of the values of the three mentioned parameters must be equal to `1`. Each of these parameters is a weight for a given type of N-gram; for example, the `bigram_lambda` parameter value will be used as a weights for bigrams.

Configuring candidate generators

In order to return possible suggestions for a term from the text provided in the `text` parameter, Elasticsearch uses so-called **candidate generators**. You can think of candidate generators as term suggesters although they are not exactly the same—they are similar, because they are used for every single term in the query provided to suggester. After the candidate terms are returned, they are scored in combination with suggestions for other terms from the text, and this way, the phrase suggestions are built.

Currently, **direct generators** are the only candidate generators available in Elasticsearch, although we can expect more of them to be present in the future. Elasticsearch allows us to provide multiple direct generators in a single phrase suggester request. We can do this by providing the list named `direct_generators`. For example, we could run the following command:

```
curl -XGET 'localhost:9200/wikipedia/_search?pretty&size=0' -d '{
  "suggest" : {
    "text" : "wordl war ii",
```

```
"generators_example_suggestion" : {
 "phrase" : {
  "analyzer" : "standard",
  "field" : "_all",
  "direct_generator" : [
   {
    "field" : "_all",
    "suggest_mode" : "always",
    "min_word_len" : 2
   },
   {
    "field" : "_all",
    "suggest_mode" : "always",
    "min_word_len" : 3
   }
  ]
 }
 }
 }
}'
```

The response should be very similar to the one previously shown, so we decided to omit it.

Configuring direct generators

Direct generators allow us to configure their behavior by using a parameter similar to that exposed by the terms suggester. These common configuration parameters are field (which is required), size, suggest_mode, max_edits, prefix_length, min_word_length (in this case, it defaults to 4), max_inspections, min_doc_freq, and max_term_freq. Refer to the term suggester description to see what these parameters mean.

In addition to the mentioned properties, direct generators allow us to use the pre_filter and post_filter properties. These two properties allow us to provide an analyzer name that Elasticsearch will use. The analyzer specified by the pre_filter property will be used for each term passed to the direct generator, and the filter specified by the post_filter property will be used after it is returned by the direct generator, just before these terms are passed to the phrase scorer for scoring.

For example, we could use the filtering functionality of the direct generators to include synonyms just before the suggestions are passed to the direct generator using the pre_filter property. For example, let's update our wikipedia index settings to include simple synonyms, and let's use them in filtering. To do this, we start with updating the settings with the following commands:

```
curl -XPOST 'localhost:9200/wikipedia/_close'
curl -XPUT 'localhost:9200/wikipedia/_settings' -d '{
  "settings" : {
   "index" : {
    "analysis": {
     "analyzer" : {
      "sample_synonyms_analyzer": {
       "tokenizer": "standard",
       "filter": [
        "sample_synonyms"
       ]
      }
     },
     "filter": {
      "sample_synonyms": {
       "type" : "synonym",
       "synonyms" : [
        "war => conflict"
       ]
      }
     }
    }
   }
  }
}'
curl -XPOST 'localhost:9200/wikipedia/_open'
```

First, we need to close the index, update the setting, and then open it again because Elasticsearch won't allow us to change analysis settings on opened indices. Now we can test our direct generator with synonyms with the following command:

```
curl -XGET 'localhost:9200/wikipedia/_search?pretty&size=0' -d '{
  "suggest" : {
   "text" : "wordl war ii",
   "generators_with_synonyms" : {
    "phrase" : {
     "analyzer" : "standard",
     "field" : "_all",
     "direct_generator" : [
      {
       "field" : "_all",
       "suggest_mode" : "always",
       "post_filter" : "sample_synonyms_analyzer"
      }
     ]
    }
   }
  }
}'
```

The response to the preceding command should be as follows:

```
{
   "took" : 47,
   "timed_out" : false,
   "_shards" : {
     "total" : 5,
     "successful" : 5,
     "failed" : 0
   },
   "hits" : {
     "total" : 7080049,
     "max_score" : 0.0,
     "hits" : [ ]
   },
   "suggest" : {
     "generators_with_synonyms" : [ {
       "text" : "wordl war ii",
```

```
      "offset" : 0,
      "length" : 12,
      "options" : [ {
        "text" : "world war ii",
        "score" : 7.055394E-5
      }, {
        "text" : "words war ii",
        "score" : 2.4085322E-5
      }, {
        "text" : "world conflicts ii",
        "score" : 1.4253577E-5
      }, {
        "text" : "words conflicts ii",
        "score" : 4.8214292E-6
      }, {
        "text" : "wordy war ii",
        "score" : 4.1216194E-6
      } ]
    } ]
  }
}
```

As you can see, instead of the `war` term, the `conflict` term was returned for some of the `phrase` suggester results. So, our synonyms' configuration was taken into consideration. However, please remember that the synonyms were taken before the scoring of the fragments, so it can happen that the suggestions with the synonyms are not the ones that are scored the most, and you will not be able to see them in the suggester results.

The completion suggester

With the release of Elasticsearch 0.90.3, we were given the possibility to use a prefix-based suggester. It allows us to create the autocomplete functionality in a very performance-effective way because of storing complicated structures in the index instead of calculating them during query time. Although this suggester is not about correcting user spelling mistakes, we thought that it will be good to show at least a simple example of this highly efficient suggester.

The logic behind the completion suggester

The prefix suggester is based on the data structure called **Finite State Transducer** (**FST**) (http://en.wikipedia.org/wiki/Finite_state_transducer). Although it is highly efficient, it may require significant resources to build on systems with large amounts of data in them: systems that Elasticsearch is perfectly suitable for. If we would like to build such a structure on the nodes after each restart or cluster state change, we may lose performance. Because of this, the Elasticsearch creators decided to use an FST-like structure during index time and store it in the index so that it can be loaded into the memory when needed.

Using the completion suggester

To use a prefix-based suggester we need to properly index our data with a dedicated field type called `completion`. It stores the FST-like structure in the index. In order to illustrate how to use this suggester, let's assume that we want to create an autocomplete feature to allow us to show book authors, which we store in an additional index. In addition to authors' names, we want to return the identifiers of the books they wrote in order to search for them with an additional query. We start with creating the `authors` index by running the following command:

```
curl -XPOST 'localhost:9200/authors' -d '{
  "mappings" : {
   "author" : {
    "properties" : {
     "name" : { "type" : "string" },
     "ac" : {
      "type" : "completion",
      "index_analyzer" : "simple",
      "search_analyzer" : "simple",
      "payloads" : true
     }
    }
   }
  }
}'
```

Our index will contain a single type called author. Each document will have two fields: the name field, which is the name of the author, and the ac field, which is the field we will use for autocomplete. The ac field is the one we are interested in; we've defined it using the completion type, which will result in storing the FST-like structure in the index. In addition to this, we've used the simple analyzer for both index and query time. The last thing is payload, which is the additional information we will return along with the suggestion; in our case, it will be an array of book identifiers.

 The type property for the field we will use for autocomplete is mandatory and should be set to completion. By default, the search_ analyzer and index_analyzer properties will be set to simple and the payloads property will be set to false.

Indexing data

To index the data, we need to provide some additional information in addition to what we usually provide during indexing. Let's look at the following commands that index two documents describing authors:

```
curl -XPOST 'localhost:9200/authors/author/1' -d '{
  "name" : "Fyodor Dostoevsky",
  "ac" : {
   "input" : [ "fyodor", "dostoevsky" ],
   "output" : "Fyodor Dostoevsky",
   "payload" : { "books" : [ "123456", "123457" ] }
  }
}'
curl -XPOST 'localhost:9200/authors/author/2' -d '{
  "name" : "Joseph Conrad",
  "ac" : {
   "input" : [ "joseph", "conrad" ],
   "output" : "Joseph Conrad",
   "payload" : { "books" : [ "121211" ] }
  }
}'
```

Notice the structure of the data for the ac field. We provide the input, output, and payload properties. The payload property is used to provide additional information that will be returned. The input property is used to provide input information that will be used to build the FST-like structure and will be used to match the user input to decide whether the document should be returned by the suggester. The output property is used to tell the suggester which data should be returned for the document.

 Please remember that the payload property must be a JSON object that starts with a { character and ends with a } character.

If the input and output property is the same in your case and you don't want to store payloads, you may index the documents just like you usually index your data. For example, the command to index our first document would look like this:

```
curl -XPOST 'localhost:9200/authors/author/3' -d '{
 "name" : "Stanislaw Lem",
 "ac" : [ "Stanislaw Lem" ]
}'
```

Querying data

Finally, let's look at how to query our indexed data. If we would like to find documents that have authors starting with fyo, we would run the following command:

```
curl -XGET 'localhost:9200/authors/_suggest?pretty' -d '{
 "authorsAutocomplete" : {
  "text" : "fyo",
  "completion" : {
   "field" : "ac"
  }
 }
}'
```

Before we look at the results, let's discuss the query. As you can see, we've run the command to the _suggest endpoint, because we don't want to run a standard query; we are just interested in autocomplete results. The rest of the query is exactly the same as the standard suggester query run against the _suggest endpoint, with the query type set to completion.

The results returned by Elasticsearch for the preceding query look as follows:

```
{
  "_shards" : {
    "total" : 5,
    "successful" : 5,
    "failed" : 0
  },
  "authorsAutocomplete" : [ {
    "text" : "fyo",
    "offset" : 0,
    "length" : 3,
    "options" : [ {
      "text" : "Fyodor Dostoevsky",
      "score" : 1.0,
      "payload":{"books":["123456","123457"]}
    } ]
  } ]
}
```

As you can see, in response, we've got the document we were looking for along with the payload information, which is the identifier of the books for that author.

Custom weights

By default, the term frequency will be used to determine the weight of the document returned by the prefix suggester. However, this may not be the best solution when you have multiple shards for your index, or your index is composed of multiple segments. In such cases, it is useful to define the weight of the suggestion by specifying the weight property for the field defined as completion; the weight property should be set to a positive integer value and not a float one like the boost for queries and documents. The higher the weight property value, the more important the suggestion is. This gives us plenty of opportunities to control how the returned suggestions will be sorted.

For example, if we would like to specify a weight for the first document in our example, we would run the following command:

```
curl -XPOST 'localhost:9200/authors/author/1' -d '{
 "name" : "Fyodor Dostoevsky",
 "ac" : {
  "input" : [ "fyodor", "dostoevsky" ],
  "output" : "Fyodor Dostoevsky",
```

```
  "payload" : { "books" : [ "123456", "123457" ] },
  "weight" : 80
 }
}'
```

Now, if we would run our example query, the results would be as follows:

```
{
  "_shards" : {
    "total" : 5,
    "successful" : 5,
    "failed" : 0
  },
  "authorsAutocomplete" : [ {
    "text" : "fyo",
    "offset" : 0,
    "length" : 3,
    "options" : [ {
      "text" : "Fyodor Dostoevsky",
      "score" : 80.0,
      "payload":{"books":["123456","123457"]}
    } ]
  } ]
}
```

See how the score of the result changed. In our initial example, it was 1.0 and, now, it is 80.0; this is because we've set the weight parameter to 80 during the indexing.

Additional parameters

There are three additional parameters supported by the suggester that we didn't mention till now. They are max_input_length, preserve_separators, and preserve_position_increments. Both preserve_separators and preserve_position_increments can be set to true or false. When setting the preserve_separators parameter to false, the suggester will omit separators such as whitespace (of course, proper analysis is required). Setting the preserve_position_increments parameter to false is needed if the first word in the suggestion is a stop word and we are using an analyzer that throws stop words away. For example, if we have The Clue as our document and the The word will be discarded by the analyzer by setting preserve_position_increments to false, the suggester will be able to return our document by specifying c as text.

The max_input_length property is set to 50 by default and specifies the maximum input length in UTF-16 characters. This limit is used at indexing time to limit the total number of characters stored in the internal structures.

Improving the query relevance

Elasticsearch and search engines in general are used for searching. Of course, some use cases may require browsing some portion of the indexed data; sometimes, it is even needed to export whole query results. However, in most cases, scoring is one of the factors that play a major role in the search process. As we said in the *Default Apache Lucene scoring explained* section of *Chapter 2, Power User Query DSL*, Elasticsearch leverages the Apache Lucene library document scoring capabilities and allows you to use different query types to manipulate the score of results returned by our queries. What's more, we can change the low-level algorithm used to calculate the score that we will describe in the *Altering Apache Lucene scoring* section of *Chapter 6, Low-level Index Control*.

Given all this, when we start designing our queries, we usually go for the simplest query that returns the documents we want. However, given all the things we can do in Elasticsearch when it comes to scoring control, such queries return results that are not the best when it comes to the user search experience. This is because Elasticsearch can't guess what our business logic is and what documents are the ones that are the best from our point of view when running a query. In this section, we will try to follow a real-life example of query relevance tuning. We want to make this chapter a bit different compared to the other ones. Instead of only giving you an insight, we have decided to give you a full example of when the query tuning process may look like. Of course, remember that this is only an example and you should adjust this process to match your organization needs. Some of the examples you find in this section may be general purpose ones, and when using them in your own application, make sure that they make sense to you.

Just to give you a little insight into what is coming, we will start with a simple query that returns the results we want, we will alter the query by introducing different Elasticsearch queries to make the results better, we will use filters, we will lower the score of the documents we think of as garbage, and finally, we will introduce faceting to render drill-down menus for users to allow the narrowing of results.

Data

Of course, in order to show you the results of the query modifications that we perform, we need data. We would love to show you the real-life data we were working with, but we can't, as our clients wouldn't like this. However, there is a solution to that: for the purpose of this section, we have decided to index Wikipedia data. To do that, we will reuse the installed Wikipedia river plugin that we installed in the *Correcting user spelling mistakes* section earlier in this chapter.

The Wikipedia river will create the `wikipedia` index for us if there is not an existing one. Because we already have such an index, we will delete it. We could go with the same index, but we know that we will need to adjust the index fields, because we need some additional analysis logic, and in order to not reindex the data, we create the index upfront.

> Remember to remove the old river before adding the new one. To remove the old river, you should just run the following command:
>
> ```
> curl -XDELETE 'localhost:9200/_river/
> wikipedia_river'
> ```

In order to reimport documents, we use the following commands:

```
curl -XDELETE 'localhost:9200/wikipedia'
curl -XPOST 'localhost:9200/wikipedia' -d'{
    "settings": {
        "index": {
            "analysis": {
                "analyzer": {
                    "keyword_ngram": {
                        "filter": [
                            "lowercase"
                        ],
                        "tokenizer": "ngram"
                    }
                }
            }
        }
    },
    "mappings": {
        "page": {
            "properties": {
                "category": {
                    "type": "string",
                    "fields": {
                        "untouched": {
```

```
            "type": "string",
            "index": "not_analyzed"
        }
    }
},
"disambiguation": {
    "type": "boolean"
},
"link": {
    "type": "string",
    "index": "not_analyzed"
},
"redirect": {
    "type": "boolean"
},
"redirect_page": {
    "type": "string"
},
"special": {
    "type": "boolean"
},
"stub": {
    "type": "boolean"
},
"text": {
    "type": "string"
},
"title": {
    "type": "string",
    "fields": {
        "ngram": {
            "type": "string",
            "analyzer": "keyword_ngram"
        },
        "simple": {
```

```
                        "type": "string",
                        "analyzer": "simple"
                }
            }
        }
    }
}
}'
```

For now, what we have to know is that we have a `page` type that we are interested in and whether that represents a Wikipedia page. We will use two fields for searching: the `text` and `title` fields. The first one holds the content of the page and the second one is responsible for holding its title.

What we have to do next is start the Wikipedia river. Because we were interested in the latest data in order to instantiate the river and start indexing, we've used the following command:

```
curl -XPUT 'localhost:9200/_river/wikipedia/_meta' -d '{
  "type" : "wikipedia"
}'
```

That's all; Elasticsearch will index the newest Wikipedia dump available to the index called `wikipedia`. All we have to do is wait. We were not patient, and we decided that we'll only index the first 10 million documents and, after our Wikipedia river hit that number of documents, we deleted it. We checked the final number of documents by running the following command:

```
curl -XGET 'localhost:9200/wikipedia/_search?q=*&size=0&pretty'
```

The response was as follows:

```
{
   "took" : 5,
   "timed_out" : false,
   "_shards" : {
     "total" : 5,
     "successful" : 5,
     "failed" : 0
   },
   "hits" : {
     "total" : 10425136,
```

```
        "max_score" : 0.0,
        "hits" : [ ]
    }
}
```

We can see that we have 10,425,136 documents in the index.

 When running examples from this chapter, please consider the fact that the data we've indexed changes over time, so the examples shown in this chapter may result in a different document if we run it after some time.

The quest for relevance improvement

After we have our indexed data, we are ready to begin the process of searching. We will start from the beginning using a simple query that will return the results we are interested in. After that, we will try to improve the query relevance. We will also try to pay attention to performance and notice the performance changes when they are most likely to happen.

The standard query

As you know, Elasticsearch includes the content of the documents in the _all field by default. So, why do we need to bother with specifying multiple fields in a query when we can use a single one, right? Going in that direction, let's assume that we've constructed the following query and now we send it to Elasticsearch to retrieve our precious documents using the following command:

```
curl -XGET 'localhost:9200/wikipedia/_search?fields=title&pretty' -d'
{
    "query": {
        "match": {
            "_all": {
                "query": "australian system",
                "operator": "OR"
            }
        }
    }
}'
```

Because we are only interested in getting the `title` field (Elasticsearch will use the _ source field to return the title field, because the title field is not stored), we've added the `fields=title` request parameter and, of course, we want it to be in a human-friendly formatting, so we added the `pretty` parameter as well.

However, the results were not as perfect as we would like them to be. The first page of documents were as follows (the whole JSON response can be found in the `response_query_standard.json` file provided with the book):

```
Australian Honours System
List of Australian Awards
Australian soccer league
Australian football league system
AANBUS
Australia Day Honours
Australian rating system
TAAATS
Australian Arbitration system
Western Australian Land Information System (WALIS)
```

While looking at the title of the documents, it seems that some of these that contain both words from the query have a lower rank than the others. Let's try to improve things.

The multi match query

What we can do first is not use the `_all` field at all. The reason for this is that we need to tell Elasticsearch what importance each of the fields has. For example, in our case, the `title` field is more important than the content of the field, which is stored in the `text` field. In order to inform this to ElasticSearch, we will use the `multi_match` query. To send such a query to Elasticsearch, we will use the following command:

```
curl -XGET 'localhost:9200/wikipedia/_search?fields=title&pretty' -d'
{
    "query": {
        "multi_match": {
            "query": "australian system",
            "fields": [
                "title^100",
                "text^10",
                "_all"
            ]
```

```
        }
    }
}'
```

The first page of results of the preceding query was as follows (the whole JSON response can be found in the `response_query_multi_match.json` file provided with the book):

```
Australian Antarctic Building System
Australian rating system
Australian Series System
Australian Arbitration system
Australian university system
Australian Integrated Forecast System
Australian Education System
The Australian electoral system
Australian preferential voting system
Australian Honours System
```

Instead of running the query against a single `_all` field, we chose to run it against the `title`, `text`, and `_all` fields. In addition to this, we introduced boosting: the higher the boost value, the more important the field will be (the default boost value for a field is `1.0`). So, we said that the `title` field is more important than the `text` field, and the `text` field is more important than `_all`.

If you look at the results now, they seem to be a bit more relevant but still not as good as we would like them to be. For example, look at the first and second documents on the results list. The first document's title is `Australian Antarctic Building System`, the second document's title is `Australian rating system`, and so on. I would like the second document to be higher than the first one.

Phrases comes into play

The next idea that should come into our minds is the introduction of phrase queries so that we can overcome the problem that was described previously. However, we still need the documents that don't have phrases included in the results just below the ones with the phrases present. So, we need to modify our query by adding the `bool` query on top. Our current query will come into the `must` section and the phrase query will go into the `should` section. An example command that sends the modified query would look as follows:

```
curl -XGET 'localhost:9200/wikipedia/_search?fields=title&pretty' -d'
{
    "query": {
```

```
      "bool": {
        "must": [
          {
            "multi_match": {
              "query": "australian system",
              "fields": [
                "title^100",
                "text^10",
                "_all"
              ]
            }
          }
        ],
        "should": [
          {
            "match_phrase": {
              "title": "australian system"
            }
          },
          {
            "match_phrase": {
              "text": "australian system"
            }
          }
        ]
      }
    }
}'
```

Now, if we look at the top results, they are as follows (the whole response can be found in the `response_query_phrase.json` file provided with the book):

```
Australian honours system
Australian Antarctic Building System
Australian rating system
Australian Series System
Australian Arbitration system
```

```
Australian university system
Australian Integrated Forecast System
Australian Education System
The Australian electoral system
Australian preferential voting system
```

We would really like to stop further query optimization, but our results are still not as good as we would like them to be, although they are a bit better. This is because we don't have all the phrases matched. What we can do is introduce the slop parameter, which will allow us to define how many words in between can be present for a match to be considered a phrase match. For example, our australian system query will be considered a phrase match for a document with the australian education system title and with a slop parameter of 1 or more. So, let's send our query with the slop parameter present by using the following command:

```
curl -XGET 'localhost:9200/wikipedia/_search?fields=title&pretty' -d'
{
    "query": {
      "bool": {
        "must": [
          {
            "multi_match": {
              "query": "australian system",
              "fields": [
                "title^100",
                "text^10",
                "_all"
              ]
            }
          }
        ],
        "should": [
          {
            "match_phrase": {
              "title": {
                "query": "australian system",
                "slop": 1
              }
            }
          }
```

```
        },
        {
            "match_phrase": {
                "text": {
                    "query": "australian system",
                    "slop": 1
                }
            }
        }
    ]
}
}
}'
```

Now, let's look at the results (the whole response can be found in the `response_query_phrase_slop.json` file provided with the book):

```
Australian Honours System
Australian honours system
Wikipedia:Articles for deletion/Australian university system
Australian rating system
Australian Series System
Australian Arbitration system
Australian university system
Australian Education System
The Australian electoral system
Australian Legal System
```

It seems that the results are now better. However, we can always do some more tweaking and see whether we can get some more improvements.

Let's throw the garbage away

What we can do now is that we can remove the garbage from our results. We can do this by removing redirect documents and special documents (for example, the ones that are marked for deletion). To do this, we will introduce a filter so that it doesn't mess with the scoring of other results (because filters are not scored). What's more, Elasticsearch will be able to cache filter results and reuse them in our queries and speed up their execution. The command that sends our query with filters will look as follows:

```
curl -XGET 'localhost:9200/wikipedia/_search?fields=title&pretty' -d'
{
```

```
"query": {
    "filtered": {
        "query": {
            "bool": {
                "must": [
                    {
                        "multi_match": {
                            "query": "australian system",
                            "fields": [
                                "title^100",
                                "text^10",
                                "_all"
                            ]
                        }
                    }
                ],
                "should": [
                    {
                        "match_phrase": {
                            "title": {
                                "query": "australian system",
                                "slop": 1
                            }
                        }
                    },
                    {
                        "match_phrase": {
                            "text": {
                                "query": "australian system",
                                "slop": 1
                            }
                        }
                    }
                ]
            }
        },
```

```
        "filter": {
          "bool": {
            "must_not": [
              {
                "term": {
                  "redirect": "true"
                }
              },
              {
                "term": {
                  "special": "true"
                }
              }
            ]
          }
        }
      }
    }
  }
}'
```

The results returned by it will look as follows:

```
Australian honours system
Australian Series System
Australian soccer league system
Australian Antarctic Building System
Australian Integrated Forecast System
Australian Defence Air Traffic System
Western Australian Land Information System
The Australian Advanced Air Traffic System
Australian archaeology
Australian Democrats
```

Isn't it better now? We think it is, but we can still make even more improvements.

Now, we boost

If you ever need to boost the importance of the phrase queries that we've introduced, we can do that by wrapping a phrase query with the `function_score` query. For example, if we want to have a phrase for the `title` field to have a boost of `1000`, we need to change the following part of the preceding query:

```
...
{
    "match_phrase": {
        "title": {
            "query": "australian system",
            "slop": 1
        }
    }
}
...
```

We need to replace the preceding part of the query with the following one:

```
...
{
    "function_score": {
        "boost_factor": 1000,
        "query": {
            "match_phrase": {
                "title": {
                    "query": "australian system",
                    "slop": 1
                }
            }
        }
    }
}
...
```

After introducing the preceding change, the documents with phrases will be scored even higher than before, but we will leave it for you to test.

Performing a misspelling-proof search

If you look back at the mappings, you will see that we have the `title` field defined as multi field and one of the fields is analyzed with a defined `ngram` analyzer. By default, it will create bigrams, so from the `system` word, it will create the `sy ys st te em` bigrams. Imagine that we could drop some of them during searches to make our search misspelling-proof. For the purpose of showing how we can do this, let's take a simple misspelled query sent with the following command:

```
curl -XGET 'localhost:9200/wikipedia/_search?fields=title&pretty' -d'
{
    "query": {
        "query_string": {
            "query": "austrelia",
            "default_field": "title",
            "minimum_should_match": "100%"
        }
    }
}'
```

The results returned by Elasticsearch would be as follows:

```
{
  "took" : 10,
  "timed_out" : false,
  "_shards" : {
    "total" : 5,
    "successful" : 5,
    "failed" : 0
  },
  "hits" : {
    "total" : 0,
    "max_score" : null,
    "hits" : [ ]
  }
}
```

We've sent a query that is misspelled against the `title` field and because there is no document with the misspelled term, we didn't get any results. So now, let's leverage the `title.ngram` field capabilities and omit some of the bigrams so that Elasticsearch can find some documents. Our command with a modified query looks as follows:

```
curl -XGET 'localhost:9200/wikipedia/_search?fields=title&pretty' -d'
{
    "query": {
      "query_string": {
         "query": "austrelia",
         "default_field": "title.ngram",
         "minimum_should_match": "85%"
      }
   }
}'
```

We changed the `default_field` property from `title` to `title.ngram` in order to inform Elasticsearch, the one with bigrams indexed. In addition to that, we've introduced the `minimum_should_match` property, and we've set it to 85 percent. This allows us to inform Elasticsearch that we don't want all the terms produced by the analysis process to match but only a percentage of them, and we don't care which terms these are.

> Lowering the value of the `minimum_should_match` property will give us more documents but a less accurate search. Setting the value of the `minimum_should_match` property to a higher one will result in the decrease of the documents returned, but they will have more bigrams similar to the query ones and, thus, they will be more relevant.

The top results returned by the preceding query are as follows (the whole result's response can be found in a file called `response_ngram.json` provided with the book):

```
Aurelia (Australia)
Australian Kestrel
Austrlia
Australian-Austrian relations
Australia-Austria relations
Australia–Austria relations
Australian religion
CARE Australia
Care Australia
Felix Austria
```

If you would like to see how to use the Elasticsearch suggester to handle spellchecking, refer to the *Correcting user spelling mistakes* section in this chapter.

Drill downs with faceting

The last thing we want to mention is faceting and aggregations. You can do multiple things with it, for example, calculating histograms, statistics for fields, geo distance ranges, and so on. However, one thing that can help your users get the data they are interested in is terms faceting. For example, if you go to `amazon.com` and enter the `kids shoes` query, you would see the following screenshot:

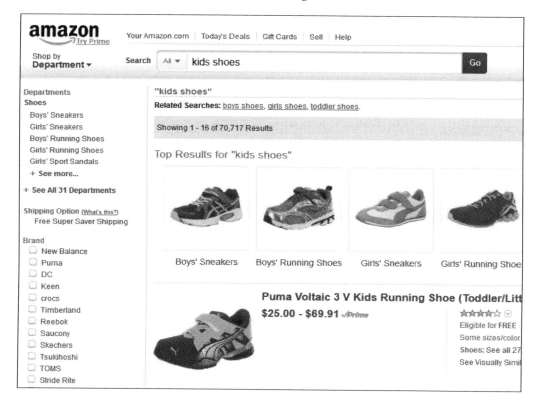

You can narrow down the results by the brand (the left-hand side of the page). The list of brands is not static and is generated on the basis of the results returned. We can achieve the same with terms faceting in Elasticsearch.

Please note that we are showing both queries with faceting and with aggregations. Faceting is deprecated and will be removed from Elasticsearch at some point. However, we know that our readers still use it and for that, we show different variants of the same query.

So now, let's get back to our Wikipedia data. Let's assume that we like to allow our users to choose the category of documents they want to see after the initial search. In order to do that, we add the facets section to our query (however, in order to simplify the example, let's use the `match_all` query instead of our complicated one) and send the new query with the following command:

```
curl -XGET 'localhost:9200/wikipedia/_search?fields=title&pretty' -d '{
    "query": {
        "match_all": {}
    },
    "facets": {
        "category_facet": {
            "terms": {
                "field": "category.untouched",
                "size": 10
            }
        }
    }
}'
```

As you can see, we've run the facet calculation on the `category.untouched` field, because terms faceting is calculated on the indexed data. If we run it on the `category` field, we will get a single term in the faceting result, and we want the whole category to be present. The faceting section of the results returned by the preceding query looks as follows (the entire result's response can be found in a file called `response_query_facets.json` provided with the book):

```
"facets" : {
  "category_facet" : {
    "_type" : "terms",
    "missing" : 6175806,
    "total" : 16732022,
    "other" : 16091291,
    "terms" : [ {
      "term" : "Living people",
```

```
          "count" : 483501
        }, {
          "term" : "Year of birth missing (living people)",
          "count" : 39413
        }, {
          "term" : "English-language films",
          "count" : 22917
        }, {
          "term" : "American films",
          "count" : 16139
        }, {
          "term" : "Year of birth unknown",
          "count" : 15561
        }, {
          "term" : "The Football League players",
          "count" : 14020
        }, {
          "term" : "Main Belt asteroids",
          "count" : 13968
        }, {
          "term" : "Black-and-white films",
          "count" : 12945
        }, {
          "term" : "Year of birth missing",
          "count" : 12442
        }, {
          "term" : "English footballers",
          "count" : 9825
        } ]
    }
  }
```

By default, we've got the faceting results sorted on the basis of the count property, which tells us how many documents belong to that particular category. Of course, we can do the same with aggregations by using the following query:

```
curl -XGET 'localhost:9200/wikipedia/_search?fields=title&pretty' -d '{
  "query": {
    "match_all": {}
  },
  "aggs": {
    "category_agg": {
```

```
        "terms": {
            "field": "category.untouched",
            "size": 10
        }
    }
}
}'
```

Now, if our user wants to narrow down its results to the `English-language films` category, we need to send the following query:

```
curl -XGET 'localhost:9200/wikipedia/_search?fields=title&pretty' -d '{
    "query": {
        "filtered": {
            "query" : {
                "match_all" : {}
            },
            "filter" : {
                "term": {
                    "category.untouched": "English-language films"
                }
            }
        }
    },
    "facets": {
        "category_facet": {
            "terms": {
                "field": "category.untouched",
                "size": 10
            }
        }
    }
}'
```

We've changed our query to include a filter and, thus, we've filtered down the documents set on which the faceting will be calculated.

Of course, we can do the same with aggregations by using the following query:

```
curl -XGET 'localhost:9200/wikipedia/_search?fields=title&pretty' -d '{
    "query": {
        "filtered": {
            "query" : {
                "match_all" : {}
            },
            "filter" : {
                "term": {
                    "category.untouched": "English-language films"
                }
            }
        }
    },
    "aggs": {
        "category_agg": {
            "terms": {
                "field": "category.untouched",
                "size": 10
            }
        }
    }
}'
```

Summary

In this chapter, we learned how to correct user spelling mistakes both by using the terms suggester and the phrase suggester, so now we know what to do in order to avoid empty pages that are a result of misspelling. In addition to that, we improved our users' query experience by improving the query relevance. We started with a simple query; we added multi match queries, phrase queries, boosts, and used query slops. We saw how to filter our garbage results and how to improve the phrase match importance. We used N-grams to avoid misspellings as an alternate method to using Elasticsearch suggesters. We've also discussed how to use faceting to allow our users to narrow down search results and thus simplify the way in which they can find the desired documents or products.

In the next chapter, we will finally get into performance-related topics, starting with discussions about Elasticsearch scaling. Then, we will discuss how to choose the right amount of shards and replicas for our deployment, and how routing can help us in our deployment. We will alter the default shard allocation logic, and we will adjust it to match our needs. Finally, we will see what Elasticsearch gives us when it comes to query execution logic and how we can control that to best match our deployment and indices architecture.

5
The Index Distribution Architecture

In the previous chapter, we were focused on improving the user search experience. We started with using the terms and phrase suggester to correct typos in user queries. In addition to that, we used the completion suggester to create an efficient, index time-calculated autocomplete functionality. Finally, we saw what Elasticsearch tuning may look like. We started with a simple query; we added multi match queries, phrase queries, boosts, and used query slops. We saw how to filter our garbage results and how to improve phrase match importance. We used n-grams to avoid misspellings as an alternate method to using Elasticsearch suggesters. We also discussed how to use faceting to allow our users to narrow down search results and thus simplify the way in which they can find the desired documents or products. By the end of this chapter, we will have covered:

- Choosing the right amount of shards and replicas
- Routing
- Shard allocation behavior adjustments
- Using query execution preference

Choosing the right amount of shards and replicas

In the beginning, when you started using Elasticsearch, you probably began by creating the index, importing your data to it and, after that, you started sending queries. We are pretty sure all worked well—at least in the beginning when the amount of data and the number of queries per second were not high. In the background, Elasticsearch created some shards and probably replicas as well (if you are using the default configuration, for example), and you didn't pay much attention to this part of the deployment.

When your application grows, you have to index more and more data and handle more and more queries per second. This is the point where everything changes. Problems start to appear (you can read about how we can handle the application's growth in *Chapter 8, Improving Performance*). It's now time to think about how you should plan your index and its configuration to rise with your application. In this chapter, we will give you some guidelines on how to handle this. Unfortunately, there is no exact recipe; each application has different characteristics and requirements, based on which, not only does the index structure depend, but also the configuration. For example, these factors can be ones like the size of the document or the whole index, query types, and the desired throughput.

Sharding and overallocation

You already know from the *Introducing Elasticsearch* section in *Chapter 1, Introduction to Elasticsearch*, what sharding is, but let's recall it. Sharding is the splitting of an Elasticsearch index to a set of smaller indices, which allows us to spread them among multiple nodes in the same cluster. While querying, the result is a sum of all the results that were returned by each shard of an index (although it's not really a sum, because a single shard may hold all the data we are interested in). By default, Elasticsearch creates five shards for every index even in a single-node environment. This redundancy is called overallocation: it seems to be totally not needed at this point and only leads to more complexity when indexing (spreading document to shards) and handling queries (querying shards and merging the results). Happily, this complexity is handled automatically, but why does Elasticsearch do this?

Let's say that we have an index that is built only of a single shard. This means that if our application grows above the capacity of a single machine, we will face a problem. In the current version of Elasticsearch, there is no possibility of splitting the index into multiple, smaller parts: we need to say how many shards the index should be built of when we create that index. What we can do is prepare a new index with more shards and reindex the data. However, such an operation requires additional time and server resources, such as CPU time, RAM, and mass storage. When it comes to the production environment, we don't always have the required time and mentioned resources. On the other hand, while using overallocation, we can just add a new server with Elasticsearch installed, and Elasticsearch will rebalance the cluster by moving parts of the index to the new machine without the additional cost of reindexing. The default configuration (which means five shards and one replica) chosen by the authors of Elasticsearch is the balance between the possibilities of growing and overhead resulting from the need to merge results from a different shard.

The default shard number of five is chosen for standard use cases. So now, this question arises: when should we start with more shards or, on the contrary, try to keep the number of shards as low as possible?

The first answer is obvious. If you have a limited and strongly defined data set, you can use only a single shard. If you do not, however, the rule of thumb dictates that the optimal number of shards be dependent on the target number of nodes. So, if you plan to use 10 nodes in the future, you need to configure the index to have 10 shards. One important thing to remember is that for high availability and query throughput, we should also configure replicas, and it also takes up room on the nodes just like the normal shard. If you have one additional copy of each shard (number_of_replicas equal to one), you end up with 20 shards — 10 with the main data and 10 with its replicas.

To sum up, our simple formula can be presented as follows:

```
max number of nodes = number of shards * (number of replicas + 1)
```

In other words, if you have planned to use 10 shards and you like to have two replicas, the maximum number of nodes that will hold the data for this setup will be 30.

A positive example of overallocation

If you carefully read the previous part of this chapter, you will have a strong conviction that you should use the minimal number of shards. However, sometimes, having more shards is handy, because a shard is, in fact, an Apache Lucene index, and more shards means that every operation executed on a single, smaller Lucene index (especially indexing) will be faster. Sometimes, this is a good enough reason to use many shards. Of course, there is the possible cost of splitting a query into multiple requests to each and every shard and merge the response from it. This can be avoided for particular types of applications where the queries are always filtered by the concrete parameter. This is the case with multitenant systems, where every query is run in the context of the defined user. The idea is simple; we can index the data of this user in a single shard and use only that shard during querying. This is in place when routing should be used (we will discuss it in detail in the *Routing explained* section in this chapter).

Multiple shards versus multiple indices

You may wonder whether, if a shard is the *de-facto* of a small Lucene index, what about true Elasticsearch indices? What is the difference between having multiple small shards and having multiple indices? Technically, the difference is not that great and, for some use cases, having more than a single index is the right approach (for example, to store time-based data such as logs in time-sliced indices). When you are using a single index with many shards, you can limit your operations to a single shard when using routing, for example. When dealing with indices, you may choose which data you are interested in; for example, choose only a few of your time-based indices using the `logs_2014-10-10,logs_2014-10-11,...` notation. More differences can be spotted in the shard and index-balancing logic, although we can configure both balancing logics.

Replicas

While sharding lets us store more data than we can fit on a single node, replicas are there to handle increasing throughput and, of course, for high availability and fault tolerance. When a node with the primary shard is lost, Elasticsearch can promote one of the available replicas to be a new primary shard. In the default configuration, Elasticsearch creates a single replica for each of the shards in the index. However, the number of replicas can be changed at any time using the Settings API. This is very convenient when we are at a point where we need more query throughput; increasing the number of replicas allows us to spread the querying load on more machine, which basically allows us to handle more parallel queries.

The drawback of using more replicas is obvious: the cost of additional space used by additional copies of each shard, the cost of indexing on nodes that host the replicas, and, of course, the cost of data copy between the primary shard and all the replicas. While choosing the number of shards, you should also consider how many replicas need to be present. If you select too many replicas, you can end up using disk space and Elasticsearch resources, when in fact, they won't be used. On the other hand, choosing to have none of the replicas may result in the data being lost if something bad happens to the primary shard.

Routing explained

In the *Choosing the right amount of shards and replicas* section in this chapter, we mentioned routing as a solution for the shards on which queries will be executed on a single one. Now it's time to look closer at this functionality.

Shards and data

Usually, it is not important how Elasticsearch divides data into shards and which shard holds the particular document. During query time, the query will be sent to all the shards of a particular index, so the only crucial thing is to use the algorithm that spreads our data evenly so that each shard contains similar amounts of data. We don't want one shard to hold 99 percent of the data while the other shard holds the rest—it is not efficient.

The situation complicates slightly when we want to remove or add a newer version of the document. Elasticsearch must be able to determine which shard should be updated. Although it may seem troublesome, in practice, it is not a huge problem. It is enough to use the sharding algorithm, which will always generate the same value for the same document identifier. If we have such an algorithm, Elasticsearch will know which shard to point to when dealing with a document.

However, there are times when it would be nice to be able to hit the same shard for some portion of data. For example, we would like to store every book of a particular type only on a particular shard and, while searching for that kind of book, we could avoid searching on many shards and merging results from them. Instead, because we know the value we used for routing, we could point Elasticsearch to the same shard we used during indexing. This is exactly what routing does. It allows us to provide information that will be used by Elasticsearch to determine which shard should be used for document storage and for querying; the same routing value will always result in the same shard. It's basically something like saying "search for documents on the shard where you've put the documents by using the provided routing value".

Let's test routing

To show you an example that will illustrate how Elasticsearch allocates shards and which documents are placed on the particular shard, we will use an additional plugin. It will help us visualize what Elasticsearch did with our data. Let's install the Paramedic plugin using the following command:

```
bin/plugin -install karmi/elasticsearch-paramedic
```

After restarting Elasticsearch, we can point our browser to `http://localhost:9200/_plugin/paramedic/index.html` and we will able to see a page with various statistics and information about indices. For our example, the most interesting information is the cluster color that indicates the cluster state and the list of shards and replicas next to every index.

Let's start two Elasticsearch nodes and create an index by running the following command:

```
curl -XPUT 'localhost:9200/documents' -d '{
  "settings": {
    "number_of_replicas": 0,
    "number_of_shards": 2
  }
}'
```

We've created an index without replicas, which is built of two shards. This means that the largest cluster can have only two nodes, and each next node cannot be filled with data unless we increase the number of replicas (you can read about this in the *Choosing the right amount of shards and replicas* section of this chapter). The next operation is to index some documents; we will do that by using the following commands:

```
curl -XPUT localhost:9200/documents/doc/1 -d '{ "title" : "Document
No. 1" }'
curl -XPUT localhost:9200/documents/doc/2 -d '{ "title" : "Document
No. 2" }'
curl -XPUT localhost:9200/documents/doc/3 -d '{ "title" : "Document
No. 3" }'
curl -XPUT localhost:9200/documents/doc/4 -d '{ "title" : "Document
No. 4" }'
```

After that, if we would look at the installed Paramedic plugin, we would see our two primary shards created and assigned.

In the information about nodes, we can also find the information that we are currently interested in. Each of the nodes in the cluster holds exactly two documents. This leads us to the conclusion that the sharding algorithm did its work perfectly, and we have an index that is built of shards that have evenly redistributed documents.

Now, let's create some chaos and let's shut down the second node. Now, using Paramedic, we should see something like this:

The first information we see is that the cluster is now in the red state. This means that at least one primary shard is missing, which tells us that some of the data is not available and some parts of the index are not available. Nevertheless, Elasticsearch allows us to execute queries; it is our decision as to what applications should do—inform the user about the possibility of incomplete results or block querying attempts. Let's try to run a simple query by using the following command:

```
curl -XGET 'localhost:9200/documents/_search?pretty'
```

The response returned by Elasticsearch will look as follows:

```
{
  "took" : 26,
  "timed_out" : false,
  "_shards" : {
    "total" : 2,
    "successful" : 1,
    "failed" : 0
  },
  "hits" : {
    "total" : 2,
    "max_score" : 1.0,
    "hits" : [ {
      "_index" : "documents",
      "_type" : "doc",
      "_id" : "2",
      "_score" : 1.0,
      "_source":{ "title" : "Document No. 2" }
    }, {
      "_index" : "documents",
      "_type" : "doc",
      "_id" : "4",
      "_score" : 1.0,
      "_source":{ "title" : "Document No. 4" }
    } ]
  }
}
```

As you can see, Elasticsearch returned the information about failures; we can see that one of the shards is not available. In the returned result set, we can only see the documents with identifiers of 2 and 4. Other documents have been lost, at least until the failed primary shard is back online. If you start the second node, after a while (depending on the network and gateway module settings), the cluster should return to the green state and all documents should be available. Now, we will try to do the same using routing, and we will try to observe the difference in the Elasticsearch behavior.

Indexing with routing

With routing, we can control the target shard Elasticsearch will choose to send the documents to by specifying the routing parameter. The value of the routing parameter is irrelevant; you can use whatever value you choose. The important thing is that the same value of the routing parameter should be used to place different documents together in the same shard. To say it simply, using the same routing value for different documents will ensure us that these documents will be placed in the same shard.

There are a few possibilities as to how we can provide the routing information to Elasticsearch. The simplest way is add the routing URI parameter when indexing a document, for example:

```
curl -XPUT localhost:9200/books/doc/1?routing=A -d '{ "title" :
"Document" }'
```

Of course, we can also provide the routing value when using bulk indexing. In such cases, routing is given in the metadata for each document by using the _routing property, for example:

```
curl -XPUT localhost:9200/_bulk --data-binary '
{ "index" : { "_index" : "books", "_type" : "doc", "_routing" : "A"
}}
{ "title" : "Document" }
'
```

Another option is to place a _routing field inside the document. However, this will work properly only when the _routing field is defined in the mappings. For example, let's create an index called books_routing by using the following command:

```
curl -XPUT 'localhost:9200/books_routing' -d '{
  "mappings": {
    "doc": {
```

```
    "_routing": {
      "required": true,
      "path": "_routing"
    },
    "properties": {
      "title" : {"type": "string" }
    }
  }
 }
}'
```

Now we can use `_routing` inside the document body, for example, like this:

```
curl -XPUT localhost:9200/books_routing/doc/1 -d '{ "title" :
"Document", "_routing" : "A" }'
```

In the preceding example, we used a `_routing` field. It is worth mentioning that the `path` parameter can point to any field that's not analyzed from the document. This is a very powerful feature and one of the main advantages of the routing feature. For example, if we extend our document with the `library_id` field's indicated library where the book is available, it is logical that all queries based on library can be more effective when we set up routing based on this `library_id` field. However, you have to remember that getting the routing value from a field requires additional parsing.

Routing in practice

Now let's get back to our initial example and do the same as what we did but now using routing. The first thing is to delete the old documents. If we do not do this and add documents with the same identifier, routing may cause that same document to now be placed in the other shard. Therefore, we run the following command to delete all the documents from our index:

```
curl -XDELETE 'localhost:9200/documents/_query?q=*:*'
```

After that, we index our data again, but this time, we add the routing information. The commands used to index our documents now look as follows:

```
curl -XPUT localhost:9200/documents/doc/1?routing=A -d '{ "title" :
"Document No. 1" }'
```

```
curl -XPUT localhost:9200/documents/doc/2?routing=B -d '{ "title" :
"Document No. 2" }'
```

```
curl -XPUT localhost:9200/documents/doc/3?routing=A -d '{ "title" :
"Document No. 3" }'
```

```
curl -XPUT localhost:9200/documents/doc/4?routing=A -d '{ "title" :
"Document No. 4" }'
```

As we said, the routing parameter tells Elasticsearch in which shard the document should be placed. Of course, it may happen that more than a single document will be placed in the same shard. That's because you usually have less shards than routing values. If we now kill one node, Paramedic will again show you the red cluster and the state. If we query for all the documents, Elasticsearch will return the following response (of course, it depends which node you kill):

```
curl -XGET 'localhost:9200/documents/_search?q=*&pretty'
```

The response from Elasticsearch would be as follows:

```
{
  "took" : 24,
  "timed_out" : false,
  "_shards" : {
    "total" : 2,
    "successful" : 1,
    "failed" : 0
  },
  "hits" : {
    "total" : 3,
    "max_score" : 1.0,
    "hits" : [ {
      "_index" : "documents",
      "_type" : "doc",
      "_id" : "1",
      "_score" : 1.0,
      "_source":{ "title" : "Document No. 1" }
    }, {
      "_index" : "documents",
      "_type" : "doc",
      "_id" : "3",
      "_score" : 1.0,
      "_source":{ "title" : "Document No. 3" }
    }, {
      "_index" : "documents",
      "_type" : "doc",
      "_id" : "4",
      "_score" : 1.0,
```

```
      "_source":{ "title" : "Document No. 4" }
    } ]
  }
}
```

In our case, the document with the identifier 2 is missing. We lost a node with the documents that had the routing value of B. If we were less lucky, we could lose three documents!

Querying

Routing allows us to tell Elasticsearch which shards should be used for querying. Why send queries to all the shards that build the index if we want to get data from a particular subset of the whole index? For example, to get the data from a shard where routing A was used, we can run the following query:

```
curl -XGET 'localhost:9200/documents/_search?pretty&q=*&routing=A'
```

We just added a routing parameter with the value we are interested in. Elasticsearch replied with the following result:

```
{
  "took" : 0,
  "timed_out" : false,
  "_shards" : {
    "total" : 1,
    "successful" : 1,
    "failed" : 0
  },
  "hits" : {
    "total" : 3,
    "max_score" : 1.0,
    "hits" : [ {
      "_index" : "documents",
      "_type" : "doc",
      "_id" : "1",
      "_score" : 1.0, "_source" : { "title" : "Document No. 1" }
    }, {
      "_index" : "documents",
      "_type" : "doc",
      "_id" : "3",
      "_score" : 1.0, "_source" : { "title" : "Document No. 3" }
    }, {
      "_index" : "documents",
```

```
          "_type" : "doc",
          "_id" : "4",
          "_score" : 1.0, "_source" : { "title" : "Document No. 4" }
      } ]
   }
}
```

Everything works like a charm. But look closer! We forgot to start the node that holds the shard with the documents that were indexed with the routing value of B. Even though we didn't have a full index view, the reply from Elasticsearch doesn't contain information about shard failures. This is proof that queries with routing hit only a chosen shard and ignore the rest. If we run the same query with routing=B, we will get an exception like the following one:

```
{
   "error" : "SearchPhaseExecutionException[Failed to execute phase
[query_fetch], all shards failed]",
   "status" : 503
}
```

We can test the preceding behavior by using the Search Shard API. For example, let's run the following command:

```
curl -XGET 'localhost:9200/documents/_search_shards?pretty&routing=A'
-d '{"query":"match_all":{}}'
```

The response from Elasticsearch would be as follows:

```
{
   "nodes" : {
     "QK5r_d5CSfaV1Wx78k633w" : {
       "name" : "Western Kid",
       "transport_address" : "inet[/10.0.2.15:9301]"
     }
   },
   "shards" : [ [ {
     "state" : "STARTED",
     "primary" : true,
     "node" : "QK5r_d5CSfaV1Wx78k633w",
     "relocating_node" : null,
     "shard" : 0,
     "index" : "documents"
   } ] ]
}
```

As we can see, only a single node will be queried.

There is one important thing that we would like to repeat. Routing ensures us that, during indexing, documents with the same routing value are indexed in the same shard. However, you need to remember that a given shard may have many documents with different routing values. Routing allows you to limit the number of shards used during queries, but it cannot replace filtering! This means that a query with routing and without routing should have the same set of filters. For example, if we use user identifiers as routing values if we search for that user's data, we should also include filters on that identifier.

Aliases

If you work as a search engine specialist, you probably want to hide some configuration details from programmers in order to allow them to work faster and not care about search details. In an ideal world, they should not worry about routing, shards, and replicas. Aliases allow us to use shards with routing as ordinary indices. For example, let's create an alias by running the following command:

```
curl -XPOST 'http://localhost:9200/_aliases' -d '{
  "actions" : [
    {
      "add" : {
        "index" : "documents",
        "alias" : "documentsA",
        "routing" : "A"
      }
    }
  ]
}'
```

In the preceding example, we created a named documentsA alias from the documents index. However, in addition to that, searching will be limited to the shard used when routing value A is used. Thanks to this approach, you can give information about the documentsA alias to developers, and they may use it for querying and indexing like any other index.

Multiple routing values

Elasticsearch gives us the possibility to search with several routing values in a single query. Depending on which shard documents with given routing values are placed, it could mean searching on one or more shards. Let's look at the following query:

```
curl -XGET 'localhost:9200/documents/_search?routing=A,B'
```

After executing it, Elasticsearch will send the search request to two shards in our index (which in our case, happens to be the whole index), because the routing value of A covers one of two shards of our index and the routing value of B covers the second shard of our index.

Of course, multiple routing values are supported in aliases as well. The following example shows you the usage of these features:

```
curl -XPOST 'http://localhost:9200/_aliases' -d '{
  "actions" : [
    {
      "add" : {
        "index" : "documents",
        "alias" : "documentsA",
        "search_routing" : "A,B",
        "index_routing" : "A"
      }
    }
  ]
}'
```

The preceding example shows you two additional configuration parameters we didn't talk about until now — we can define different values of routing for searching and indexing. In the preceding case, we've defined that during querying (the search_routing parameter) two values of routing (A and B) will be applied. When indexing (index_routing parameter), only one value (A) will be used. Note that indexing doesn't support multiple routing values, and you should also remember proper filtering (you can add it to your alias).

Altering the default shard allocation behavior

In *Elasticsearch Server Second Edition*, published by *Packt Publishing*, we talked about a number of things related to the shard allocation functionality provided by Elasticsearch. We discussed the Cluster Reroute API, shard rebalancing, and shard awareness. Although now very commonly used, these topics are very important if you want to be in full control of your Elasticsearch cluster. Because of that, we decided to extend the examples provided in *Elasticsearch Server Second Edition* and provide you with guidance on how to use Elasticsearch shards awareness and alter the default shard allocation mechanism.

Let's start with a simple example. We assume that we have a cluster built of four nodes that looks as follows:

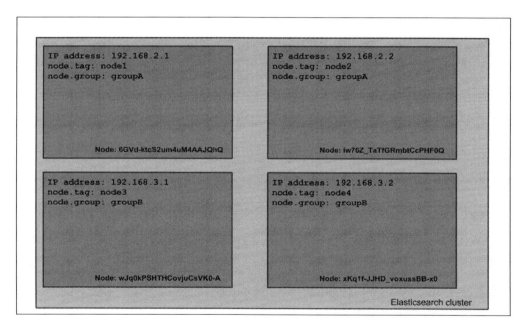

As you can see, our cluster is built of four nodes. Each node was bound to a specific IP address, and each node was given the `tag` property and a `group` property (added to `elasticsearch.yml` as `node.tag` and `node.group` properties). This cluster will serve the purpose of showing you how shard allocation filtering works. The `group` and `tag` properties can be given whatever names you want; you just need to prefix your desired property name with the `node` name; for example, if you would like to use a `party` property name, you would just add `node.party: party1` to your `elasticsearch.yml` file.

Allocation awareness

Allocation awareness allows us to configure shards and their replicas' allocation with the use of generic parameters. In order to illustrate how allocation awareness works, we will use our example cluster. For the example to work, we should add the following property to the elasticsearch.yml file:

```
cluster.routing.allocation.awareness.attributes: group
```

This will tell Elasticsearch to use the node.group property as the awareness parameter.

> One can specify multiple attributes when setting the cluster.routing.allocation.awareness.attributes property, for example:
> ```
> cluster.routing.allocation.awareness.attributes:
> group,
> node
> ```

After this, let's start the first two nodes, the ones with the node.group parameter equal to groupA, and let's create an index by running the following command:

```
curl -XPOST 'localhost:9200/mastering' -d '{
  "settings" : {
   "index" : {
    "number_of_shards" : 2,
    "number_of_replicas" : 1
   }
  }
}'
```

After this command, our two nodes' cluster will look more or less like this:

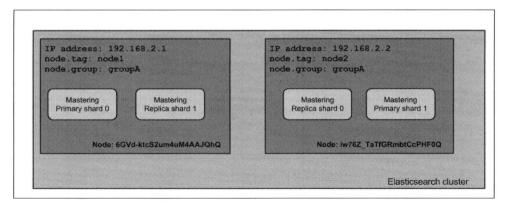

As you can see, the index was divided evenly between two nodes. Now let's see what happens when we launch the rest of the nodes (the ones with `node.group` set to `groupB`):

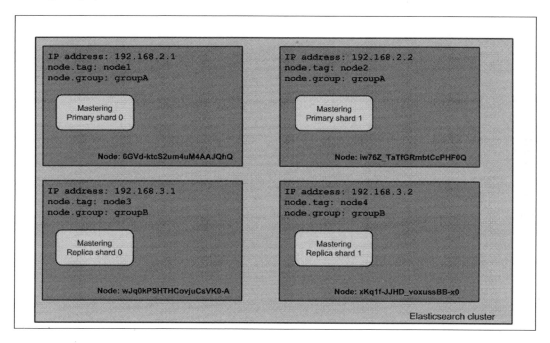

Notice the difference: the primary shards were not moved from their original allocation nodes, but the replica shards were moved to the nodes with a different `node.group` value. That's exactly right—when using shard allocation awareness, Elasticsearch won't allocate shards and replicas to the nodes with the same value of the property used to determine the allocation awareness (which, in our case, is `node.group`). One of the example usages of this functionality is to divide the cluster topology between virtual machines or physical locations in order to be sure that you don't have a single point of failure.

> Please remember that when using allocation awareness, shards will not be allocated to the node that doesn't have the expected attributes set. So, in our example, a node without the `node.group` property set will not be taken into consideration by the allocation mechanism.

Forcing allocation awareness

Forcing allocation awareness can come in handy when we know, in advance, how many values our awareness attributes can take, and we don't want more replicas than needed to be allocated in our cluster, for example, not to overload our cluster with too many replicas. To do this, we can force allocation awareness to be active only for certain attributes. We can specify these values using the `cluster.routing.allocation.awareness.force.zone.values` property and providing a list of comma-separated values to it. For example, if we would like allocation awareness to only use the `groupA` and `groupB` values of the `node.group` property, we would add the following to the `elasticsearch.yml` file:

```
cluster.routing.allocation.awareness.attributes: group
cluster.routing.allocation.awareness.force.zone.values: groupA,
groupB
```

Filtering

Elasticsearch allows us to configure the allocation for the whole cluster or for the index level. In the case of cluster allocation, we can use the properties prefixes:

- `cluster.routing.allocation.include`
- `cluster.routing.allocation.require`
- `cluster.routing.allocation.exclude`

When it comes to index-specific allocation, we can use the following properties prefixes:

- `index.routing.allocation.include`
- `index.routing.allocation.require`
- `index.routing.allocation.exclude`

The previously mentioned prefixes can be used with the properties that we've defined in the `elasticsearch.yml` file (our `tag` and `group` properties) and with a special property called `_ip` that allows us to match or exclude IPs using nodes' IP address, for example, like this:

```
cluster.routing.allocation.include._ip: 192.168.2.1
```

If we would like to include nodes with a `group` property matching the `groupA` value, we would set the following property:

```
cluster.routing.allocation.include.group: groupA
```

Notice that we've used the `cluster.routing.allocation.include` prefix, and we've concatenated it with the name of the property, which is `group` in our case.

What include, exclude, and require mean

If you look closely at the parameters mentioned previously, you would notice that there are three kinds:

- `include`: This type will result in the inclusion of all the nodes with this parameter defined. If multiple `include` conditions are visible, then all the nodes that match at least one of these conditions will be taken into consideration when allocating shards. For example, if we would add two `cluster.routing.allocation.include.tag` parameters to our configuration, one with a property to the value of `node1` and the second with the `node2` value, we would end up with indices (actually, their shards) being allocated to the first and second node (counting from left to right). To sum up, the nodes that have the `include` allocation parameter type will be taken into consideration by Elasticsearch when choosing the nodes to place shards on, but that doesn't mean that Elasticsearch will put shards on them.

- `require`: This was introduced in the Elasticsearch 0.90 type of allocation filter, and it requires all the nodes to have the value that matches the value of this property. For example, if we would add one `cluster.routing.allocation.require.tag` parameter to our configuration with the value of `node1` and a `cluster.routing.allocation.require.group` parameter, the value of `groupA` would end up with shards allocated only to the first node (the one with the IP address of `192.168.2.1`).

- `exclude`: This allows us to exclude nodes with given properties from the allocation process. For example, if we set `cluster.routing.allocation.include.tag` to `groupA`, we would end up with indices being allocated only to nodes with IP addresses `192.168.3.1` and `192.168.3.2` (the third and fourth node in our example).

 Property values can use simple wildcard characters. For example, if we would like to include all the nodes that have the `group` parameter value beginning with `group`, we could set the `cluster.routing.allocation.include.group` property to `group*`. In the example cluster case, it would result in matching nodes with the `groupA` and `groupB` group parameter values.

Runtime allocation updating

In addition to setting all discussed properties in the `elasticsearch.yml` file, we can also use the update API to update these settings in real-time when the cluster is already running.

Index level updates

In order to update settings for a given index (for example, our `mastering` index), we could run the following command:

```
curl -XPUT 'localhost:9200/mastering/_settings' -d '{
  "index.routing.allocation.require.group": "groupA"
}'
```

As you can see, the command was sent to the `_settings` end-point for a given index. You can include multiple properties in a single call.

Cluster level updates

In order to update settings for the whole cluster, we could run the following command:

```
curl -XPUT 'localhost:9200/_cluster/settings' -d '{
  "transient" : {
    "cluster.routing.allocation.require.group": "groupA"
  }
}'
```

As you can see, the command was sent to the `cluster/_settings` end-point. You can include multiple properties in a single call. Please remember that the `transient` name in the preceding command means that the property will be forgotten after the cluster restart. If you want to avoid this and set this property as a permanent one, use `persistent` instead of the `transient` one. An example command, which will keep the settings between restarts, could look like this:

```
curl -XPUT 'localhost:9200/_cluster/settings' -d '{
  "persistent" : {
    "cluster.routing.allocation.require.group": "groupA"
  }
}'
```

 Please note that running the preceding commands, depending on the command and where your indices are located, can result in shards being moved between nodes.

Defining total shards allowed per node

In addition to the previously mentioned properties, we are also allowed to define how many shards (primaries and replicas) for an index can by allocated per node. In order to do that, one should set the `index.routing.allocation.total_shards_per_node` property to a desired value. For example, in `elasticsearch.yml` we could set this:

```
index.routing.allocation.total_shards_per_node: 4
```

This would result in a maximum of four shards per index being allocated to a single node.

This property can also be updated on a live cluster using the Update API, for example, like this:

```
curl -XPUT 'localhost:9200/mastering/_settings' -d '{
  "index.routing.allocation.total_shards_per_node": "4"
}'
```

Now, let's see a few examples of what the cluster would look like when creating a single index and having the allocation properties used in the `elasticsearch.yml` file.

Defining total shards allowed per physical server

One of the properties that can be useful when having multiple nodes on a single physical server is `cluster.routing.allocation.same_shard.host`. When set to `true`, it prevents Elasticsearch from placing a primary shard and its replica (or replicas) on the same physical host. We really advise that you set this property to `true` if you have very powerful servers and that you go for multiple Elasticsearch nodes per physical server.

Inclusion

Now, let's use our example cluster to see how the allocation inclusion works. Let's start by deleting and recreating the `mastering` index by using the following commands:

```
curl -XDELETE 'localhost:9200/mastering'
curl -XPOST 'localhost:9200/mastering' -d '{
 "settings" : {
  "index" : {
```

```
    "number_of_shards" : 2,
    "number_of_replicas" : 0
  }
 }
}'
```

After this, let's try to run the following command:

```
curl -XPUT 'localhost:9200/mastering/_settings' -d '{
 "index.routing.allocation.include.tag": "node1",
 "index.routing.allocation.include.group": "groupA",
 "index.routing.allocation.total_shards_per_node": 1
}'
```

If we visualize the response of the index status, we would see that the cluster looks like the one in the following image:

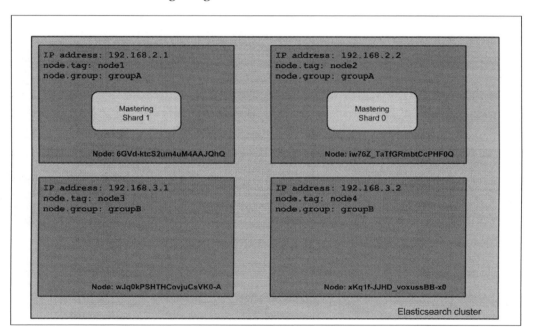

As you can see, the `mastering` index shards are allocated to nodes with the `tag` property set to `node1` or the `group` property set to `groupA`.

Requirement

Now, let's reuse our example cluster and try running the following command:

```
curl -XPUT 'localhost:9200/mastering/_settings' -d '{
  "index.routing.allocation.require.tag": "node1",
  "index.routing.allocation.require.group": "groupA"
}'
```

If we visualize the response of the index status command, we would see that the cluster looks like this:

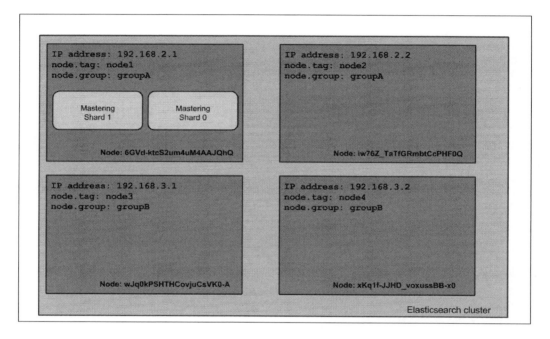

As you can see, the view is different than the one when using `include`. This is because we tell Elasticsearch to allocate shards of the `mastering` index only to the nodes that match both the `require` parameters, and in our case, the only node that matches both is the first node.

Exclusion

Let's now look at exclusions. To test it, we try to run the following command:

```
curl -XPUT 'localhost:9200/mastering/_settings' -d '{
 "index.routing.allocation.exclude.tag": "node1",
 "index.routing.allocation.require.group": "groupA"
}'
```

Again, let's look at our cluster now:

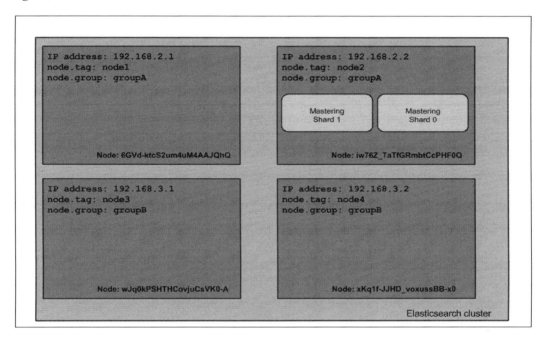

As you can see, we said that we require the group property to be equal to groupA, and we want to exclude the node with a tag equal to node1. This resulted in the shard of the mastering index being allocated to the node with the 192.168.2.2 IP address, which is what we wanted.

Disk-based allocation

Of course, the mentioned properties are not the only ones that can be used. With the release of Elasticsearch 1.3.0 we got the ability to configure awareness on the basis of the disk usage. By default, disk-based allocation is turned on, and if we want, we can turn it off by setting the cluster.routing.allocation.disk.threshold_enabled property to false.

There are three additional properties that can help us configure disk-based allocation. The `cluster.routing.allocation.disk.watermark.low` cluster controls when Elasticsearch does not allow you to allocate new shards on the node. By default, it is set to 85 percent and it means that when the disk usage is equal or higher than 85 percent, no new shards will be allocated on that node. The second property is `cluster.routing.allocation.disk.watermark.high`, which controls when Elasticsearch will try to move the shards out of the node and is set to 90 percent by default. This means that Elasticsearch will try to move the shard out of the node if the disk usage is 90 percent or higher.

Both `cluster.routing.allocation.disk.watermark.low` and `cluster.routing.allocation.disk.watermark.high` can be set to absolute values, for example, 1024mb.

Query execution preference

Let's forget about the shard placement and how to configure it—at least for a moment. In addition to all the fancy stuff that Elasticsearch allows us to set for shards and replicas, we also have the possibility to specify where our queries (and other operations, for example, the real-time GET) should be executed.

Before we get into the details, let's look at our example cluster:

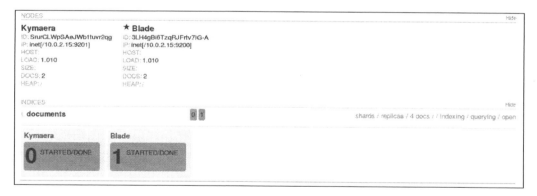

As you can see, we have three nodes and a single index called `mastering`. Our index is divided into two primary shards, and there is one replica for each primary shard.

Introducing the preference parameter

In order to control where the query (and other operations) we are sending will be executed, we can use the `preference` parameter, which can be set to one of the following values:

- `_primary`: Using this property, the operations we are sending will only be executed on primary shards. So, if we send a query against `mastering` index with the preference parameter set to the `_primary` value, we would have it executed on the nodes with the names `node1` and `node2`. For example, if you know that your primary shards are in one rack and the replicas are in other racks, you may want to execute the operation on primary shards to avoid network traffic.

- `_primary_first`: This option is similar to the `_primary` value's behavior but with a failover mechanism. If we ran a query against the `mastering` index with the preference parameter set to the `_primary_first` value, we would have it executed on the nodes with the names `node1` and `node2`; however, if one (or more) of the primary shards fails, the query will be executed against the other shard, which in our case is allocated to a node named `node3`. As we said, this is very similar to the `_primary` value but with additional fallback to replicas if the primary shard is not available for some reason.

- `_local`: Elasticsearch will prefer to execute the operation on a local node, if possible. For example, if we send a query to `node3` with the preference parameter set to `_local`, we would end up having that query executed on that node. However, if we send the same query to `node2`, we would end up with one query executed against the primary shard numbered 1 (which is located on that node) and the second part of the query will be executed against `node1` or `node3` where the shard numbered 0 resides. This is especially useful while trying to minimize the network latency; while using the `_local` preference, we ensure that our queries are executed locally whenever possible (for example, when running a client connection from a local node or sending a query to a node).

- `_only_node:wJq0kPSHTHCovjuCsVK0-A`: This operation will be only executed against a node with the provided identifier (which is `wJq0kPSHTHCovjuCsVK0-A` in this case). So in our case, the query would be executed against two replicas located on `node3`. Please remember that if there aren't enough shards to cover all the index data, the query will be executed against only the shard available in the specified node. For example, if we set the preference parameter to `_only_node:6GVd-ktcS2um4uM4AAJQhQ`, we would end up having our query executed against a single shard. This can be useful for examples where we know that one of our nodes is more powerful than the other ones and we want some of the queries to be executed only on that node.

- `_prefer_node:wJq0kPSHTHCovjuCsVK0-A`: This option sets the preference parameter to `_prefer_node`: the value followed by a node identifier (which is `wJq0kPSHTHCovjuCsVK0-A` in our case) will result in Elasticsearch preferring the mentioned node while executing the query, but if some shards are not available on the preferred node, Elasticsearch will send the appropriate query parts to nodes where the shards are available. Similar to the `_only_node` option, `_prefer_node` can be used while choosing a particular node, with a fall back to other nodes, however.

- `_shards:0,1`: This is the preference value that allows us to identify which shards the operation should be executed against (in our case, it will be all the shards, because we only have shards `0` and `1` in the `mastering` index). This is the only preference parameter value that can be combined with the other mentioned values. For example, in order to locally execute our query against the `0` and `1` shard, we should concatenate the `0,1` value with `_local` using the `;` character, so the final value of the preference parameter should look like this: `0,1;_local`. Allowing us to execute the operation against a single shard can be useful for diagnosis purposes.

- custom, string value: Setting the `_preference` parameter to a custom value will guarantee that the query with the same custom value will be executed against the same shards. For example, if we send a query with the `_preference` parameter set to the `mastering_elasticsearch` value, we would end up having the query executed against primary shards located on nodes named `node1` and `node2`. If we send another query with the same preference parameter value, then the second query will again be executed against the shards located on nodes named `node1` and `node2`. This functionality can help us in cases where we have different refresh rates and we don't want our users to see different results while repeating requests. There is one more thing missing, which is the default behavior. What Elasticsearch will do by default is that it will randomize the operation between shards and replicas. If we sent many queries, we would end up having the same (or almost the same) number of queries run against each of the shards and replicas.

Summary

In this chapter, we talked about general shards and the index architecture. We chose the right amount of shards and replicas for our deployment, and we used routing during indexing and querying and in conjunction with aliases. We also discussed shard-allocation behavior adjustments, and finally, we looked at what query execution preference can bring us.

In the next chapter, we will take a deeper look, altering the Apache Lucene scoring mechanism by providing different similarity models. We will adjust our inverted index format by using codecs. We will discuss near real-time indexing and querying, flush and refresh operations, and transaction log configuration. We will talk about throttling and segment merges. Finally, we will discuss Elasticsearch caching—field data, filter, and query shard caches.

6
Low-level Index Control

In the previous chapter, we talked about general shards and the index architecture. We started by learning how to choose the right amount of shards and replicas, and we used routing during indexing and querying, and in conjunction with aliases. We also discussed shard allocation behavior adjustments, and finally, we looked at what query execution preference can bring us.

In this chapter, we will take a deeper dive into more low-level aspects of handling shards in Elasticsearch. By the end of this chapter, you will have learned:

- Altering the Apache Lucene scoring by using different similarity models
- Altering index writing by using codes
- Near real-time indexing and querying
- Data flushing, index refresh, and transaction log handling
- I/O throttling
- Segment merge control and visualization
- Elasticsearch caching

Altering Apache Lucene scoring

With the release of Apache Lucene 4.0 in 2012, all the users of this great full text search library were given the opportunity to alter the default TF/IDF-based algorithm. The Lucene API was changed to allow easier modification and extension of the scoring formula. However, this was not the only change that was made to Lucene when it comes to documents' score calculation. Lucene 4.0 was shipped with additional similarity models, which basically allows us to use a different scoring formula for our documents. In this section, we will take a deeper look at what Lucene 4.0 brings and how these features were incorporated into Elasticsearch.

Available similarity models

As already mentioned, the original and default similarity model available before Apache Lucene 4.0 was the TF/IDF model. We already discussed it in detail in the *Default Apache Lucene scoring explained* section in *Chapter 2, Power User Query DSL*.

The five new similarity models that we can use are:

- **Okapi BM25**: This similarity model is based on a probabilistic model that estimates the probability of finding a document for a given query. In order to use this similarity in Elasticsearch, you need to use the BM25 name. The Okapi BM25 similarity is said to perform best when dealing with short text documents where term repetitions are especially hurtful to the overall document score.

- **Divergence from randomness (DFR)**: This similarity model is based on the probabilistic model of the same name. In order to use this similarity in Elasticsearch, you need to use the DFR name. It is said that the divergence from the randomness similarity model performs well on text similar to natural language text.

- **Information-based**: This is very similar to the model used by Divergence from randomness. In order to use this similarity in Elasticsearch, you need to use the IB name. Similar to the DFR similarity, it is said that the information-based model performs well on data similar to natural language text.

- **LM Dirichlet**: This similarity model uses Bayesian smoothing with Dirichlet priors. To use this similarity, we need to use the LMDirichlet name. More information about it can be found at https://lucene.apache. org/core/4_9_0/core/org/apache/lucene/search/similarities/ LMDirichletSimilarity.html.

- **LM Jelinek Mercer**: This similarity model is based on the Jelinek Mercer smoothing method. To use this similarity, we need to use the LMJelinekMercer name. More information about it can be found at https://lucene.apache.org/core/4_9_0/core/org/apache/lucene/ search/similarities/LMJelinekMercerSimilarity.html.

All the mentioned similarity models require mathematical knowledge to fully understand them and a deep explanation of these models is far beyond the scope of this book. However, if you would like to explore these models and increase your knowledge about them, please go to http://en.wikipedia.org/wiki/Okapi_BM25 for the Okapi BM25 similarity and http://terrier.org/docs/v3.5/dfr_ description.html for divergence from the randomness similarity.

Setting a per-field similarity

Since Elasticsearch 0.90, we are allowed to set a different similarity for each of the fields we have in our mappings. For example, let's assume that we have the following simple mappings that we use in order to index blog posts (stored in the `posts_no_similarity.json` file):

```
{
  "mappings" : {
    "post" : {
      "properties" : {
        "id" : { "type" : "long", "store" : "yes" },
        "name" : { "type" : "string", "store" : "yes", "index" :
"analyzed" },
        "contents" : { "type" : "string", "store" : "no", "index" :
"analyzed" }
      }
    }
  }
}
```

What we would like to do is use the BM25 similarity model for the `name` field and the `contents` field. In order to do this, we need to extend our field definitions and add the similarity property with the value of the chosen similarity name. Our changed mappings (stored in the `posts_similarity.json` file) would look like this:

```
{
  "mappings" : {
    "post" : {
      "properties" : {
        "id" : { "type" : "long", "store" : "yes" },
        "name" : { "type" : "string", "store" : "yes", "index" :
"analyzed", "similarity" : "BM25" },
        "contents" : { "type" : "string", "store" : "no", "index" :
"analyzed", "similarity" : "BM25" }
      }
    }
  }
}
```

That's all; nothing more is needed. After the preceding change, Apache Lucene will use the BM25 similarity to calculate the score factor for the `name` and `contents` fields.

Please note that in the case of the Divergence from randomness and Information-based similarities, we need to configure some additional properties to specify these similarities' behavior. How to do that is covered in the next part of the current section.

Similarity model configuration

As we now know how to set the desired similarity for each field in our index, it's time to see how to configure them if we need them, which is actually pretty easy. What we need to do is use the index settings section to provide an additional similarity section, for example, like this (this example is stored in the `posts_custom_similarity.json` file):

```
{
  "settings" : {
   "index" : {
    "similarity" : {
     "mastering_similarity" : {
      "type" : "default",
      "discount_overlaps" : false
     }
    }
   }
  },
  "mappings" : {
   "post" : {
    "properties" : {
     "id" : { "type" : "long", "store" : "yes" },
     "name" : { "type" : "string", "store" : "yes", "index" :
"analyzed", "similarity" : "mastering_similarity" },
     "contents" : { "type" : "string", "store" : "no", "index" :
"analyzed" }
    }
   }
  }
}
```

You can, of course, have more than one similarity configuration, but let's focus on the preceding example. We've defined a new similarity model named `mastering_similarity`, which is based on the default similarity, which is the TF/IDF one. We've set the `discount_overlaps` property to `false` for this similarity, and we've used it as the similarity for the `name` field. We'll talk about what properties can be used for different similarities further in this section. Now, let's see how to change the default similarity model Elasticsearch will use.

Choosing the default similarity model

In order to change the similarity model used by default, we need to provide a configuration of a similarity model that will be called `default`. For example, if we would like to use our `mastering_similarity` "name" as the default one, we would have to change the preceding configuration to the following one (the whole example is stored in the `posts_default_similarity.json` file):

```
{
  "settings" : {
   "index" : {
    "similarity" : {
     "default" : {
      "type" : "default",
      "discount_overlaps" : false
     }
    }
   }
  },
  ...
}
```

Because of the fact that the query norm and coordination factors (which were explained in the *Default Apache Lucene scoring explained* section in *Chapter 2, Power User Query DSL*) are used by all similarity models globally and are taken from the default similarity, Elasticsearch allows us to change them when needed. To do this, we need to define another similarity—one called base. It is defined exactly the same as what we've shown previously, but instead of setting its name to default, we set it to base, just like this (the whole example is stored in the `posts_base_similarity.json` file):

```
{
  "settings" : {
   "index" : {
    "similarity" : {
     "base" : {
      "type" : "default",
      "discount_overlaps" : false
     }
    }
   }
  },
  ...
}
```

If the base similarity is present in the index configuration, Elasticsearch will use it to calculate the `query norm` and `coord` factors when calculating the score using other similarity models.

Configuring the chosen similarity model

Each of the newly introduced similarity models can be configured to match our needs. Elasticsearch allows us to use the default and BM25 similarities without any configuration, because they are preconfigured for us. In the case of DFR and IB, we need to provide the configuration in order to use them. Let's now see what properties each of the similarity models' implementation provides.

Configuring the TF/IDF similarity

In the case of the TF/IDF similarity, we are allowed to set only a single parameter — `discount_overlaps`, which defaults to `true`. By default, the tokens that have their position increment set to `0` (and therefore, are placed at the same position as the one before them) will not be taken into consideration when calculating the score. If we want them to be taken into consideration, we need to configure the similarity with the `discount_overlaps` property set to `false`.

Configuring the Okapi BM25 similarity

In the case of the Okapi BM25 similarity, we have these parameters: we can configure `k1` (controls the saturation — nonlinear term frequency normalization) as a float value, `b` (controls how the document length affects the term frequency values) as a float value, and `discount_overlaps`, which is exactly the same as in TF/IDF similarity.

Configuring the DFR similarity

In the case of the DFR similarity, we have these parameters that we can configure: `basic_model` (which can take the value `be`, `d`, `g`, `if`, `in`, or `ine`), `after_effect` (with values of `no`, `b`, and `l`), and the normalization (which can be `no`, `h1`, `h2`, `h3`, or `z`). If we choose a normalization other than `no`, we need to set the normalization factor. Depending on the chosen normalization, we should use `normalization.h1.c` (the float value) for the `h1` normalization, `normalization.h2.c` (the float value) for the `h2` normalization, `normalization.h3.c` (the float value) for the `h3` normalization, and `normalization.z.z` (the float value) for the `z` normalization. For example, this is what the example similarity configuration could look like:

```
"similarity" : {
 "esserverbook_dfr_similarity" : {
  "type" : "DFR",
  "basic_model" : "g",
```

```
  "after_effect" : "l",
  "normalization" : "h2",
  "normalization.h2.c" : "2.0"
 }
}
```

Configuring the IB similarity

In the case of the IB similarity, we have these parameters that we can configure: the distribution property (which can take the value of ll or spl) and the lambda property (which can take the value of df or tff). In addition to this, we can choose the normalization factor, which is the same as the one used for the DFR similarity, so we'll omit describing it for the second time. This is what the example IB similarity configuration could look like:

```
"similarity" : {
 "esserverbook_ib_similarity" : {
  "type" : "IB",
  "distribution" : "ll",
  "lambda" : "df",
  "normalization" : "z",
  "normalization.z.z" : "0.25"
 }
}
```

Configuring the LM Dirichlet similarity

In the case of the LM Dirichlet similarity, we have the mu property that we can configure the mu property, which is by default set to 2000. An example configuration of this could look as follows:

```
"similarity" : {
 "esserverbook_lm_dirichlet_similarity" : {
  "type" : "LMDirichlet",
  "mu" : "1000"
 }
}
```

Configuring the LM Jelinek Mercer similarity

When it comes to the LM Jelinek Mercer similarity, we can configure the lambda property, which is set to 0.1 by default. An example configuration of this could look as follows:

```
"similarity" : {
 "esserverbook_lm_jelinek_mercer_similarity" : {
  "type" : "LMJelinekMercer",
```

```
    "lambda" : "0.7"
  }
}
```

 It is said that for short fields (like the document title) the optimal lambda value is around `0.1`, while for long fields the lambda should be set to `0.7`.

Choosing the right directory implementation – the store module

The store module is one of the modules that we usually don't pay much attention to when configuring our cluster; however, it is very important. It is an abstraction between the I/O subsystem and Apache Lucene itself. All the operation that Lucene does with the hard disk drive is done using the store module. Most of the store types in Elasticsearch are mapped to an appropriate Apache Lucene Directory class (http://lucene.apache.org/core/4_9_0/core/org/apache/lucene/store/Directory.html). The directory is used to access all the files the index is built of, so it is crucial to properly configure it.

The store type

Elasticsearch exposes five store types that we can use. Let's see what they provide and how we can leverage their features.

The simple filesystem store

The simplest implementation of the `Directory` class that is available is implemented using a random access file (Java `RandomAccessFile`—http://docs.oracle.com/javase/7/docs/api/java/io/RandomAccessFile.html) and maps to `SimpleFSDirectory` (http://lucene.apache.org/core/4_9_0/core/org/apache/lucene/store/SimpleFSDirectory.html) in Apache Lucene. It is sufficient for very simple applications. However, the main bottleneck will be multithreaded access, which has poor performance. In the case of Elasticsearch, it is usually better to use the new I/O-based system store instead of the Simple filesystem store. However, if you would like to use this system store, you should set `index.store.type` to `simplefs`.

The new I/O filesystem store

This store type uses the Directory class implementation based on the `FileChannel` class (http://docs.oracle.com/javase/7/docs/api/java/nio/channels/FileChannel.html) from `java.nio package` and maps to `NIOFSDirectory` in Apache Lucene (http://lucene.apache.org/core/4_9_0/core/org/apache/lucene/store/NIOFSDirectory.html). The discussed implementation allows multiple threads to access the same files concurrently without performance degradation. In order to use this store, one should set `index.store.type` to `niofs`.

> Please remember that because of some bugs that exist in the JVM machine for Microsoft Windows, it is very probable that the new I/O filesystem store will suffer from performance problems when running on Microsoft Windows. More information about this bug can be found at http://bugs.sun.com/bugdatabase/view_bug.do?bug_id=6265734.

The MMap filesystem store

This store type uses Apache Lucene's `MMapDirectory` (http://lucene.apache.org/core/4_9_0/core/org/apache/lucene/store/MMapDirectory.html) implementation. It uses the `mmap` system call (http://en.wikipedia.org/wiki/Mmap) for reading, and it uses random access files for writing. It uses a portion of the available virtual memory address space in the process equal to the size of the file being mapped. It doesn't have any locking, so it is scalable when it comes to multithread access. When using `mmap` to read index files for the operating system, it looks like it is already cached (it was mapped to the virtual space). Because of this, when reading a file from the Apache Lucene index, this file doesn't need to be loaded into the operating system cache and thus, the access is faster. This basically allows Lucene and thus Elasticsearch to directly access the I/O cache, which should result in fast access to index files.

It is worth noting that the MMap filesystem store works best on 64-bit environments and should only be used on 32-bit machines when you are sure that the index is small enough and the virtual address space is sufficient. In order to use this store, one should set `index.store.type` to `mmapfs`.

The hybrid filesystem store

Introduced in Elasticsearch 1.3.0, the hybrid file store uses both NIO and MMap access depending on the file type. A the time of writing this, only term dictionary and doc values were read and written using MMap, and all the other files of the index were opened using NIOFSDirectory. In order to use this store, one should set `index.store.type` to `default`.

The memory store

This is the second store type that is not based on the Apache Lucene Directory (the first one is the hybrid filesystem store). The memory store allows us to store all the index files in the memory, so the files are not stored on the disk. This is crucial, because it means that the index data is not persistent—it will be removed whenever a full cluster restart will happen. However, if you need a small, very fast index that can have multiple shards and replicas and can be rebuilt very fast, the memory store type may be the thing you are looking for. In order to use this store, one should set `index.store.type` to `memory`.

> The data stored in the memory store, like all the other stores, is replicated among all the nodes that can hold data.

Additional properties

When using the memory store type, we also have some degree of control over the caches, which are very important when using the memory store. Please remember that all the following settings are set per node:

- `cache.memory.direct`: This defaults to `true` and specifies whether the memory store should be allocated outside of the JVM heap memory. It is usually a good idea to leave it to the default value so that the heap is not overloaded with data.

- `cache.memory.small_buffer_size`: This defaults to `1kb` and defines a small buffer size—the internal memory structure used to hold segments' information and deleted documents' information.

- `cache.memory.large_buffer_size`: This defaults to `1mb` and defines a large buffer size—the internal memory structure used to hold index files other than segments' information and deleted documents.

- `cache.memory.small_cache_size`: The objects' small cache size—the internal memory structure used for the caching of index segments' information and deleted documents' information. It defaults to `10mb`.

- `cache.memory.large_cache_size`: The objects' large cache size—the internal memory structure used to cache information about the index other than the index segments' information and deleted documents' information. It defaults to `500mb`.

The default store type

There are differences when it comes to the default store of Elasticsearch 1.3.0 and the newer and older versions.

The default store type for Elasticsearch 1.3.0 and higher

Starting from Elasticsearch 1.3.0, the new default Elasticsearch store type is the hybrid one that we can choose by setting `index.store.type` to `default`.

The default store type for Elasticsearch versions older than 1.3.0

By default, Elasticsearch versions older than 1.3.0 use filesystem-based storage. However different store types are chosen for different operating systems. For example, for a 32-bit Microsoft Windows system, the `simplefs` type will be used; `mmapfs` will be used when Elasticsearch is running on Solaris and Microsoft Windows 64 bit, and `niofs` will be used for the rest of the world.

> If you are looking for some information from experts on how they see which Directory implementation to use, please look at the `http://blog.thetaphi.de/2012/07/use-lucenes-mmapdirectory-on-64bit.html` post written by Uwe Schindler and `http://jprante.github.io/lessons/2012/07/26/Mmap-with-Lucene.html` by Jörg Prante.

Usually, the default store type will be the one that you want to use. However, sometimes, it is worth considering using the MMap file system store type, especially when you have plenty of memory and your indices are big. This is because when using `mmap` to access the index file, it will cause the index files to be cached only once and be reused both by Apache Lucene and the operating system.

NRT, flush, refresh, and transaction log

In an ideal search solution, when new data is indexed, it is instantly available for searching. When you start Elasticsearch, this is exactly how it works even in distributed environments. However, this is not the whole truth, and we will show you why it is like this.

Let's start by indexing an example document to the newly created index using the following command:

```
curl -XPOST localhost:9200/test/test/1 -d '{ "title": "test" }'
```

Now, let's replace this document, and let's try to find it immediately. In order to do this, we'll use the following command chain:

```
curl -XPOST localhost:9200/test/test/1 -d '{ "title": "test2" }' ;
curl -XGET 'localhost:9200/test/test/_search?pretty'
```

The preceding command will probably result in a response that is very similar to the following one:

```
{"_index":"test","_type":"test","_id":"1","_version":2,"created":f
alse}{
  "took" : 1,
  "timed_out" : false,
  "_shards" : {
    "total" : 5,
    "successful" : 5,
    "failed" : 0
  },
  "hits" : {
    "total" : 1,
    "max_score" : 1.0,
    "hits" : [ {
      "_index" : "test",
      "_type" : "test",
      "_id" : "1",
      "_score" : 1.0,
      "_source":{ "title": "test" }
    } ]
  }
}
```

We see two responses glued together. The first line starts with a response to the indexing command — the first command we've sent. As you can see, everything is correct — we've updated the document (look at _version). With the second command, our search query should return the document with the title field set to test2; however, as you can see, it returned the first document. What happened? Before we give you the answer to this question, we will take a step back and discuss how the underlying Apache Lucene library makes the newly indexed documents available for searching.

Updating the index and committing changes

As we already know from the *Introducing Apache Lucene* section in *Chapter 1, Introduction to Elasticsearch,* during the indexing process, new documents are written into segments. The segments are independent indices, which means that queries that are run in parallel to indexing should add newly created segments from time to time to the set of these segments that are used for searching. Apache Lucene does this by creating subsequent (because of the write-once nature of the index) segments_N files, which list segments in the index. This process is called committing. Lucene can do this in a secure way — we are sure that all changes or none of them hit the index. If a failure happens, we can be sure that the index will be in a consistent state.

Let's return to our example. The first operation adds the document to the index but doesn't run the commit command to Lucene. This is exactly how it works. However, a commit is not enough for the data to be available for searching. The Lucene library uses an abstraction class called Searcher to access the index, and this class needs to be refreshed.

After a commit operation, the Searcher object should be reopened in order for it to be able to see the newly created segments. This whole process is called refresh. For performance reasons, Elasticsearch tries to postpone costly refreshes and, by default, refresh is not performed after indexing a single document (or a batch of them), but the Searcher is refreshed every second. This happens quite often, but sometimes, applications require the refresh operation to be performed more often than once every second. When this happens, you can consider using another technology, or the requirements should be verified. If required, there is a possibility of forcing the refresh by using the Elasticsearch API. For example, in our example, we can add the following command:

```
curl -XGET localhost:9200/test/_refresh
```

If we add the preceding command before the search, Elasticsearch would respond as we had expected.

Changing the default refresh time

The time between automatic Searcher refresh operations can be changed by using the `index.refresh_interval` parameter either in the Elasticsearch configuration file or by using the Update Settings API, for example:

```
curl -XPUT localhost:9200/test/_settings -d '{
  "index" : {
    "refresh_interval" : "5m"
  }
}'
```

The preceding command will change the automatic refresh to be performed every 5 minutes. Please remember that the data that is indexed between refreshes won't be visible by queries.

> As we said, the refresh operation is costly when it comes to resources. The longer the period of the refresh, the faster your indexing will be. If you are planning for a very high indexing procedure when you don't need your data to be visible until the indexing ends, you can consider disabling the refresh operation by setting the `index.refresh_interval` parameter to `-1` and setting it back to its original value after the indexing is done.

The transaction log

Apache Lucene can guarantee index consistency and all or nothing indexing, which is great. However, this fact cannot ensure us that there will be no data loss when failure happens while writing data to the index (for example, when there isn't enough space on the device, the device is faulty, or there aren't enough file handlers available to create new index files). Another problem is that frequent commit is costly in terms of performance (as you may recall, a single commit will trigger a new segment creation, and this can trigger the segments to merge). Elasticsearch solves these issues by implementing the transaction log. The transaction log holds all uncommitted transactions and, from time to time, Elasticsearch creates a new log for subsequent changes. When something goes wrong, the transaction log can be replayed to make sure that none of the changes were lost. All of these tasks are happening automatically, so the user may not be aware of the fact that the commit was triggered at a particular moment. In Elasticsearch, the moment where the information from the transaction log is synchronized with the storage (which is the Apache Lucene index) and the transaction log is cleared is called **flushing**.

Please note the difference between flush and refresh operations. In most of the cases, refresh is exactly what you want. It is all about making new data available for searching. On the other hand, the flush operation is used to make sure that all the data is correctly stored in the index and the transaction log can be cleared.

In addition to automatic flushing, it can be forced manually using the flush API. For example, we can run a command to flush all the data stored in the transaction log for all indices by running the following command:

```
curl -XGET localhost:9200/_flush
```

Or, we can run the `flush` command for the particular index, which in our case is the one called `library`:

```
curl -XGET localhost:9200/library/_flush
```

```
curl -XGET localhost:9200/library/_refresh
```

In the second example, we used it together with the refresh, which after flushing the data, opens a new searcher.

The transaction log configuration

If the default behavior of the transaction log is not enough, Elasticsearch allows us to configure its behavior when it comes to the transaction log handling. The following parameters can be set in the `elasticsearch.yml` file as well as using index settings' Update API to control the transaction log behavior:

- `index.translog.flush_threshold_period`: This defaults to 30 minutes (`30m`). It controls the time after which the flush will be forced automatically even if no new data was being written to it. In some cases, this can cause a lot of I/O operation, so sometimes it's better to perform the flush more often with less data stored in it.

- `index.translog.flush_threshold_ops`: This specifies the maximum number of operations after which the flush operation will be performed. By default, Elasticsearch does not limit these operations.

- `index.translog.flush_threshold_size`: This specifies the maximum size of the transaction log. If the size of the transaction log is equal to or greater than the parameter, the flush operation will be performed. It defaults to `200` MB.

- `index.translog.interval`: This defaults to `5s` and describes the period between consecutive checks if the flush is needed. Elasticsearch randomizes this value to be greater than the defined one and less than double of it.

- `index.gateway.local.sync`: This defines how often the transaction log should be sent to the disk using the `fsync` system call. The default is `5s`.

- `index.translog.disable_flush`: This option allows us to disable the automatic flush. By default, flushing is enabled, but sometimes, it is handy to disable it temporarily, for example, during the import of a large amount of documents.

 All of the mentioned parameters are specified for an index of our choice, but they define the behavior of the transaction log for each of the index shards.

In addition to setting the previously mentioned properties in the `elasticsearch.yml` file, we can also set them by using the Settings Update API. For example, the following command will result in disabling flushing for the `test` index:

```
curl -XPUT localhost:9200/test/_settings -d '{
  "index" : {
    "translog.disable_flush" : true
  }
}'
```

The previous command was run before the import of a large amount of data, which gave us a performance boost for indexing. However, one should remember to turn on flushing when the import is done.

Near real-time GET

Transaction logs give us one more feature for free, that is, the real-time GET operation, which provides us with the possibility of returning the previous version of the document, including noncommitted versions. The real-time GET operation fetches data from the index, but first, it checks whether a newer version of this document is available in the transaction log. If there is no flushed document, the data from the index is ignored and a newer version of the document is returned—the one from the transaction log.

In order to see how it works, you can replace the search operation in our example with the following command:

```
curl -XGET localhost:9200/test/test/1?pretty
```

Elasticsearch should return a result similar to the following:

```
{
    "_index" : "test",
    "_type" : "test",
    "_id" : "1",
    "_version" : 2,
    "exists" : true, "_source" : { "title": "test2" }
}
```

If you look at the result, you would see that, again, the result was just as we expected and no trick with refresh was required to obtain the newest version of the document.

Segment merging under control

As you already know (we've discussed it throughout *Chapter 1, Introduction to Elasticsearch*), every Elasticsearch index is built out of one or more shards and can have zero or more replicas. You also know that each of the shards and replicas are actual Apache Lucene indices that are built of multiple segments (at least one segment). If you recall, the segments are written once and read many times, and data structures, apart from the information about the deleted documents that are held in one of the files, can be changed. After some time, when certain conditions are met, the contents of some segments can be copied to a bigger segment, and the original segments are discarded and thus deleted from the disk. Such an operation is called **segment merging**.

You may ask yourself, why bother about segment merging? There are a few reasons. First of all, the more segments the index is built of, the slower the search will be and the more memory Lucene will need. In addition to this, segments are immutable, so the information is not deleted from it. If you happen to delete many documents from your index, until the merge happens, these documents are only marked as deleted and are not deleted physically. So, when segment merging happens, the documents that are marked as deleted are not written into the new segment, and this way, they are removed, which decreases the final segment size.

 Many small changes can result in a large number of small segments, which can lead to problems with a large number of opened files. We should always be prepared to handle such situations, for example, by having the appropriate opened files' limit set.

So, just to quickly summarize, segments merging takes place and from the user's point of view, it will result in two effects:

- It will reduce the number of segments in order to allow faster searching when a few segments are merged into a single one

- It will reduce the size of the index because of removing the deleted documents when the merge is finalized

However, you have to remember that segment merging comes with a price: the price of I/O operations, which can affect performance on slower systems. Because of this, Elasticsearch allows us to choose the merge policy and the store level throttling.

Choosing the right merge policy

Although segment merging is Apache Lucene's duty, Elasticsearch allows us to configure which merge policy we would like to use. There are three policies that we are currently allowed to use:

- `tiered` (the default one)
- `log_byte_size`
- `log_doc`

Each of the preceding mentioned policies have their own parameters, which define their behavior and the default values that we can override (please look at the section dedicated to the policy of your choice to see what those parameters are).

In order to tell Elasticsearch which merge policy we want to use, we should set `index.merge.policy.type` to the desired type, shown as follows:

```
index.merge.policy.type: tiered
```

 Once the index is created with the specified merge policy type, it can't be changed. However, all the properties defining the merge policy behavior can be changed using the Index Update API.

Let's now look at the different merge policies and the functionality that they provide. After this, we will discuss all the configuration options provided by the policies.

The tiered merge policy

The tiered merge policy is the default merge policy that Elasticsearch uses. It merges segments of approximately similar size, taking into account the maximum number of segments allowed per tier. It is also possible to differentiate the number of segments that are allowed to be merged at once from how many segments are allowed to be present per tier. During indexing, this merge policy will compute how many segments are allowed to be present in the index, which is called **budget**. If the number of segments the index is built of is higher than the computed budget, the tiered policy will first sort the segments by the decreasing order of their size (taking into account the deleted documents). After that, it will find the merge that has the lowest cost. The merge cost is calculated in a way that merges are reclaiming more deletions, and having a smaller size is favored.

If the merge produces a segment that is larger than the value specified by the `index.merge.policy.max_merged_segment` property, the policy will merge fewer segments to keep the segment size under the budget. This means that for indices that have large shards, the default value of the `index.merge.policy.max_merged_segment` property may be too low and will result in the creation of many segments, slowing down your queries. Depending on the volume of your data, you should monitor your segments and adjust the merge policy setting to match your needs.

The log byte size merge policy

The log byte size merge policy is a merge policy, which over time, will produce an index that will be built of a logarithmic size of indices. There will be a few large segments, then there will be a few merge factor smaller segments, and so on. You can imagine that there will be a few segments of the same level of size when the number of segments will be lower than the merge factor. When an extra segment is encountered, all the segments within that level are merged. The number of segments an index will contain is proportional to the logarithm of the next size in bytes. This merge policy is generally able to keep the low number of segments in your index while minimizing the cost of segments merging.

The log doc merge policy

The log doc merge policy is similar to the `log_byte_size` merge policy, but instead of operating on the actual segment size in bytes, it operates on the number of documents in the index. This merge policy will perform well when the documents are similar in terms of size or if you want segments of similar sizes in terms of the number of documents.

Merge policies' configuration

We now know how merge policies work, but we lack the knowledge about the configuration options. So now, let's discuss each of the merge policies and see what options are exposed to us. Please remember that the default values will usually be OK for most of the deployments and they should be changed only when needed.

The tiered merge policy

When using the `tiered` merge policy, the following options can be altered:

- `index.merge.policy.expunge_deletes_allowed`: This defaults to `10` and specifies the percentage of deleted documents in a segment in order for it to be considered to be merged when running `expungeDeletes`.

- `index.merge.policy.floor_segment`: This is a property that enables us to prevent the frequent flushing of very small segments. Segments smaller than the size defined by this property are treated by the merge mechanism, as they would have the size equal to the value of this property. It defaults to `2MB`.

- `index.merge.policy.max_merge_at_once`: This specifies the maximum number of segments that will be merged at the same time during indexing. By default, it is set to `10`. Setting the value of this property to higher values can result in multiple segments being merged at once, which will need more I/O resources.

- `index.merge.policy.max_merge_at_once_explicit`: This specifies the maximum number of segments that will be merged at the same time during the optimize operation or `expungeDeletes`. By default, this is set to `30`. This setting will not affect the maximum number of segments that will be merged during indexing.

- `index.merge.policy.max_merged_segment`: This defaults to `5GB` and specifies the maximum size of a single segment that will be produced during segment merging when indexing. This setting is an approximate value, because the merged segment size is calculated by summing the size of segments that are going to be merged minus the size of the deleted documents in these segments.

- `index.merge.policy.segments_per_tier`: This specifies the allowed number of segments per tier. Smaller values of this property result in less segments, which means more merging and lower indexing performance. It defaults to `10` and should be set to a value higher than or equal to `index.merge.policy.max_merge_at_once`, or you'll be facing too many merges and performance issues.

- `index.reclaim_deletes_weight`: This defaults to `2.0` and specifies how many merges that reclaim deletes are favored. When setting this value to `0.0`, the reclaim deletes will not affect the merge selection. The higher the value, the more favored the merge that reclaims deletes will be.

- `index.compund_format`: This is a Boolean value that specifies whether the index should be stored in a compound format or not. It defaults to `false`. If set to `true`, Lucene will store all the files that build the index in a single file. Sometimes, this is useful for systems running constantly out of file handlers, but it will decrease the searching and indexing performance.

The log byte size merge policy

When using the `log_byte_size` merge policy, the following options can be used to configure its behavior:

- `merge_factor`: This specifies how often segments are merged during indexing. With a smaller `merge_factor` value, the searches are faster and less memory is used, but this comes with the cost of slower indexing. With larger `merge_factor` values, it is the opposite—the indexing is faster (because of less merging being done), but the searches are slower and more memory is used. By default, `merge_factor` is given the value of `10`. It is advised to use larger values of `merge_factor` for batch indexing and lower values of this parameter for normal index maintenance.

- `min_merge_size`: This defines the size (the total size of the segment files in bytes) of the smallest segment possible. If a segment is lower in size than the number specified by this property, it will be merged if the `merge_factor` property allows us to do that. This property defaults to `1.6MB` and is very useful in order to avoid having many very small segments. However, one should remember that setting this property to a large value will increase the merging cost.

- `max_merge_size`: This defines the maximum size (the total size of the segment files in bytes) of the segment that can be merged with other segments. By default, it is not set, so there is no limit on the maximum size a segment can be in order to be merged.

- `maxMergeDocs`: This defines the maximum number of documents a segment can have in order to be merged with other segments. By default, it is not set, so there is no limit to the maximum number of documents a segment can have.

- `calibrate_size_by_deletes`: This is a Boolean value, which is set to `true` and specifies whether the size of the deleted documents should be taken into consideration when calculating the segment size.

The mentioned properties we just saw should be prefixed with the `index.merge.policy` prefix. So if we would like to set the `min_merge_docs` property, we should use the `index.merge.policy.min_merge_docs` property.

In addition to this, the `log_byte_size` merge policy accepts the `index.merge.async` and `index.merge.async_interval` properties just like the `tiered` merge policy does.

The log doc merge policy

When using the `log_doc` merge policy, the following options can be used to configure its behavior:

- `merge_factor`: This is same as the property that is present in the `log_byte_size` merge policy, so please refer to this policy for the explanation.

- `min_merge_docs`: This defines the minimum number of documents for the smallest segment. If a segment contains a lower document count than the number specified by this property, it will be merged if the `merge_factor` property allows this. This property defaults to `1000` and is very useful in order to avoid having many very small segments. However, one should remember that setting this property to a large value will increase the merging cost.

- `max_merge_docs`: This defines the maximum number of documents a segment can have in order to be merged with other segments. By default, it is not set, so there is no limit to the maximum number of documents a segment can have.

- `calibrate_size_by_deletes`: This is a Boolean value that defaults to `true` and specifies whether the size of deleted documents should be taken into consideration when calculating the segment size.

Similar to the previous merge policy, the previously mentioned properties should be prefixed with the `index.merge.policy` prefix. So if we would like to set the `min_merge_docs` property, we should use the `index.merge.policy.min_merge_docs` property.

Scheduling

In addition to having control over how the merge policy is behaving, Elasticsearch allows us to define the execution of the merge policy once a merge is needed. There are two merge schedulers available, with the default being `ConcurrentMergeScheduler`.

The concurrent merge scheduler

This is a merge scheduler that will use multiple threads in order to perform segments' merging. This scheduler will create a new thread until the maximum number of threads is reached. If the maximum number of threads is reached and a new thread is needed (because segments' merge needs to be performed), all the indexing will be paused until at least one merge is completed.

In order to control the maximum threads allowed, we can alter the `index.merge.scheduler.max_thread_count` property. By default, it is set to the value calculated by the following equation:

```
maximum_value(1, minimum_value(3, available_processors / 2)
```

So, if our system has eight processors available, the maximum number of threads that the concurrent merge scheduler is allowed to use will be equal to four.

You should also remember that this is especially not good for spinning disks. You want to be sure that merging won't saturate your disks' throughput. Because of this, if you see extensive merging, you should lower the number of merging threads. It is usually said that for spinning disks, the number of threads used by the concurrent merge scheduler should be set to 1.

The serial merge scheduler

A simple merge scheduler uses the same thread for merging. It results in a merge that stops all the other document processing that was happening on the same thread, which in this case, means the stopping of indexing. This merge scheduler is only provided for backwards compatibility and, in fact, uses the concurrent merge scheduler with the number of threads equal to one.

Setting the desired merge scheduler

In order to set the desired merge scheduler, one should set the `index.merge.scheduler.type` property to the value of `concurrent` or `serial`. For example, in order to use the concurrent merge scheduler, one should set the following property:

```
index.merge.scheduler.type: concurrent
```

In order to use the serial merge scheduler, one should set the following property:

```
index.merge.scheduler.type: serial
```

When talking about the merge policy and merge schedulers, it would be nice to visualize them. If one needs to see how the merges are done in the underlying Apache Lucene library, we suggest that you visit Mike McCandless' blog post at `http://blog.mikemccandless.com/2011/02/visualizing-lucenes-segment-merges.html`.

In addition to this, there is a plugin that allows us to see what is happening to the segments called SegmentSpy. Refer to the following URL for more information:

`https://github.com/polyfractal/elasticsearch-segmentspy`

When it is too much for I/O – throttling explained

In the *Choosing the right directory implementation* section, we've talked about the store type, which means we are now able to configure the store module to match our needs. However, we didn't write everything about the store module—we didn't write about throttling.

Controlling I/O throttling

As you remember from the *Segment merging under control* section, Apache Lucene stores the data in immutable segment files that can be read many times but can be written only once. The merge process is asynchronous and, in general, it should not interfere with indexing and searching, looking from the Lucene point of view. However, problems may occur because merging is expensive when it comes to I/O—it requires you to read the segments that are going to be merged and write new ones. If searching and indexing happen concurrently, this can be too much for the I/O subsystem, especially on systems with low I/O. This is where throttling kicks in—we can control how much I/O Elasticsearch will use.

Configuration

Throttling can be configured both on a node-level and on the index-level, so you can either configure how many resources a node will use or how many resources will be used for the index.

The throttling type

In order to configure the throttling type on the node-level, one should use the `indices.store.throttle.type` property, which can take the value of `none`, `merge`, and `all`. The `none` value will tell Elasticsearch that no limiting should take place. The `merge` value tells Elasticsearch that we want to limit the I/O usage for the merging of nodes (and it is the default value) and the `all` value specifies that we want to limit all store module-based operations.

In order to configure the throttling type on the index-level, one should use the `index.store.throttle.type` property, which can take the same values as the `indices.store.throttle.type` property with an additional one — `node`. The `node` value will tell Elasticsearch that instead of using per-index throttling limiting, we will use the node-level configuration. This is the default value.

Maximum throughput per second

In both cases, when using index or node-level throttling, we are able to set the maximum bytes per second that I/O can use. For the value of this property, we can use `10mb`, `500mb`, or anything that we need. For the index-level configuration, we should use the `index.store.throttle.max_bytes_per_sec` property and for the node-level configuration, we should use `indices.store.throttle.max_bytes_per_sec`.

> The previously mentioned properties can be set both in the `elasticsearch.yml` file and can also be updated dynamically using the cluster update settings for the node-level configuration and using the index update settings for the index-level configuration.

Node throttling defaults

On the node-level, since Elasticsearch 0.90.1, throttling is enabled by default. The `indices.store.throttle.type` property is set to `merge` and the `indices.store.throttle.max_bytes_per_sec` property is set to `20mb`. Elasticsearch versions before 0.90.1 don't have throttling enabled by default.

Performance considerations

When using **SSD** (**solid state drives**) or when query speed matters only a little (or you are not searching when you index your data), it is worth considering disabling throttling completely. We can do this by setting the `indices.store.throttle.type` property to `none`. This causes Elasticsearch to not use any store-level throttling and use full disk throughput for store-based operations.

The configuration example

Now, let's imagine that we have a cluster that consists of four Elasticsearch nodes and we want to configure throttling for the whole cluster. By default, we want the merge operation not to process more than 50 megabytes per second for a node. We know that we can handle such operations without affecting the search performance, and this is what we are aiming at. In order to achieve this, we would run the following request:

```
curl -XPUT 'localhost:9200/_cluster/settings' -d '{
 "persistent" : {
  "indices.store.throttle.type" : "merge",
  "indices.store.throttle.max_bytes_per_sec" : "50mb"
 }
}'
```

In addition to this, we have a single index called payments that is very rarely used, and we've placed it in the smallest machine in the cluster. This index doesn't have replicas and is built of a single shard. What we would like to do for this index is limit the merges to process a maximum of 10 megabytes per second. So, in addition to the preceding command, we would run one like this:

```
curl -XPUT 'localhost:9200/payments/_settings' -d '{
 "index.store.throttle.type" : "merge",
 "index.store.throttle.max_bytes_per_sec" : "10mb"
}'
```

After running the preceding commands, we can check our index settings by running the following command:

```
curl -XGET 'localhost:9200/payments/_settings?pretty'
```

In response, we should get the following JSON:

```
{
  "payments" : {
    "settings" : {
      "index" : {
        "creation_date" : "1414072648520",
        "store" : {
          "throttle" : {
            "type" : "merge",
            "max_bytes_per_sec" : "10mb"
```

```
      }
    },
    "number_of_shards" : "5",
    "number_of_replicas" : "1",
    "version" : {
      "created" : "1040001"
    },
    "uuid" : "M3lePTOvSN2jnDz1J0t4Uw"
      }
    }
  }
}
```

As you can see, after updating the index setting, closing the index, and opening it again, we've finally got our settings working.

Understanding Elasticsearch caching

One of the very important parts of Elasticsearch, although not always visible to the users, is caching. It allows Elasticsearch to store commonly used data in memory and reuse it on demand. Of course, we can't cache everything—we usually have way more data than we have memory, and creating caches may be quite expensive when it comes to performance. In this chapter, we will look at the different caches exposed by Elasticsearch, and we will discuss how they are used and how we can control their usage. Hopefully, such information will allow you to better understand how this great search server works internally.

The filter cache

The filter cache is the simplest of all the caches available in Elasticsearch. It is used during query time to cache the results of filters that are used in queries. We already talked about filters in section *Handling filters and why it matters* of *Chapter 2, Power User Query DSL*, but let's look at a simple example. Let's assume that we have the following query:

```
{
  "query" : {
   "filtered" : {
    "query" : {
     "match_all" : {}
    },
    "filter" : {
     "term" : {
```

```
        "category" : "romance"
      }
     }
    }
   }
  }
```

The preceding query will return all the documents that have the romance term in the category field. As you can see, we've used the match_all query combined with a filter. Now, after the initial query, every query with the same filter present in it will reuse the results of our filter and save the precious I/O and CPU resources.

Filter cache types

There are two types of filter caches available in Elasticsearch: node-level and index-level filter caches. This gives us the possibility of choosing the filter cache to be dependent on the index or on a node (which is the default behavior). As we can't always predict where the given index will be allocated (actually, its shards and replicas), it is not recommended that you use the index-level filter cache because we can't predict the memory usage in such cases.

Node-level filter cache configuration

The default and recommended filter cache type is configured for all shards allocated to a given node (set using the index.cache.filter.type property to the node value or not setting that property at all). Elasticsearch allows us to use the indices.cache.filter.size property to configure the size of this cache. We can either use a percentage value as 10% (which is the default value), or a static memory value as 1024mb. If we use the percentage value, Elasticsearch will calculate it as a percentage of the maximum heap memory given to a node.

The node-level filter cache is a **Least Recently Used** cache type (**LRU**), which means that while removing cache entries, the ones that were used the least number of times will be thrown away in order to make place for the newer entries.

Index-level filter cache configuration

The second type of filter cache that Elasticsearch allows us to use is the index-level filter cache. We can configure its behavior by configuring the following properties:

- `index.cache.filter.type`: This property sets the type of the cache, which can take the values of `resident`, `soft`, `weak`, and `node` (the default one). By using this property, Elasticsearch allows us to choose the implementation of the cache. The entries in the `resident` cache can't be removed by JVM unless we want them to be removed (either by using the API or by setting the maximum size or expiration time) and is basically recommended because of this (filling up the filter cache can be expensive). The `soft` and `weak` filter cache types can be cleared by JVM when it lacks memory, with the difference that when clearing up memory, JVM will choose the weaker reference objects first and then choose the one that uses the soft reference. The `node` value tells Elasticsearch to use the node-level filter cache.

- `index.cache.filter.max_size`: This property specifies the maximum number of cache entries that can be stored in the filter cache (the default is `-1`, which means unbounded). You need to remember that this setting is not applied for the whole index but for a single segment of a shard for the index, so the memory usage will differ depending on how many shards (and replicas) there are (for the given index) and how many segments the index contains. Generally, the default, unbounded filter cache is fine with the `soft` type and the proper queries that are paying attention in order to make the caches reusable.

- `index.cache.filter.expire`: This property specifies the expiration time of an entry in the filter cache, which is unbounded (set to `-1`) by default. If we want our filter cache to expire if not accessed, we can set the maximum time of inactivity. For example, if we would like our cache to expire after 60 minutes, we should set this property to `60m`.

If you want to read more about the soft and weak references in Java, please refer to the Java documentation, especially the Javadocs, for these two types: `http://docs.oracle.com/javase/8/docs/api/java/lang/ref/SoftReference.html` and `http://docs.oracle.com/javase/8/docs/api/java/lang/ref/WeakReference.html`.

The field data cache

The field data cache is used when we want to send queries that involve operations that work on uninverted data. What Elasticsearch needs to do is load all the values for a given field and store that in the memory—you can call this field data cache. This cache is used by Elasticsearch when we use faceting, aggregations, scripting, or sorting on the field value. When first executing an operation that requires data uninverting, Elasticsearch loads all the data for that field into the memory. Yes, that's right; all the data from a given field is loaded into the memory by default and is never removed from it. Elasticsearch does this to be able to provide fast document-based access to values in a field. Remember that the field data cache is usually expensive to build from the hardware resource's point of view, because the data for the whole field needs to be loaded into the memory, and this requires both I/O operations and CPU resources.

> One should remember that for every field that we sort on or use faceting on, the data needs to be loaded into the memory each and every term. This can be expensive, especially for the fields that are high cardinality ones: the ones with numerous different terms in them.

Field data or doc values

Lucene doc values and their implementation in Elasticsearch is getting better and better with each release. With the release of Elasticsearch 1.4.0, they are almost, or as fast as, the field data cache. The thing is that doc values are calculated during indexing time and are stored on the disk along with the index, and they don't require as much memory as the field data cache. In fact, they require very little heap space and are almost as fast as the field data cache. If you are using operations that require large amounts of field data cache, you should consider using doc values for such fields. You only need to add the `doc_values` property and set it to `true` for such fields, and Elasticsearch will do the rest.

> At the time of writing this, Elasticsearch does not allow using doc values on analyzed string fields. You can use doc values with all the other field types.

For example, if we would like to set our year field to use doc values, we would change its configuration to the following one:

```
"year" : {
 "type" : "long",
 "ignore_malformed" : false,
```

```
"index" : "analyzed",
"doc_values" : true
}
```

If you reindex your data, Elasticsearch would use the doc values (instead of the field data cache) for the operations that require uninverted data in the `year` field, for example, aggregations.

Node-level field data cache configuration

Since Elasticsearch 0.90.0, we are allowed to use the following properties to configure the node-level field data cache, which is the default field data cache if we don't alter the configuration:

- `indices.fielddata.cache.size`: This specifies the maximum size of the field data cache either as a percentage value such as 20%, or an absolute memory size such as 10gb. If we use the percentage value, Elasticsearch will calculate it as a percentage of the maximum heap memory given to a node. By default, the field data cache size is unbounded and should be monitored, as it can consume a vast amount of memory given to the JVM.

- `indices.fielddata.cache.expire`: This property specifies the expiration time of an entry in the field data cache, which is set to -1 by default, which means that the entries in the cache won't be expired. If we want our field data cache to expire if not accessed, we can set the maximum time of inactivity. For example, if we like our cache to expire after 60 minutes, we should set this property to 60m. Please remember that the field data cache is very expensive to rebuild, and the expiration should be considered with caution.

 If we want to be sure that Elasticsearch will use the node-level field data cache, we should set the `index.fielddata.cache.type` property to the `node` value or not set that property at all.

Index-level field data cache configuration

Similar to index-level filter cache, we can also use the index-level field data cache, but again, it is not recommended that you do because of the same reasons: it is hard to predict which shards or which indices will be allocated to which nodes. Because of this, we can't predict the amount of memory that will be used for the field data cache for each index, and we can run into memory-related issues when Elasticsearch does the rebalancing, for example.

However, if you know what you are doing and what you want to use—resident or soft field data cache—you can use the `index.fielddata.cache.type` property and set it to `resident` or `soft`. As we already discussed during the filter cache's description, the entries in the resident cache can't be removed by JVM unless we want them to be, and it is basically recommended that you use this cache type when we want to use the index-level field data cache. Rebuilding the field data cache is expensive and will affect the Elasticsearch query's performance. The `soft` field data cache types can be cleared by JVM when it lacks memory.

The field data cache filtering

In addition to the previously mentioned configuration options, Elasticsearch allows us to choose which field values are loaded into the field data cache. This can be useful in some cases, especially if you remember that sorting, faceting, and aggregations use the field data cache to calculate the results. Elasticsearch allows us to use three types of field data loading filtering: by term frequency, by using `regex`, or a combination of both methods.

Let's talk about one of the examples where field data filtering can be useful and where you may want to exclude the terms with lower frequency from the results of faceting. For example, we may need to do this because we know that we have some terms in the index that have spelling mistakes, and these are lower cardinality terms for sure. We don't want to bother calculating aggregations for them, so we can remove them from the data, correct them in our data source, or remove them from the field data cache by filtering. This will not only exclude them from the results returned by Elasticsearch, but it will also make the field data memory footprint lower, because less data will be stored in the memory. Now let's look at the filtering possibilities.

Adding field data filtering information

In order to introduce the field data cache filtering information, we need to add an additional object to our mappings field definition: the `fielddata` object with its child object—`filter`. So our extended field definition for some abstract `tag` field would look as follows:

```
"tag" : {
 "type" : "string",
 "index" : "not_analyzed",
 "fielddata" : {
  "filter" : {
  ...
  }
 }
}
```

We will see what to put in the `filter` object in the upcoming sections.

Filtering by term frequency

Filtering by term frequency allows us to only load the terms that have a frequency higher than the specified minimum (the min parameter) and lower than the specified maximum (the max parameter). The term frequency bounded by the min and max parameters is not specified for the whole index but per segment, which is very important, because these frequencies will differ. The min and max parameters can be specified either as a percentage (for example, 1 percent is 0.01 and 50 percent is 0.5), or as an absolute number.

In addition to this, we can include the min_segment_size property that specifies the minimum number of documents a segment should contain in order to be taken into consideration while building the field data cache.

For example, if we would like to store only the terms that come from segments with at least 100 documents and the terms that have a segment term frequency between 1 percent to 20 percent in the field data cache, we should have mappings similar to the following ones:

```
{
  "book" : {
    "properties" : {
      "tag" : {
        "type" : "string",
        "index" : "not_analyzed",
        "fielddata" : {
          "filter" : {
            "frequency" : {
              "min" : 0.01,
              "max" : 0.2,
              "min_segment_size" : 100
            }
          }
        }
      }
    }
  }
}
```

Filtering by regex

In addition to filtering by the term frequency, we can also filter by the `regex` expression. In such a case, only the terms that match the specified `regex` will be loaded into the field data cache. For example, if we only want to load the data from the `tag` field, which probably has Twitter tags (starting with the # character), we should have the following mappings:

```
{
  "book" : {
    "properties" : {
      "tag" : {
        "type" : "string",
        "index" : "not_analyzed",
        "fielddata" : {
          "filter" : {
            "regex" : "^#.*"
          }
        }
      }
    }
  }
}
```

Filtering by regex and term frequency

Of course, we can combine the previously discussed filtering methods. So, if we want to have the field data cache responsible for holding the `tag` field data of only those terms that start with the # character, this comes from a segment with at least 100 documents and has a segment term frequency between 1 to 20 percent; we should have the following mappings:

```
{
  "book" : {
    "properties" : {
      "tag" : {
        "type" : "string",
        "index" : "not_analyzed",
        "fielddata" : {
          "filter" : {
            "frequency" : {
              "min" : 0.1,
              "max" : 0.2,
```

```
          "min_segment_size" : 100
        },
        "regex" : "^#.*"
      }
    }
  }
 }
}
}
```

> Remember that the field data cache is not built during indexing but can be rebuilt while querying and, because of that, we can change filtering during runtime by updating the `fieldata` section using the Mappings API. However, one has to remember that after changing the field data loading filtering settings, the cache should be cleared using the clear cache API described in the *Clearing the caches* section in this chapter.

The filtering example

So now, let's go back to the example from the beginning of the filtering section. What we want to do is exclude the terms with the lowest frequency from faceting results. In our case, the lowest ones are the ones that have the frequency lower than 50 percent. Of course, this frequency is very high, but in our example, we only use four documents. In production, you'd like to have different values: lower ones. In order to do this, we will create a `books` index with the following commands:

```
curl -XPOST 'localhost:9200/books' -d '{
  "settings" : {
   "number_of_shards" : 1,
   "number_of_replicas" : 0
  },
  "mappings" : {
   "book" : {
    "properties" : {
     "tag" : {
      "type" : "string",
      "index" : "not_analyzed",
      "fielddata" : {
       "filter" : {
        "frequency" : {
          "min" : 0.5,
          "max" : 0.99
```

```
            }
           }
          }
         }
        }
       }
      }
     }
   }'
```

Now, let's index some sample documents using the bulk API (the code is stored in the regex.json file provided with the book):

```
curl -s -XPOST 'localhost:9200/_bulk' --data-binary '
{ "index": {"_index": "books", "_type": "book", "_id": "1"}}
{"tag":["one"]}
{ "index": {"_index": "books", "_type": "book", "_id": "2"}}
{"tag":["one"]}
{ "index": {"_index": "books", "_type": "book", "_id": "3"}}
{"tag":["one"]}
{ "index": {"_index": "books", "_type": "book", "_id": "4"}}
{"tag":["four"]}
'
```

Now, let's check a simple term's faceting by running the following query (because as we already discussed, faceting and aggregations use the field data cache to operate):

```
curl -XGET 'localhost:9200/books/_search?pretty' -d ' {
 "query" : {
  "match_all" : {}
 },
 "aggregations" : {
  "tag" : {
   "terms" : {
    "field" : "tag"
   }
  }
 }
}'
```

The response for the preceding query would be as follows:

```
{
  "took" : 1,
  "timed_out" : false,
  "_shards" : {
    "total" : 1,
    "successful" : 1,
    "failed" : 0
  },
  .
  .
  .
  "aggregations" : {
  "tag" : {
        "doc_count_error_upper_bound" : 0,
        "sum_other_doc_count" : 0,
        "buckets" : [ {
          "key" : "one",
"doc_count" : 3 }]
  }
}
}
```

As you can see, the `terms` aggregation was only calculated for the `one` term, and the `four` term was omitted. If we assume that the `four` term was misspelled, then we have achieved what we wanted.

Field data formats

Field data cache is not a simple functionality and is implemented to save as much memory as possible. Because of this, Elasticsearch exposes a few formats for the field data cache depending on the data type. We can set the format of the internal data stored in the field data cache by specifying the `format` property inside a `fielddata` object for a field, for example:

```
"tag" : {
 "type" : "string",
 "fielddata" : {
  "format" : "paged_bytes"
 }
}
```

Let's now look at the possible formats.

String-based fields

For string-based fields, Elasticsearch exposes three formats of the field data cache. The default format is `paged_bytes`, which stores unique occurrences of the terms sequentially and maps documents to these terms. This data is stored in the memory. The second format is `fst`, which stores the field data cache in a structure called **Finite State Transducer (FST** — http://en.wikipedia.org/wiki/Finite_state_transducer), which results in lower memory usage compared to the default format, but it is also slower compared to it. Finally, the third format is `doc_values`, which results in computing the field data cache entries during indexing and storing them on the disk along with the index files. This format is almost as fast as the default one, but its memory footprint is very low. However, it can't be used with analyzed string fields. Field data filtering is not supported for the `doc_values` format.

Numeric fields

For numeric-based fields, we have two options when it comes to the format of the field data cache. The default `array` format stores the data in an in-memory array. The second type of format is `doc_values`, which uses doc values to store the field data, which means that the field data cache entries will be computed during indexing and stored on the disk along with the index files. Field data filtering is not supported for the `doc_values` format.

Geographical-based fields

For geo-point based fields, we have options similar to the numeric fields: the default `array` format, which stores longitudes and latitudes in an array, or `doc_values`, which uses doc values to store the field data. Of course, field data filtering is not supported for the `doc_values` format.

Field data loading

In addition to what we wrote already, Elasticsearch allows us to configure how the field data cache is loaded. As we already mentioned, the field data cache is loaded by default when the cache is needed for the first time — during the first query execution that needs uninverted data. We can change this behavior by including the `loading` property and setting it to `eager`. This will make Elasticsearch load the field data cache eagerly whenever new data appears to be loaded into the cache. Therefore, to make the field data cache for the `tag` field to be loaded eagerly, we would configure it the following way:

```
"tag" : {
  "type" : "string",
  "fielddata" : {
```

```
    "loading" : "eager"
  }
}
```

We can also completely disable the field data cache loading by setting the `format` property to `disabled`. For example, to disable loading the field data cache for our `tag` field, we can change its configuration to the following one:

```
"tag" : {
 "type" : "string",
 "fielddata" : {
  "format" : "disabled"
 }
}
```

Please note that functionalities that require uninverted data (such as aggregations) won't work on such defined fields.

The shard query cache

A new cache introduced in Elasticsearch 1.4.0 can help with query performance. The shard query cache is responsible for caching local results for each shard. As you remember, when Elasticsearch executes a query, it is sent to all the relevant shards and is executed on them. The results are returned to the node that requested them and are combined. The shard query cache is about caching these partial results on the shard level.

 At the time of writing this, the only cached `search_type` query was `count`. Therefore, the documents returned by the query will not be cached, but the total number of hits, aggregations, and suggestions returned by each shard will be cached, speeding up proceeding queries. Note that this is likely to be changed in future versions of Elasticsearch.

The shard query cache is not enabled by default. However, we have two options that show you how to enable it. We can do this by adding the `index.cache.query. enable` property and setting it to `true` in the settings of our index or by updating the indices settings in real-time with a command like this:

```
curl -XPUT 'localhost:9200/mastering/_settings' -d '{
 "index.cache.query.enable" : true
}'
```

The second option is to enable the shard query cache per request. We can do this by using the `query_cache` URI parameter set to true on a per-query basis. The thing to remember is that passing this parameter overwrites the index-level settings. An example request could look as follows:

```
curl -XGET
'localhost:9200/books/_search?search_type=count&query_cache=true' -d
'{
 "query" : {
  "match_all" : {}
 },
 "aggregations" : {
  "tags" : {
   "terms" : {
    "field" : "tag"
   }
  }
 }
}'
```

The good thing about shard query cache is that it is invalidated and updated automatically. Whenever a shard's contents changes, Elasticsearch will update the contents of the cache automatically, so the results of the cached and not cached query will always be the same.

Setting up the shard query cache

By default, Elasticsearch will use up to 1 percent of the heap size given to a node for the shard query cache. This means that all indices present on a node can use up to 1 percent of the total heap memory for the query cache. We can change this by setting the `indices.cache.query.size` property in the `elasticsearch.yml` file.

In addition to this, we can control the expiration time of the cache by setting the `indices.cache.query.expire` property. For example, if we would like the cache to be automatically expired after 60 minutes, we should set the property to `60m`.

Using circuit breakers

Because queries can put a lot of pressure on Elasticsearch resources, they allow us to use so-called circuit breakers that prevent Elasticsearch from using too much memory in certain functionalities. Elasticsearch estimates the memory usage and rejects the query execution if certain thresholds are met. Let's look at the available circuit breakers and what they can help us with.

The field data circuit breaker

The field data circuit breaker will prevent request execution if the estimated memory usage for the request is higher than the configured values. By default, Elasticsearch sets `indices.breaker.fielddata.limit` to `60%`, which means that no more than 60 percent of the JVM heap is allowed to be used for the field data cache.

We can also configure the multiplier that Elasticsearch uses for estimates (the estimated values are multiplied by this property value) by using the `indices.breaker.fielddata.overhead` property. By default, it is set to `1.03`.

 Please note than before Elasticsearch 1.4.0, `indices.breaker.fielddata.limit` was called `indices.fielddata.breaker.limit` and `indices.breaker.fielddata.overhead` was called `indices.fielddatabreaker.overhead`.

The request circuit breaker

Introduced in Elasticsearch 1.4.0, the request circuit breaker allows us to configure Elasticsearch to reject the execution of the request if the total estimated memory used by it will be higher than the `indices.breaker.request.limit` property (set to `40%` of the total heap memory assigned to the JVM by default).

Similar to the field data circuit breaker, we can set the overhead by using the `indices.breaker.request.overhead` property, which defaults to `1`.

The total circuit breaker

In addition to the previously described circuit breakers, Elasticsearch 1.4.0 introduced a notion of the total circuit breaker, which defines the total amount of memory that can be used along all the other circuit breakers. We can configure it using `indices.breaker.total.limit`, and it defaults to `70%` of the JVM heap.

Please remember that all the circuit breakers can be dynamically changed on a working cluster using the Cluster Update Settings API.

Clearing the caches

As we've mentioned earlier, sometimes it is necessary to clear the caches. Elasticsearch allows us to clear the caches using the _cache REST endpoint. Let's look at the usage possibilities.

Index, indices, and all caches clearing

The simplest thing we can do is just clear all the caches by running the following command:

```
curl -XPOST 'localhost:9200/_cache/clear'
```

Of course, as we are used to, we can choose a single index or multiple indices to clear the caches for them. For example, if we want to clear the cache for the mastering index, we should run the following command:

```
curl -XPOST 'localhost:9200/mastering/_cache/clear'
```

If we want to clear caches for the mastering and books indices, we should run the following command:

```
curl -XPOST 'localhost:9200/mastering,books/_cache/clear'
```

Clearing specific caches

By default, Elasticsearch clears all the caches when running the cache clear request. However, we are allowed to choose which caches should be cleared and which ones should be left alone. Elasticsearch allows us to choose the following behavior:

- Filter caches can be cleared by setting the filter parameter to true. In order to exclude this cache type from the clearing one, we should set this parameter to false. Note that the filter cache is not cleared immediately, but it is scheduled by Elasticsearch to be cleared in the next 60 seconds.

- The field data cache can be cleared by setting the field_data parameter to true. In order to exclude this cache type from the clearing one, we should set this parameter to false.

- To clear the caches of identifiers used for parent-child relationships, we can set the id_cache parameter to true. Setting this property to false will exclude that cache from being cleared.

- The shard query cache can be cleared by setting the query_cache parameter to true. Setting this parameter to false will exclude the shard query cache from being cleared.

For example, if we want all caches apart from the filter and shard query caches for the mastering index, we could run the following command:

```
curl -XPOST
'localhost:9200/mastering/_cache/clear?field_data=true&filter=false&query_cache=false'
```

Summary

In this chapter, we started by discussing how to alter the Apache Lucene scoring by using different similarity methods. We altered our index postings format writing by using codecs. We indexed and searched our data in a near real-time manner, and we also learned how to flush and refresh our data. We configured the transaction log and throttled the I/O subsystem. We talked about segment merging and how to visualize it. Finally, we discussed federated search and the usage of tribe nodes in Elasticsearch.

In the next chapter, we will focus on the Elasticsearch administration. We will configure discovery and recovery, and we will use the human-friendly Cat API. In addition to this, we will back up and restore our indices, finalizing what federated search is, and how to search and index data to multiple clusters while still using all the functionalities of Elasticsearch.

Elasticsearch Administration

7

In the previous chapter, we discussed how to alter the Apache Lucene scoring by using different similarity methods. We indexed and searched our data in a near real-time manner, and we also learned how to flush and refresh our data. We configured the transaction log and the throttled I/O subsystem. We talked about segment merging and how to visualize it. Finally, we discussed federated search and the usage of tribe nodes in Elasticsearch.

In this chapter, we will talk more about the Elasticsearch configuration and new features introduced in Elasticsearch 1.0 and higher. By the end of this chapter, you will have learned:

- Configuring the discovery and recovery modules
- Using the Cat API that allows a human-readable insight into the cluster status
- The backup and restore functionality
- Federated search

Discovery and recovery modules

When starting your Elasticsearch node, one of the first things that Elasticsearch does is look for a master node that has the same cluster name and is visible in the network. If a master node is found, the starting node gets joined into an already formed cluster. If no master is found, then the node itself is selected as a master (of course, if the configuration allows such behavior). The process of forming a cluster and finding nodes is called **discovery**. The module responsible for discovery has two main purposes—electing a master and discovering new nodes within a cluster.

After the cluster is formed, a process called **recovery** is started. During the recovery process, Elasticsearch reads the metadata and the indices from the gateway, and prepares the shards that are stored there to be used. After the recovery of the primary shards is done, Elasticsearch should be ready for work and should continue with the recovery of all the replicas (if they are present).

In this section, we will take a deeper look at these two modules and discuss the possibilities of configuration Elasticsearch gives us and what the consequences of changing them are.

 Note that the information provided in the *Discovery and recovery modules* section is an extension of what we already wrote in *Elasticsearch Server Second Edition*, published by *Packt Publishing*.

Discovery configuration

As we have already mentioned multiple times, Elasticsearch was designed to work in a distributed environment. This is the main difference when comparing Elasticsearch to other open source search and analytics solutions available. With such assumptions, Elasticsearch is very easy to set up in a distributed environment, and we are not forced to set up additional software to make it work like this. By default, Elasticsearch assumes that the cluster is automatically formed by the nodes that declare the same `cluster.name` setting and can communicate with each other using multicast requests. This allows us to have several independent clusters in the same network.

There are a few implementations of the discovery module that we can use, so let's see what the options are.

Zen discovery

Zen discovery is the default mechanism that's responsible for discovery in Elasticsearch and is available by default. The default Zen discovery configuration uses multicast to find other nodes. This is a very convenient solution: just start a new Elasticsearch node and everything works—this node will be joined to the cluster if it has the same cluster name and is visible by other nodes in that cluster. This discovery method is perfectly suited for development time, because you don't need to care about the configuration; however, it is not advised that you use it in production environments. Relying only on the cluster name is handy but can also lead to potential problems and mistakes, such as the accidental joining of nodes. Sometimes, multicast is not available for various reasons or you don't want to use it for these mentioned reasons. In the case of bigger clusters, the multicast discovery may generate too much unnecessary traffic, and this is another valid reason why it shouldn't be used for production.

For these cases, Zen discovery allows us to use the unicast mode. When using the unicast Zen discovery, a node that is not a part of the cluster will send a ping request to all the addresses specified in the configuration. By doing this, it informs all the specified nodes that it is ready to be a part of the cluster and can be either joined to an existing cluster or can form a new one. Of course, after the node joins the cluster, it gets the cluster topology information, but the initial connection is only done to the specified list of hosts. Remember that even when using unicast Zen discovery, the Elasticsearch node still needs to have the same cluster name as the other nodes.

 If you want to know more about the differences between multicast and unicast ping methods, refer to these URLs: `http://en.wikipedia.org/wiki/Multicast` and `http://en.wikipedia.org/wiki/Unicast`.

If you still want to learn about the configuration properties of multicast Zen discovery, let's look at them.

Multicast Zen discovery configuration

The multicast part of the Zen discovery module exposes the following settings:

- `discovery.zen.ping.multicast.address` (the default: all available interfaces): This is the interface used for the communication given as the address or interface name.

- `discovery.zen.ping.multicast.port` (the default: `54328`): This port is used for communication.

- `discovery.zen.ping.multicast.group` (the default: `224.2.2.4`): This is the multicast address to send messages to.

- `discovery.zen.ping.multicast.buffer_size` (the default: `2048`): This is the size of the buffer used for multicast messages.

- `discovery.zen.ping.multicast.ttl` (the default: `3`): This is the time for which a multicast message lives. Every time a packet crosses the router, the TTL is decreased. This allows for the limiting area where the transmission can be received. Note that routers can have the threshold values assigned compared to TTL, which causes that TTL value to not match exactly the number of routers that a packet can jump over.

- `discovery.zen.ping.multicast.enabled` (the default: `true`): Setting this property to `false` turns off the multicast. You should disable multicast if you are planning to use the unicast discovery method.

The unicast Zen discovery configuration

The unicast part of Zen discovery provides the following configuration options:

- `discovery.zen.ping.unicats.hosts`: This is the initial list of nodes in the cluster. The list can be defined as a list or as an array of hosts. Every host can be given a name (or an IP address) or have a port or port range added. For example, the value of this property can look like this: `["master1", "master2:8181", "master3[80000-81000]"]`. So, basically, the hosts' list for the unicast discovery doesn't need to be a complete list of Elasticsearch nodes in your cluster, because once the node is connected to one of the mentioned nodes, it will be informed about all the others that form the cluster.

- `discovery.zen.ping.unicats.concurrent_connects` (the default: 10): This is the maximum number of concurrent connections unicast discoveries will use. If you have a lot of nodes that the initial connection should be made to, it is advised that you increase the default value.

Master node

One of the main purposes of discovery apart from connecting to other nodes is to choose a master node—a node that will take care of and manage all the other nodes. This process is called **master election** and is a part of the discovery module. No matter how many master eligible nodes there are, each cluster will only have a single master node active at a given time. If there is more than one master eligible node present in the cluster, they can be elected as the master when the original master fails and is removed from the cluster.

Configuring master and data nodes

By default, Elasticsearch allows every node to be a master node and a data node. However, in certain situations, you may want to have worker nodes, which will only hold the data or process the queries and the master nodes that will only be used as cluster-managed nodes. One of these situations is to handle a massive amount of data, where data nodes should be as performant as possible, and there shouldn't be any delay in master nodes' responses.

Configuring data-only nodes

To set the node to only hold data, we need to instruct Elasticsearch that we don't want such a node to be a master node. In order to do this, we add the following properties to the `elasticsearch.yml` configuration file:

```
node.master: false
node.data: true
```

Configuring master-only nodes

To set the node not to hold data and only to be a master node, we need to instruct Elasticsearch that we don't want such a node to hold data. In order to do that, we add the following properties to the elasticsearch.yml configuration file:

```
node.master: true
node.data: false
```

Configuring the query processing-only nodes

For large enough deployments, it is also wise to have nodes that are only responsible for aggregating query results from other nodes. Such nodes should be configured as nonmaster and nondata, so they should have the following properties in the elasticsearch.yml configuration file:

```
node.master: false
node.data: false
```

 Please note that the node.master and the node.data properties are set to true by default, but we tend to include them for configuration clarity.

The master election configuration

We already wrote about the master election configuration in *Elasticsearch Server Section Edition*, but this topic is very important, so we decided to refresh our knowledge about it.

Imagine that you have a cluster that is built of 10 nodes. Everything is working fine until, one day, your network fails and three of your nodes are disconnected from the cluster, but they still see each other. Because of the Zen discovery and the master election process, the nodes that got disconnected elect a new master and you end up with two clusters with the same name with two master nodes. Such a situation is called a **split-brain** and you must avoid it as much as possible. When a split-brain happens, you end up with two (or more) clusters that won't join each other until the network (or any other) problems are fixed. If you index your data during this time, you may end up with data loss and unrecoverable situations when the nodes get joined together after the network split.

In order to prevent split-brain situations or at least minimize the possibility of their occurrences, Elasticsearch provides a `discovery.zen.minimum_master_nodes` property. This property defines a minimum amount of master eligible nodes that should be connected to each other in order to form a cluster. So now, let's get back to our cluster; if we set the `discovery.zen.minimum_master_nodes` property to 50 percent of the total nodes available plus one (which is six, in our case), we would end up with a single cluster. Why is that? Before the network failure, we would have 10 nodes, which is more than six nodes, and these nodes would form a cluster. After the disconnections of the three nodes, we would still have the first cluster up and running. However, because only three nodes disconnected and three is less than six, these three nodes wouldn't be allowed to elect a new master and they would wait for reconnection with the original cluster.

Zen discovery fault detection and configuration

Elasticsearch runs two detection processes while it is working. The first process is to send ping requests from the current master node to all the other nodes in the cluster to check whether they are operational. The second process is a reverse of that—each of the nodes sends ping requests to the master in order to verify that it is still up and running and performing its duties. However, if we have a slow network or our nodes are in different hosting locations, the default configuration may not be sufficient. Because of this, the Elasticsearch discovery module exposes three properties that we can change:

- `discovery.zen.fd.ping_interval`: This defaults to `1s` and specifies the interval of how often the node will send ping requests to the target node.

- `discovery.zen.fd.ping_timeout`: This defaults to `30s` and specifies how long the node will wait for the sent ping request to be responded to. If your nodes are 100 percent utilized or your network is slow, you may consider increasing that property value.

- `discovery.zen.fd.ping_retries`: This defaults to `3` and specifies the number of ping request retries before the target node will be considered not operational. You can increase this value if your network has a high number of lost packets (or you can fix your network).

There is one more thing that we would like to mention. The master node is the only node that can change the state of the cluster. To achieve a proper cluster state updates sequence, Elasticsearch master nodes process single cluster state update requests one at a time, make the changes locally, and send the request to all the other nodes so that they can synchronize their state. The master nodes wait for the given time for the nodes to respond, and if the time passes or all the nodes are returned, with the current acknowledgment information, it proceeds with the next cluster state update request processing. To change the time, the master node waits for all the other nodes to respond, and you should modify the default 30 seconds time by setting the `discovery.zen.publish_timeout` property. Increasing the value may be needed for huge clusters working in an overloaded network.

The Amazon EC2 discovery

Amazon, in addition to selling goods, has a few popular services such as selling storage or computing power in a pay-as-you-go model. So-called Amazon Elastic Compute Cloud (EC2) provides server instances and, of course, they can be used to install and run Elasticsearch clusters (among many other things, as these are normal Linux machines). This is convenient—you pay for instances that are needed in order to handle the current traffic or to speed up calculations, and you shut down unnecessary instances when the traffic is lower. Elasticsearch works well on EC2, but due to the nature of the environment, some features may work slightly differently. One of these features that works differently is discovery, because Amazon EC2 doesn't support multicast discovery. Of course, we can switch to unicast discovery, but sometimes, we want to be able to automatically discover nodes and, with unicast, we need to at least provide the initial list of hosts. However, there is an alternative— we can use the Amazon EC2 plugin, a plugin that combines the multicast and unicast discovery methods using the Amazon EC2 API.

> Make sure that during the set up of EC2 instances, you set up communication between them (on port 9200 and 9300 by default). This is crucial in order to have Elasticsearch nodes communicate with each other and, thus, cluster functioning is required. Of course, this communication depends on `network.bind_host` and `network.publish_host` (or `network.host`) settings.

The EC2 plugin installation

The installation of a plugin is as simple as with most of the plugins. In order to install it, we should run the following command:

```
bin/plugin install elasticsearch/elasticsearch-cloud-aws/2.4.0
```

The EC2 plugin's generic configuration

This plugin provides several configuration settings that we need to provide in order for the EC2 discovery to work:

- `cluster.aws.access_key`: Amazon access key — one of the credential values you can find in the Amazon configuration panel

- `cluster.aws.secret_key`: Amazon secret key — similar to the previously mentioned `access_key` setting, it can be found in the EC2 configuration panel

The last thing is to inform Elasticsearch that we want to use a new discovery type by setting the `discovery.type` property to `ec2` value and turn off multicast.

Optional EC2 discovery configuration options

The previously mentioned settings are sufficient to run the EC2 discovery, but in order to control the EC2 discovery plugin behavior, Elasticsearch exposes additional settings:

- `cloud.aws.region`: This region will be used to connect with Amazon EC2 web services. You can choose a region that's adequate for the region where your instance resides, for example, `eu-west-1` for Ireland. The possible values during the writing of the book were `eu-west`, `sa-east`, `us-east`, `us-west-1`, `us-west-2`, `ap-southeast-1`, and `ap-southeast-1`.

- `cloud.aws.ec2.endpoint`: If you are using EC2 API services, instead of defining a region, you can provide an address of the AWS endpoint, for example, `ec2.eu-west-1.amazonaws.com`.

- `cloud.aws.protocol`: This is the protocol that should be used by the plugin to connect to Amazon Web Services endpoints. By default, Elasticsearch will use the HTTPS protocol (which means setting the value of the property to `https`). We can also change this behavior and set the property to `http` for the plugin to use HTTP without encryption. We are also allowed to overwrite the `cloud.aws.protocol` settings for each service by using the `cloud.aws.ec2.protocol` and `cloud.aws.s3.protocol` properties (the possible values are the same — `https` and `http`).

- `cloud.aws.proxy_host`: Elasticsearch allows us to define a proxy that will be used to connect to AWS endpoints. The `cloud.aws.proxy_host` property should be set to the address to the proxy that should be used.

- `cloud.aws.proxy_port`: The second property related to the AWS endpoints proxy allows us to specify the port on which the proxy is listening. The `cloud.aws.proxy_port` property should be set to the port on which the proxy listens.

- `discovery.ec2.ping_timeout` (the default: `3s`): This is the time to wait for the response for the ping message sent to the other node. After this time, the nonresponsive node will be considered dead and removed from the cluster. Increasing this value makes sense when dealing with network issues or we have a lot of EC2 nodes.

The EC2 nodes scanning configuration

The last group of settings we want to mention allows us to configure a very important thing when building cluster working inside the EC2 environment— the ability to filter available Elasticsearch nodes in our Amazon Elastic Cloud Computing network. The Elasticsearch EC2 plugin exposes the following properties that can help us configure its behavior:

- `discovery.ec2.host_type`: This allows us to choose the host type that will be used to communicate with other nodes in the cluster. The values we can use are `private_ip` (the default one; the private IP address will be used for communication), `public_ip` (the public IP address will be used for communication), `private_dns` (the private hostname will be used for communication), and `public_dns` (the public hostname will be used for communication).

- `discovery.ec2.groups`: This is a comma-separated list of security groups. Only nodes that fall within these groups can be discovered and included in the cluster.

- `discovery.ec2.availability_zones`: This is array or command-separated list of availability zones. Only nodes with the specified availability zones will be discovered and included in the cluster.

- `discovery.ec2.any_group` (this defaults to `true`): Setting this property to `false` will force the EC2 discovery plugin to discover only those nodes that reside in an Amazon instance that falls into all of the defined security groups. The default value requires only a single group to be matched.

- `discovery.ec2.tag`: This is a prefix for a group of EC2-related settings. When you launch your Amazon EC2 instances, you can define tags, which can describe the purpose of the instance, such as the customer name or environment type. Then, you use these defined settings to limit discovery nodes. Let's say you define a tag named `environment` with a value of `qa`. In the configuration, you can now specify the following:

    - `discovery.ec2.tag.environment`: `qa` and only nodes running on instances with this tag will be considered for discovery.

    - `cloud.node.auto_attributes`: When this is set to `true`, Elasticsearch will add EC2-related node attributes (such as the availability zone or group) to the node properties and will allow us to use them, adjusting the Elasticsearch shard allocation and configuring the shard placement. You can find more about shard placement in the *Altering the default shard allocation behavior* section of *Chapter 5, The Index Distribution Architecture*.

Other discovery implementations

The Zen discovery and EC2 discovery are not the only discovery types that are available. There are two more discovery types that are developed and maintained by the Elasticsearch team, and these are:

- Azure discovery: `https://github.com/elasticsearch/elasticsearch-cloud-azure`
- Google Compute Engine discovery: `https://github.com/elasticsearch/elasticsearch-cloud-gce`

In addition to these, there are a few discovery implementations provided by the community, such as the ZooKeeper discovery for older versions of Elasticsearch (`https://github.com/sonian/elasticsearch-zookeeper`).

The gateway and recovery configuration

The gateway module allows us to store all the data that is needed for Elasticsearch to work properly. This means that not only is the data in Apache Lucene indices stored, but also all the metadata (for example, index allocation settings), along with the mappings configuration for each index. Whenever the cluster state is changed, for example, when the allocation properties are changed, the cluster state will be persisted by using the gateway module. When the cluster is started up, its state will be loaded using the gateway module and applied.

One should remember that when configuring different nodes and different gateway types, indices will use the gateway type configuration present on the given node. If an index state should not be stored using the gateway module, one should explicitly set the index gateway type to none.

The gateway recovery process

Let's say explicitly that the recovery process is used by Elasticsearch to load the data stored with the use of the gateway module in order for Elasticsearch to work. Whenever a full cluster restart occurs, the gateway process kicks in to load all the relevant information we've mentioned — the metadata, the mappings, and of course, all the indices. When the recovery process starts, the primary shards are initialized first, and then, depending on the replica state, they are initialized using the gateway data, or the data is copied from the primary shards if the replicas are out of sync.

Elasticsearch allows us to configure when the cluster data should be recovered using the gateway module. We can tell Elasticsearch to wait for a certain number of master eligible or data nodes to be present in the cluster before starting the recovery process. However, one should remember that when the cluster is not recovered, all the operations performed on it will not be allowed. This is done in order to avoid modification conflicts.

Configuration properties

Before we continue with the configuration, we would like to say one more thing. As you know, Elasticsearch nodes can play different roles — they can have a role of data nodes — the ones that hold data — they can have a master role, or they can be only used for request handing, which means not holding data and not being master eligible. Remembering all this, let's now look at the gateway configuration properties that we are allowed to modify:

- `gateway.recover_after_nodes`: This is an integer number that specifies how many nodes should be present in the cluster for the recovery to happen. For example, when set to 5, at least 5 nodes (doesn't matter whether they are data or master eligible nodes) must be present for the recovery process to start.

- `gateway.recover_after_data_nodes`: This is an integer number that allows us to set how many data nodes should be present in the cluster for the recovery process to start.

- `gateway.recover_after_master_nodes`: This is another gateway configuration option that allows us to set how many master eligible nodes should be present in the cluster for the recovery to start.

- `gateway.recover_after_time`: This allows us to set how much time to wait before the recovery process starts after the conditions defined by the preceding properties are met. If we set this property to `5m`, we tell Elasticsearch to start the recovery process 5 minutes after all the defined conditions are met. The default value for this property is `5m`, starting from Elasticsearch 1.3.0.

Let's imagine that we have six nodes in our cluster, out of which four are data eligible. We also have an index that is built of three shards, which are spread across the cluster. The last two nodes are master eligible and they don't hold the data. What we would like to configure is the recovery process to be delayed for 3 minutes after the four data nodes are present. Our gateway configuration could look like this:

```
gateway.recover_after_data_nodes: 4
gateway.recover_after_time: 3m
```

Expectations on nodes

In addition to the already mentioned properties, we can also specify properties that will force the recovery process of Elasticsearch. These properties are:

- `gateway.expected_nodes`: This is the number of nodes expected to be present in the cluster for the recovery to start immediately. If you don't need the recovery to be delayed, it is advised that you set this property to the number of nodes (or at least most of them) with which the cluster will be formed from, because that will guarantee that the latest cluster state will be recovered.

- `gateway.expected_data_nodes`: This is the number of expected data eligible nodes to be present in the cluster for the recovery process to start immediately.

- `gateway.expected_master_nodes`: This is the number of expected master eligible nodes to be present in the cluster for the recovery process to start immediately.

Now, let's get back to our previous example. We know that when all six nodes are connected and are in the cluster, we want the recovery to start. So, in addition to the preceeding configuration, we would add the following property:

```
gateway.expected_nodes: 6
```

So the whole configuration would look like this:

```
gateway.recover_after_data_nodes: 4
gateway.recover_after_time: 3m
gateway.expected_nodes: 6
```

The preceding configuration says that the recovery process will be delayed for 3 minutes once four data nodes join the cluster and will begin immediately after six nodes are in the cluster (doesn't matter whether they are data nodes or master eligible nodes).

The local gateway

With the release of Elasticsearch 0.20 (and some of the releases from 0.19 versions), all the gateway types, apart from the default `local gateway type`, were deprecated. It is advised that you do not use them, because they will be removed in future versions of Elasticsearch. This is still not the case, but if you want to avoid full data reindexation, you should only use the `local` gateway type, and this is why we won't discuss all the other types.

The `local` gateway type uses a local storage available on a node to store the metadata, mappings, and indices. In order to use this gateway type and the local storage available on the node, there needs to be enough disk space to hold the data with no memory caching.

The persistence to the local gateway is different from the other gateways that are currently present (but deprecated). The writes to this gateway are done in a synchronous manner in order to ensure that no data will be lost during the write process.

> In order to set the type of gateway that should be used, one should use the `gateway.type` property, which is set to `local` by default.

There is one additional thing regarding the local gateway of Elasticsearch that we didn't talk about—dangling indices. When a node joins a cluster, all the shards and indices that are present on the node, but are not present in the cluster, will be included in the cluster state. Such indices are called **dangling indices**, and we are allowed to choose how Elasticsearch should treat them.

Elasticsearch exposes the `gateway.local.auto_import_dangling` property, which can take the value of `yes` (the default value that results in importing all dangling indices into the cluster), `close` (results in importing the dangling indices into the cluster state but keeps them closed by default), and `no` (results in removing the dangling indices). When setting the `gateway.local.auto_import_dangling` property to `no`, we can also set the `gateway.local.dangling_timeout` property (defaults to `2h`) to specify how long Elasticsearch will wait while deleting the dangling indices. The dangling indices feature can be nice when we restart old Elasticsearch nodes, and we don't want old indices to be included in the cluster.

Low-level recovery configuration

We discussed that we can use the gateway to configure the behavior of the Elasticsearch recovery process, but in addition to that, Elasticsearch allows us to configure the recovery process itself. We mentioned some of the recovery configuration options already when talking about shard allocation in the *Altering The default shard allocation behavior* section of *Chapter 5, The Index Distribution Architecture;* however, we decided that it would be good to mention the properties we can use in the section dedicated to gateway and recovery.

Cluster-level recovery configuration

The recovery configuration is specified mostly on the cluster level and allows us to set general rules for the recovery module to work with. These settings are:

- `indices.recovery.concurrent_streams`: This defaults to `3` and specifies the number of concurrent streams that are allowed to be opened in order to recover a shard from its source. The higher the value of this property, the more pressure will be put on the networking layer; however, the recovery may be faster, depending on your network usage and throughput.

- `indices.recovery.max_bytes_per_sec`: By default, this is set to `20MB` and specifies the maximum number of data that can be transferred during shard recovery per second. In order to disable data transfer limiting, one should set this property to `0`. Similar to the number of concurrent streams, this property allows us to control the network usage of the recovery process. Setting this property to higher values may result in higher network utilization and a faster recovery process.

- `indices.recovery.compress`: This is set to `true` by default and allows us to define whether ElasticSearch should compress the data that is transferred during the recovery process. Setting this to `false` may lower the pressure on the CPU, but it will also result in more data being transferred over the network.

- `indices.recovery.file_chunk_size`: This is the chunk size used to copy the shard data from the source shard. By default, it is set to `512KB` and is compressed if the `indices.recovery.compress` property is set to `true`.

- `indices.recovery.translog_ops`: This defaults to `1000` and specifies how many transaction log lines should be transferred between shards in a single request during the recovery process.

- `indices.recovery.translog_size`: This is the chunk size used to copy the shard transaction log data from the source shard. By default, it is set to `512KB` and is compressed if the `indices.recovery.compress` property is set to `true`.

> In the versions prior to Elasticsearch 0.90.0, there was the `indices.recovery.max_size_per_sec` property that could be used, but it was deprecated, and it is suggested that you use the `indices.recovery.max_bytes_per_sec` property instead. However, if you are using an Elasticsearch version older than 0.90.0, it may be worth remembering this.

All the previously mentioned settings can be updated using the Cluster Update API, or they can be set in the `elasticsearch.yml` file.

Index-level recovery settings

In addition to the values mentioned previously, there is a single property that can be set on a per-index basis. The property can be set both in the `elasticsearch.yml` file and using the indices Update Settings API, and it is called `index.recovery.initial_shards`. In general, Elasticsearch will only recover a particular shard when there is a quorum of shards present and if that quorum can be allocated. A quorum is 50 percent of the shards for the given index plus one. By using the `index.recovery.initial_shards` property, we can change what Elasticsearch will take as a quorum. This property can be set to the one of the following values:

- `quorum`: 50 percent, plus one shard needs to be present and be allocable. This is the default value.

- `quorum-1`: 50 percent of the shards for a given index need to be present and be allocable.

- `full`: All of the shards for the given index need to be present and be allocable.

- `full-1`: 100 percent minus one shards for the given index need to be present and be allocable.

- **integer** value: Any integer such as 1, 2, or 5 specifies the number of shards that are needed to be present and that can be allocated. For example, setting this value to 2 will mean that at least two shards need to be present and Elasticsearch needs at least 2 shards to be allocable.

It is good to know about this property, but in most cases, the default value will be sufficient for most deployments.

The indices recovery API

With the introduction of the indices recovery API, we are no longer limited to only looking at the cluster state and the output similar to the following one:

```
curl 'localhost:9200/_cluster/health?pretty'
{
  "cluster_name" : "mastering_elasticsearch",
  "status" : "red",
  "timed_out" : false,
  "number_of_nodes" : 10,
  "number_of_data_nodes" : 10,
  "active_primary_shards" : 9,
  "active_shards" : 9,
  "relocating_shards" : 0,
  "initializing_shards" : 0,
  "unassigned_shards" : 1
}
```

By running an HTTP GET request to the _recovery endpoint (for all the indices or for a particular one), we can get the information about the state of the indices' recovery. For example, let's look at the following request:

```
curl -XGET 'localhost:9200/_recovery?pretty'
```

The preceding request will return information about ongoing and finished recoveries of all the shards in the cluster. In our case, the response was as follows (we had to cut it):

```
{
  "test_index" : {
    "shards" : [ {
      "id" : 3,
      "type" : "GATEWAY",
```

```
  "stage" : "START",
  "primary" : true,
  "start_time_in_millis" : 1414362635212,
  "stop_time_in_millis" : 0,
  "total_time_in_millis" : 175,
  "source" : {
    "id" : "3M_ErmCNTR-huTqOTv5smw",
    "host" : "192.168.1.10",
    "transport_address" : "inet[/192.168.1.10:9300]",
    "ip" : "192.168.10",
    "name" : "node1"
  },
  "target" : {
    "id" : "3M_ErmCNTR-huTqOTv5smw",
    "host" : "192.168.1.10",
    "transport_address" : "inet[/192.168.1.10:9300]",
    "ip" : "192.168.1.10",
    "name" : "node1"
  },
  "index" : {
    "files" : {
      "total" : 400,
      "reused" : 400,
      "recovered" : 400,
      "percent" : "100.0%"
    },
    "bytes" : {
      "total" : 2455604486,
      "reused" : 2455604486,
      "recovered" : 2455604486,
      "percent" : "100.0%"
    },
    "total_time_in_millis" : 28
  },
  "translog" : {
    "recovered" : 0,
    "total_time_in_millis" : 0
  },
  "start" : {
    "check_index_time_in_millis" : 0,
    "total_time_in_millis" : 0
  }
}, {
  "id" : 9,
```

```
"type" : "GATEWAY",
"stage" : "DONE",
"primary" : true,
"start_time_in_millis" : 1414085189696,
"stop_time_in_millis" : 1414085189729,
"total_time_in_millis" : 33,
"source" : {
  "id" : "nNw_k7_XSOivvPCJLHVE5A",
  "host" : "192.168.1.11",
  "transport_address" : "inet[/192.168.1.11:9300]",
  "ip" : "192.168.1.11",
  "name" : "node3"
},
"target" : {
  "id" : "nNw_k7_XSOivvPCJLHVE5A",
  "host" : "192.168.1.11",
  "transport_address" : "inet[/192.168.1.11:9300]",
  "ip" : "192.168.1.11",
  "name" : "node3"
},
"index" : {
  "files" : {
    "total" : 0,
    "reused" : 0,
    "recovered" : 0,
    "percent" : "0.0%"
  },
  "bytes" : {
    "total" : 0,
    "reused" : 0,
    "recovered" : 0,
    "percent" : "0.0%"
  },
  "total_time_in_millis" : 0
},
"translog" : {
  "recovered" : 0,
  "total_time_in_millis" : 0
},
"start" : {
  "check_index_time_in_millis" : 0,
  "total_time_in_millis" : 33
},
.
```

```
            .
            .
      ]
    }
  }
}
```

The preceding response contains information about two shards for test_index (the information for the rest of the shards was removed for clarity). We can see that one of the shards is during the recovery process ("stage" : "START") and the second one already finished the recovery process ("stage" : "DONE"). We can see a lot of information about the recovery process, and the information is provided on the index shard level, which allows us to clearly see at what stage our Elasticsearch cluster is. We can also limit the information to only shards that are currently being recovered by adding the active_only=true parameter to our request, so it would look as follows:

```
curl -XGET 'localhost:9200/_recovery?active_only=true&pretty'
```

If we want to get even more detailed information, we can add the detailed=true parameter to our request, so it would look like this:

```
curl -XGET 'localhost:9200/_recovery?detailed=true&pretty'
```

The human-friendly status API – using the Cat API

The Elasticsearch Admin API is quite extensive and covers almost every part of its architecture—from low-level information about Lucene to high-level information about the cluster nodes and their health. All this information is available both using the Elasticsearch Java API as well as using the REST API; however, the data is returned in the JSON format. What's more—the returned data can sometimes be hard to analyze without further parsing. For example, try to run the following request on your Elasticsearch cluster:

```
curl -XGET 'localhost:9200/_stats?pretty'
```

On our local, single node cluster, Elasticsearch returns the following information (we cut it down drastically; the full response can be found in the stats.json file provided with the book):

```
{
  "_shards" : {
    "total" : 60,
```

```
        "successful" : 30,
        "failed" : 0
      },
      "_all" : {
        "primaries" : {
          .

          .

          .
        },
        "total" : {
          .

          .

          .
        }
      },
      "indices" : {
        .

        .

        .
      }
    }
}
```

If you look at the provided stats.json file, you would see that the response is about 1,350 lines long. This isn't quite convenient for analysis by a human without additional parsing. Because of this, Elasticsearch provides us with a more human-friendly API—the Cat API. The special Cat API returns data in a simple text, tabular format, and what's more, it provides aggregated data that is usually usable without any further processing.

 Remember that we've told you that Elasticsearch allows you to get information not just in the JSON format? If you don't remember this, please try to add the format=yaml request parameter to your request.

The basics

The base endpoint for the Cat API is quite obvious—it is /_cat. Without any parameters, it shows us all the available endpoints for that API. We can check this by running the following command:

```
curl -XGET 'localhost:9200/_cat'
```

The response returned by Elasticsearch should be similar or identical (depending on your Elasticsearch version) to the following one:

```
=^.^=
/_cat/allocation
/_cat/shards
/_cat/shards/{index}
/_cat/master
/_cat/nodes
/_cat/indices
/_cat/indices/{index}
/_cat/segments
/_cat/segments/{index}
/_cat/count
/_cat/count/{index}
/_cat/recovery
/_cat/recovery/{index}
/_cat/health
/_cat/pending_tasks
/_cat/aliases
/_cat/aliases/{alias}
/_cat/thread_pool
/_cat/plugins
/_cat/fielddata
/_cat/fielddata/{fields}
```

So, looking for the top Elasticsearch allows us to get the following information using the Cat API:

- Shard allocation-related information
- All shard-related information (limited to a given index)
- Nodes information, including elected master indication
- Indices' statistics (limited to a given index)
- Segments' statistics (limited to a given index)
- Documents' count (limited to a given index)
- Recovery information (limited to a given index)
- Cluster health
- Tasks pending execution
- Index aliases and indices for a given alias

- The thread pool configuration
- Plugins installed on each node
- The field data cache size and field data cache sizes for individual fields

Using the Cat API

Let's start using the Cat API through an example. We can start with checking the cluster health of our Elasticsearch cluster. To do this, we just run the following command:

```
curl -XGET 'localhost:9200/_cat/health'
```

The response returned by Elasticsearch to the preceding command should be similar to the following one:

```
1414347090 19:11:30 elasticsearch yellow 1 1 47 47 0 0 47
```

It is clean and nice. Because it is in a tabular format, it is also easier to use the response in tools such as grep, awk, or sed—a standard set of tools for every administrator. It is also more readable once you know what it is all about. To add a header describing each column purpose, we just need to add an additional v parameter just like this:

```
curl -XGET 'localhost:9200/_cat/health?v'
```

The response is very similar to what we've seen previously, but it now contains a header describing each column:

```
epoch      timestamp cluster       status node.total node.data shards
pri relo init unassign
1414347107 19:11:47  elasticsearch yellow          1         1     47
47   0    0       47
```

Common arguments

Every Cat API endpoint has its own arguments, but there are a few common options that are shared among all of them:

- v: This adds a header line to response with names of presented items.
- h: This allows us to show only chosen columns (refer to the next section).
- help: This lists all possible columns that this particular endpoint is able to show. The command shows the name of the parameter, its abbreviation, and the description.

- bytes: This is the format for information representing values in bytes. As we said, the Cat API is designed to be used by humans and, because of that, these values are represented in a human-readable form by default, for example, 3.5kB or 40GB. The bytes option allows us to set the same base for all numbers, so sorting or numerical comparison will be easier. For example, bytes=b presents all values in bytes, bytes=k in kilobytes, and so on.

 For the full list of arguments for each Cat API endpoint, refer to the official Elasticsearch documentation available at http://www.elasticsearch.org/guide/en/elasticsearch/reference/current/cat.html.

The examples

When we wrote this book, the Cat API had 21 endpoints. We don't want to describe them all—it would be a repetition of information contained in the documentation or chapters about the administration API. However, we didn't want to leave this section without any example regarding the usage of the Cat API. Because of this, we decided to show you how easily you can get information using the Cat API compared to the standard JSON API exposed by Elasticsearch.

Getting information about the master node

The first example shows you how easy it is to get information about which node in our cluster is the master node. By calling the /_cat/master REST endpoint, we can get information about the nodes and which one of them is currently being elected as a master. For example, let's run the following command:

```
curl -XGET 'localhost:9200/_cat/master?v'
```

The response returned by Elasticsearch for my local two nodes cluster looks as follows:

```
id                      host         ip       node
8gfdQlV-SxKB0uUxkjbxSg Banshee.local 10.0.1.3 Siege
```

As you can see in the response, we've got the information about which node is currently elected as the master—we can see its identifier, IP address, and name.

Getting information about the nodes

The `/_cat/nodes` REST endpoint provides information about all the nodes in the cluster. Let's see what Elasticsearch will return after running the following command:

```
curl -XGET 'localhost:9200/_cat/nodes?v&h=name,node.role,load,uptime'
```

In the preceding example, we have used the possibility of choosing what information we want to get from the approximately 70 options for this endpoint. We have chosen to get only the node name, its role—whether a node is a data or client node— node load, and its uptime.

The response returned by Elasticsearch looks as follows:

```
name            node.role load uptime
Alicia Masters d          6.09  6.7m
Siege          d          6.09   1h
```

As you can see the `/_cat/nodes` REST endpoint provides all requested information about the nodes in the cluster.

Backing up

One of the most important tasks for the administrator is to make sure that no data will be lost in the case of a system failure. Elasticsearch, in its assumptions, is a resistant and well-configured cluster of nodes and can survive even a few simultaneous disasters. However, even the most properly configured cluster is vulnerable to network splits and network partitions, which in some very rare cases can result in data corruption or loss. In such cases, being able to get data restored from the backup is the only solution that can save us from recreating our indices. You probably already know what we want to talk about: the snapshot / restore functionality provided by Elasticsearch. However, as we said earlier, we don't want to repeat ourselves—this is a book for more advanced Elasticsearch users, and basics of the snapshot and restore API were already described in *Elasticsearch Server Second Edition* by *Packt Publishing* and in the official documentation. Now, we want to focus on the functionalities that were added after the release of Elasticsearch 1.0 and thus omitted in the previous book—let's talk about the cloud capabilities of the Elasticsearch backup functionality.

Saving backups in the cloud

The central concept of the snapshot / restore functionality is a **repository**. It is a place where the data—our indices and the related meta information—is safely stored (assuming that the storage is reliable and highly available). The assumption is that every node that is a part of the cluster has access to the repository and can both write to it and read from it. Because of the need for high availability and reliability, Elasticsearch, with the help of additional plugins, allows us to push our data outside of the cluster—to the cloud. There are three possibilities where our repository can be located, at least using officially supported plugins:

- The **S3 repository**: Amazon Web Services
- The **HDFS repository**: Hadoop clusters
- The **Azure repository**: Microsoft's cloud platform

Because we didn't discuss any of the plugins related to the snapshot / restore functionality, let's get through them to see where we can push our backup data.

The S3 repository

The S3 repository is a part of the Elasticsearch AWS plugin, so to use S3 as the repository for snapshotting, we need to install the plugin first:

```
bin/plugin -install elasticsearch/elasticsearch-cloud-aws/2.4.0
```

After installing the plugin on every Elasticsearch node in the cluster, we need to alter their configuration (the elasticsearch.yml file) so that the AWS access information is available. The example configuration can look like this:

```
cloud:
  aws:
    access_key: YOUR_ACCESS_KEY
    secret_key: YOUT_SECRET_KEY
```

To create the S3 repository that Elasticsearch will use for snapshotting, we need to run a command similar to the following one:

```
curl -XPUT 'http://localhost:9200/_snapshot/s3_repository' -d '{
 "type": "s3",
 "settings": {
  "bucket": "bucket_name"
 }
}'
```

The following settings are supported when defining an S3-based repository:

- bucket: This is the required parameter describing the Amazon S3 bucket to which the Elasticsearch data will be written and from which Elasticsearch will read the data.

- region: This is the name of the AWS region where the bucket resides. By default, the US Standard region is used.

- base_path: By default, Elasticsearch puts the data in the root directory. This parameter allows you to change it and alter the place where the data is placed in the repository.

- server_side_encryption: By default, encryption is turned off. You can set this parameter to true in order to use the AES256 algorithm to store data.

- chunk_size: By default, this is set to 100m and specifies the size of the data chunk that will be sent. If the snapshot size is larger than chunk_size, Elasticsearch will split the data into smaller chunks that are not larger than the size specified in chunk_size.

- buffer_size: The size of this buffer is set to 5m (which is the lowest possible value) by default. When the chunk size is greater than the value of buffer_size, Elasticsearch will split it into buffer_size fragments and use the AWS multipart API to send it.

- max_retries: This specifies the number of retries Elasticsearch will take before giving up on storing or retrieving the snapshot. By default, it is set to 3.

In addition to the preceding properties, we are allowed to set two additional properties that can overwrite the credentials stored in elasticserch.yml, which will be used to connect to S3. This is especially handy when you want to use several S3 repositories—each with its own security settings:

- access_key: This overwrites cloud.aws.access_key from elasticsearch.yml

- secret_key: This overwrites cloud.aws.secret_key from elasticsearch.yml

The HDFS repository

If you use Hadoop and its HDFS (http://wiki.apache.org/hadoop/HDFS) filesystem, a good alternative to back up the Elasticsearch data is to store it in your Hadoop cluster. As with the case of S3, there is a dedicated plugin for this. To install it, we can use the following command:

```
bin/plugin -i elasticsearch/elasticsearch-repository-hdfs/2.0.2
```

Note that there is an additional plugin version that supports Version 2 of Hadoop. In this case, we should append `hadoop2` to the plugin name in order to be able to install the plugin. So for Hadoop 2, our command that installs the plugin would look as follows:

```
bin/plugin -i elasticsearch/elasticsearch-repository-hdfs/2.0.2-hadoop2
```

There is also a lite version that can be used in a situation where Hadoop is installed on the system with Elasticsearch. In this case, the plugin does not contain Hadoop libraries and are already available to Elasticsearch. To install the lite version of the plugin, the following command can be used:

```
bin/plugin -i elasticsearch/elasticsearch-repository-hdfs/2.0.2-light
```

After installing the plugin on each Elasticsearch (no matter which version of the plugin was used) and restarting the cluster, we can use the following command to create a repository in our Hadoop cluster:

```
curl -XPUT 'http://localhost:9200/_snapshot/hdfs_repository' -d '{
 "type": "hdfs"
 "settings": {
  "path": "snapshots"
 }
}'
```

The available settings that we can use are as follows:

- `uri`: This is the optional parameter that tells Elasticsearch where HDFS resides. It should have a format like `hdfs://HOST:PORT/`.
- `path`: This is the information about the path where snapshot files should be stored. It is a required parameter.
- `load_default`: This specifies whether the default parameters from the Hadoop configuration should be loaded and set to `false` if the reading of the settings should be disabled.
- `conf_location`: This is the name of the Hadoop configuration file to be loaded. By default, it is set to `extra-cfg.xml`.
- `chunk_size`: This specifies the size of the chunk that Elasticsearch will use to split the snapshot data; by default, it is set to `10m`. If you want the snapshotting to be faster, you can use smaller chunks and more streams to push the data to HDFS.

- conf.<key>: This is where key is any Hadoop argument. The value provided using this property will be merged with the configuration.

- concurrent_streams: By default, this is set to 5 and specifies the number of concurrent streams used by a single node to write and read to HDFS.

The Azure repository

The last of the repositories we wanted to mention is Microsoft's Azure cloud. Just like Amazon S3, we are able to use a dedicated plugin to push our indices and metadata to Microsoft cloud services. To do this, we need to install a plugin, which we can do by running the following command:

```
bin/plugin -install elasticsearch/elasticsearch-cloud-azure/2.4.0
```

The configuration is also similar to the Amazon S3 plugin configuration. Our elasticsearch.yml file should contain the following section:

```
cloud:
    azure:
        storage_account: YOUR_ACCOUNT
        storage_key: YOUT_SECRET_KEY
```

After Elasticsearch is configured, we need to create the actual repository, which we do by running the following command:

```
curl -XPUT 'http://localhost:9200/_snapshot/azure_repository' -d '{
 "type": "azure"
}'
```

The following settings are supported by the Elasticsearch Azure plugin:

- container: As with the bucket in Amazon S3, every piece of information must reside in the container. This setting defines the name of the container in the Microsoft Azure space. The default value is elasticserch-snapshots.

- base_path: This allows us to change the place where Elasticsearch will put the data. By default, Elasticsearch puts the data in the root directory.

- chunk_size: This is the maximum chunk size used by Elasticsearch (set to 64m by default, and this is also the maximum value allowed). You can change it to change the size when the data should be split into smaller chunks.

Federated search

Sometimes, having data in a single cluster is not enough. Imagine a situation where you have multiple locations where you need to index and search your data—for example, local company divisions that have their own clusters for their own data. The main center of your company would also like to search the data—not in each location but all at once. Of course, in your search application, you can connect to all these clusters and merge the results manually, but from Elasticsearch 1.0, it is also possible to use the so-called **tribe node** that works as a federated Elasticsearch client and can provide access to more than a single Elasticsearch cluster. What the tribe node does is fetch all the cluster states from the connected clusters and merge these states into one global cluster state available on the tribe node. In this section, we will take a look at tribe nodes and how to configure and use them.

 Remember that the described functionality was introduced in Elasticsearch 1.0 and is still marked as experimental. It can be changed or even removed in future versions of Elasticsearch.

The test clusters

For the purpose of showing you how tribe nodes work, we will create two clusters that hold data. The first cluster is named mastering_one (as you remember to set the cluster name, you need to specify the cluster.name property in the elasticsearch.yml file) and the second cluster is named mastering_two. To keep it as simple as it can get, each of the clusters contain only a single Elasticsearch node. The node in the cluster named mastering_one is available at the 192.168.56.10 IP address and the cluster named mastering_one is available at the 192.168.56.40 IP address.

Cluster one was indexed with the following documents:

```
curl -XPOST '192.168.56.10:9200/index_one/doc/1' -d '{"name" : "Test document 1 cluster 1"}'
curl -XPOST '192.168.56.10:9200/index_one/doc/2' -d '{"name" : "Test document 2 cluster 1"}'
```

For the second cluster the following data was indexed:

```
curl -XPOST '192.168.56.40:9200/index_two/doc/1' -d '{"name" : "Test document 1 cluster 2"}'
curl -XPOST '192.168.56.40:9200/index_two/doc/2' -d '{"name" : "Test document 2 cluster 2"}'
```

Creating the tribe node

Now, let's try to create a simple tribe node that will use the multicast discovery by default. To do this, we need a new Elasticsearch node. We also need to provide a configuration for this node that will specify which clusters our tribe node should connect together—in our case, these are our two clusters that we created earlier. To configure our tribe node, we need the following configuration in the `elasticsearch.yml` file:

```
tribe.mastering_one.cluster.name: mastering_one
tribe.mastering_two.cluster.name: mastering_two
```

All the configurations for the tribe node are prefixed with the `tribe` prefix. In the preceding configuration, we told Elasticsearch that we will have two tribes: one named `mastering_one` and the second one named `mastering_two`. These are arbitrary names that are used to distinguish the clusters that are a part of the tribe cluster.

We can start our tribe node, which we will start on a server with the `192.168.56.50` IP address. After starting Elasticsearch, we will try to use the default multicast discovery to find the `mastering_one` and `mastering_two` clusters and connect to them. You should see the following in the logs of the tribe node:

```
[2014-10-30 17:28:04,377] [INFO ] [cluster.service         ]
[Feron] added {{[mastering_one_node_1][mGF6HHoORQGYkVTzuPd4Jw]
[ragnar][inet[/192.168.56.10:9300]]{tribe.name=mastering_one},},
reason: cluster event from mastering_one, zen-disco-receive(from
master [[mastering_one_node_1][mGF6HHoORQGYkVTzuPd4Jw][ragnar]
[inet[/192.168.56.10:9300]]])
[2014-10-30 17:28:08,288] [INFO ] [cluster.service         ]
[Feron] added {{[mastering_two_node_1][ZqvDAsY1RmylH46hqCTEnw]
[ragnar][inet[/192.168.56.40:9300]]{tribe.name=mastering_two},},
reason: cluster event from mastering_two, zen-disco-receive(from
master [[mastering_two_node_1][ZqvDAsY1RmylH46hqCTEnw][ragnar]
[inet[/192.168.56.40:9300]]])
```

As we can see, our tribe node joins two clusters together.

Using the unicast discovery for tribes

Of course, multicast discovery is not the only possibility to connect multiple clusters together using the tribe node; we can also use the unicast discovery if needed. For example, to change our tribe node configuration to use unicast, we would change the `elasticsearch.yml` file to look as follows:

```
tribe.mastering_one.cluster.name: mastering_one
tribe.mastering_one.discovery.zen.ping.multicast.enabled: false
```

```
tribe.mastering_one.discovery.zen.ping.unicast.hosts:
["192.168.56.10:9300"]
tribe.mastering_two.cluster.name: mastering_two
tribe.mastering_two.discovery.zen.ping.multicast.enabled: false
tribe.mastering_two.discovery.zen.ping.unicast.hosts:
["192.168.56.40:9300"]
```

As you can see, for each tribe cluster, we disabled the multicast and we specified the unicast hosts. Also note the thing we already wrote about—each property for the tribe node is prefixed with the `tribe` prefix.

Reading data with the tribe node

We said in the beginning that the tribe node fetches the cluster state from all the connected clusters and merges it into a single cluster state. This is done in order to enable read and write operations on all the clusters when using the tribe node. Because the cluster state is merged, almost all operations work in the same way as they would on a single cluster, for example, searching.

Let's try to run a single query against our tribe now to see what we can expect. To do this, we use the following command:

```
curl -XGET '192.168.56.50:9200/_search?pretty'
```

The results of the preceding query look as follows:

```
{
  "took" : 9,
  "timed_out" : false,
  "_shards" : {
    "total" : 10,
    "successful" : 10,
    "failed" : 0
  },
  "hits" : {
    "total" : 4,
    "max_score" : 1.0,
    "hits" : [ {
      "_index" : "index_two",
      "_type" : "doc",
      "_id" : "1",
      "_score" : 1.0,
      "_source":{"name" : "Test document 1 cluster 2"}
    }, {
      "_index" : "index_one",
```

```
            "_type" : "doc",
            "_id" : "2",
            "_score" : 1.0,
            "_source":{"name" : "Test document 2 cluster 1"}
         }, {
            "_index" : "index_two",
            "_type" : "doc",
            "_id" : "2",
            "_score" : 1.0,
            "_source":{"name" : "Test document 2 cluster 2"}
         }, {
            "_index" : "index_one",
            "_type" : "doc",
            "_id" : "1",
            "_score" : 1.0,
            "_source":{"name" : "Test document 1 cluster 1"}
         } ]
      }
   }
```

As you can see, we have documents coming from both clusters—yes, that's right; our tribe node was about to automatically get data from all the connected tribes and return the relevant results. We can, of course, do the same with more sophisticated queries; we can use percolation functionality, suggesters, and so on.

Master-level read operations

Read operations that require the master to be present, such as reading the cluster state or cluster health, will be performed on the tribe cluster. For example, let's look at what cluster health returns for our tribe node. We can check this by running the following command:

```
curl -XGET '192.168.56.50:9200/_cluster/health?pretty'
```

The results of the preceding command will be similar to the following one:

```
{
   "cluster_name" : "elasticsearch",
   "status" : "yellow",
   "timed_out" : false,
   "number_of_nodes" : 5,
   "number_of_data_nodes" : 2,
   "active_primary_shards" : 10,
   "active_shards" : 10,
   "relocating_shards" : 0,
```

```
    "initializing_shards" : 0,
    "unassigned_shards" : 10
}
```

As you can see, our tribe node reported 5 nodes to be present. We have a single node for each of the connected clusters: one tribe node and two internal nodes that are used to provide connectivity to the connected clusters. This is why there are 5 nodes and not three of them.

Writing data with the tribe node

We talked about querying and master-level read operations, so it is time to write some data to Elasticsearch using the tribe node. We won't say much; instead of talking about indexing, let's just try to index additional documents to one of our indices that are present on the connected clusters. We can do this by running the following command:

```
curl -XPOST '192.168.56.50:9200/index_one/doc/3' -d '{"name" : "Test
document 3 cluster 1"}'
```

The execution of the preceding command will result in the following response:

```
{"_index":"index_one","_type":"doc","_id":"3","_
version":1,"created":true}
```

As we can see, the document has been created and, what's more, it was indexed in the proper cluster. The tribe node just did its work by forwarding the request internally to the proper cluster. All the write operations that don't require the cluster state to change, such as indexing, will be properly executed using the tribe node.

Master-level write operations

Master-level write operations can't be executed on the tribe node—for example, we won't be able to create a new index using the tribe node. Operations such as index creation will fail when executed on the tribe node, because there is no global master present. We can test this easily by running the following command:

```
curl -XPOST '192.168.56.50:9200/index_three'
```

The preceding command will return the following error after about 30 seconds of waiting:

```
{"error":"MasterNotDiscoveredException[waited for
[30s]]","status":503}
```

As we can see, the index was not created. We should run the master-level write commands on the clusters that are a part of the tribe.

Handling indices conflicts

One of the things that the tribe node can't handle properly is indices with the same names present in multiple connected clusters. What the Elasticsearch tribe node will do by default is that it will choose one and only one index with the same name. So, if all your clusters have the same index, only a single one will be chosen.

Let's test this by creating the index called `test_conflicts` on the `mastering_one` cluster and the same index on the `mastering_two` cluster. We can do this by running the following commands:

```
curl -XPOST '192.168.56.10:9200/test_conflicts'
curl -XPOST '192.168.56.40:9200/test_conflicts'
```

In addition to this, let's index two documents—one to each cluster. We do this by running the following commands:

```
curl -XPOST '192.168.56.10:9200/test_conflicts/doc/11' -d '{"name" :
"Test conflict cluster 1"}'
curl -XPOST '192.168.56.40:9201/test_conflicts/doc/21' -d '{"name" :
"Test conflict cluster 2"}'
```

Now, let's run our tribe node and try to run a simple search command:

```
curl -XGET '192.168.56.50:9202/test_conflicts/_search?pretty'
```

The output of the command will be as follows:

```
{
  "took" : 1,
  "timed_out" : false,
  "_shards" : {
    "total" : 5,
    "successful" : 5,
    "failed" : 0
  },
  "hits" : {
    "total" : 1,
    "max_score" : 1.0,
    "hits" : [ {
      "_index" : "test_conflicts",
      "_type" : "doc",
```

```
        "_id" : "11",
        "_score" : 1.0,
        "_source":{"name" : "Test conflict cluster 1"}
    } ]
  }
}
```

As you can see, we only got a single document in the result. This is because the Elasticsearch tribe node can't handle indices with the same names coming from different clusters and will choose only one index. This is quite dangerous, because we don't know what to expect.

The good thing is that we can control this behavior by specifying the `tribe.on_conflict` property in `elasticsearch.yml` (introduced in Elasticsearch 1.2.0). We can set it to one of the following values:

- `any`: This is the default value that results in Elasticsearch choosing one of the indices from the connected tribe clusters.
- `drop`: Elasticsearch will ignore the index and won't include it in the global cluster state. This means that the index won't be visible when using the cluster node (both for write and read operations) but still will be present on the connected clusters themselves.
- `prefer_TRIBE_NAME`: Elasticsearch allows us to choose the tribe cluster from which the indices should be taken. For example, if we set our property to `prefer_mastering_one`, it would mean that Elasticsearch will load the conflicting indices from the cluster named `mastering_one`.

Blocking write operations

The tribe node can also be configured to block all write operations and all the metadata change requests. To block all the write operations, we need to set the `tribe.blocks.write` property to `true`. To disallow metadata change requests, we need to set the `tribe.blocks.metadata` property to `true`. By default, these properties are set to `false`, which means that write and metadata altering operations are allowed. Disallowing these operations can be useful when our tribe node should only be used for searching and nothing else.

In addition to this, Elasticsearch 1.2.0 introduced the ability to block write operations on defined indices. We do this by using the `tribe.blocks.indices.write` property and setting its value to the name of the indices. For example, if we want our tribe node to block write operations on all the indices starting with `test` and `production`, we set the following property in the `elasticsearch.yml` file of the tribe node:

```
tribe.blocks.indices.write: test*, production*
```

Summary

In this chapter, we focused more on the Elasticsearch configuration and new features that were introduced in Elasticsearch 1.0. We configured discovery and recovery, and we used the human-friendly Cat API. In addition to that, we used the backup and restore functionality, which allowed easy backup and recovery of our indices. Finally, we looked at what federated search is and how to search and index data to multiple clusters, while still using all the functionalities of Elasticsearch and being connected to a single node.

In the next chapter, we will focus on the performance side of Elasticsearch. We will start by optimizing our queries with filters. We will discuss the garbage collector work, and we will benchmark our queries with the new benchmarking capabilities of Elasticsearch. We will use warming queries to speed up the query execution time, and we will use the Hot Threads API to see what is happening inside Elasticsearch. Finally, we will discuss Elasticsearch scaling and prepare Elasticsearch for high indexing and querying use cases.

8
Improving Performance

In the previous chapter, we looked at the discovery and recovery modules' configuration. We configured these modules and learned why they are important. We also saw additional discovery implementations available through plugins. We used the human-friendly Cat API to get information about the cluster in a human-readable form. We backed up our data to the external cloud storage, and we discussed tribe nodes—a federated search functionality allowing you to connect several Elasticsearch clusters together. By the end of this chapter, you will have learned the following things:

- What doc values can help us with when it comes to queries that are based on field data cache
- How garbage collector works
- How to benchmark your queries and fix performance problems before going to production
- What is the Hot Threads API and how it can help you with problems' diagnosis
- How to scale Elasticsearch and what to look at when doing that
- Preparing Elasticsearch for high querying throughput use cases
- Preparing Elasticsearch for high indexing throughput use cases

Using doc values to optimize your queries

In the *Understanding Elasticsearch caching* section of *Chapter 6, Low-level Index Control* we described caching: one of many ways that allow us to improve Elasticsearch's outstanding performance. Unfortunately, caching is not a silver bullet and, sometimes, it is better to avoid it. If your data is changing rapidly and your queries are very unique and not repeatable, then caching won't really help and can even make your performance worse sometimes.

The problem with field data cache

Every cache is based on a simple principle. The main assumption is that to improve performance, it is worth storing some part of the data in the memory instead of fetching from slow sources such as spinning disks, or to save the system a need to recalculate some processed data. However, caching is not free and it has its price—in terms of Elasticsearch, the cost of caching is mostly memory. Depending on the cache type, you may only need to store recently used data, but again, that's not always possible. Sometimes, it is necessary to hold all the information at once, because otherwise, the cache is just useless. For example, the field data cache used for sorting or aggregations—to make this functionality work, all values for a given field must be uninverted by Elasticsearch and placed in this cache. If we have a large number of documents and our shards are very large, we can be in trouble. The signs of such troubles may be something such as those in the response returned by Elasticsearch when running queries:

```
{
    "error": "ReduceSearchPhaseException[Failed to execute phase
    [fetch], [reduce] ; shardFailures {[vWD3FNVoTy-
    64r2vf6NwAw][dvt1][1]: ElasticsearchException[Java heap space];
    nested: OutOfMemoryError[Java heap space]; }{[vWD3FNVoTy-
    64r2vf6NwAw][dvt1][2]: ElasticsearchException[Java heap space];
    nested: OutOfMemoryError[Java heap space]; }]; nested:
    OutOfMemoryError[Java heap space]; ",
    "status": 500
}
```

The other indications of memory-related problems may be present in Elasticsearch logs and look as follows:

```
[2014-11-29 23:21:32,991] [DEBUG] [action.search.type       ]
    [Abigail Brand] [dvt1][2], node[vWD3FNVoTy-64r2vf6NwAw], [P],
    s[STARTED]: Failed to execute
    [org.elasticsearch.action.search.SearchRequest@49d609d3]
    lastShard [true]
```

```
org.elasticsearch.ElasticsearchException: Java heap space
    at org.elasticsearch.ExceptionsHelper.convertToRuntime
    (ExceptionsHelper.java:46)
    at org.elasticsearch.search.SearchService.executeQueryPhase
    (SearchService.java:304)
    at org.elasticsearch.search.action.
    SearchServiceTransportAction$5.call
    (SearchServiceTransportAction.java:231)
    at org.elasticsearch.search.action.
    SearchServiceTransportAction$5.call
    (SearchServiceTransportAction.java:228)
    at org.elasticsearch.search.action.
    SearchServiceTransportAction$23.run
    (SearchServiceTransportAction.java:559)
    at java.util.concurrent.ThreadPoolExecutor.runWorker
    (ThreadPoolExecutor.java:1145)
    at java.util.concurrent.ThreadPoolExecutor$Worker.run
    (ThreadPoolExecutor.java:615)
    at java.lang.Thread.run(Thread.java:744)
Caused by: java.lang.OutOfMemoryError: Java heap space
```

This is where doc values can help us. Doc values are data structures in Lucene that are column-oriented, which means that they do not store the data in inverted index but keep them in a document-oriented data structure that is stored on the disk and calculated during the indexation. Because of this, doc values allow us to avoid keeping uninverted data in the field data cache and instead use doc values that access the data from the index, and since Elasticsearch 1.4.0, values are as fast as you would use in the memory field data cache.

The example of doc values usage

To show you the difference in memory consumption between the doc values-based approach and the field data cache-based approach, we indexed some simple documents into Elasticsearch. We indexed the same data to two indices: dvt1 and dvt2. Their structure is identical; the only difference is highlighted in the following code:

```
{
  "t": {
    "properties": {
      "token": {
        "type": "string",
        "index": "not_analyzed",
```

```
            "doc_values": true
        }
      }
    }
  }
}
```

The `dvt2` index uses `doc_values`, while `dtv1` doesn't use it, so the queries run against them (if they use sorting or aggregations) will use the field data cache.

> For the purpose of the tests, we've set the JVM heap lower than the default values given to Elasticsearch. The example Elasticsearch instance was run using:
>
> ```
> bin/elasticsearch -Xmx16m -Xms16m
> ```
>
> This seems somewhat insane for the first sight, but who said that we can't run Elasticsearch on the embedded device? The other way to simulate this problem is, of course, to index way more data. However, for the purpose of the test, keeping the memory low is more than enough.

Let's now see how Elasticsearch behaves when hitting our example indices. The query does not look complicated but shows the problem very well. We will try to sort our data on the basis of our single field in the document: the `token` type. As we know, sorting requires uninverted data, so it will use either the field data cache or doc values if they are available. The query itself looks as follows:

```
{
  "sort": [
    {
      "token": {
        "order": "desc"
      }
    }
  ]
}
```

It is a simple sort, but it is sufficient to take down our server when we try to search in the `dvt1` index. At the same time, a query run against the `dvt2` index returns the expected results without any sign of problems.

The difference in memory usage is significant. We can compare the memory usage for both indices after restarting Elasticsearch and removing the memory limit from the startup parameters. After running the query against both `dvt1` and `dvt2`, we use the following command to check the memory usage:

```
curl -XGET 'localhost:9200/dvt1,dvt2/_stats/fielddata?pretty'
```

The response returned by Elasticsearch in our case was as follows:

```
{
  "_shards" : {
    "total" : 20,
    "successful" : 10,
    "failed" : 0
  },
  "_all" : {
    "primaries" : {
      "fielddata" : {
        "memory_size_in_bytes" : 17321304,
        "evictions" : 0
      }
    },
    "total" : {
      "fielddata" : {
        "memory_size_in_bytes" : 17321304,
        "evictions" : 0
      }
    }
  },
  "indices" : {
    "dvt2" : {
      "primaries" : {
        "fielddata" : {
          "memory_size_in_bytes" : 0,
          "evictions" : 0
        }
      },
      "total" : {
        "fielddata" : {
          "memory_size_in_bytes" : 0,
          "evictions" : 0
        }
      }
    },
    "dvt1" : {
      "primaries" : {
        "fielddata" : {
          "memory_size_in_bytes" : 17321304,
          "evictions" : 0
        }
      },
```

```
        "total" : {
          "fielddata" : {
            "memory_size_in_bytes" : 17321304,
            "evictions" : 0
          }
        }
      }
    }
  }
```

The most interesting parts are highlighted. As we can see, the indexes without doc_ values use 17321304 bytes (16 MB) of memory for the field data cache. At the same time, the second index uses nothing; exactly no RAM memory is used to store the uninverted data.

Of course, as with most optimizations, doc values are not free to use when it comes to resources. Among the drawbacks of using doc values are speed—doc values are slightly slower compared to field data cache. The second drawback is the additional space needed for doc_values. For example, in our simple test case, the index with doc values was 41 MB, while the index without doc values was 34 MB. This gives us a bit more than 20 percent increase in the index size, but that usually depends on the data you have in your index. However, remember that if you have memory problems related to queries and field data cache, you may want to turn on doc values, reindex your data, and not worry about out-of-memory exceptions related to the field data cache anymore.

Knowing about garbage collector

You know that Elasticsearch is a Java application and, because of that, it runs in the Java Virtual Machine. Each Java application is compiled into a so-called **byte code**, which can be executed by the JVM. In the most general way of thinking, you can imagine that the JVM is just executing other programs and controlling their behavior. However, this is not what you will care about unless you develop plugins for Elasticsearch, which we will discuss in *Chapter 9, Developing Elasticsearch Plugins*. What you will care about is the **garbage collector**—the piece of JVM that is responsible for memory management. When objects are de-referenced, they can be removed from the memory by the garbage collector. When the memory is running, the low garbage collector starts working and tries to remove objects that are no longer referenced. In this section, we will see how to configure the garbage collector, how to avoid memory swapping, how to log the garbage collector behavior, how to diagnose problems, and how to use some Java tools that will show you how it all works.

You can learn more about the architecture of JVM in many places you find on the World Wide Web, for example, on Wikipedia: http://en.wikipedia.org/wiki/Java_virtual_machine.

Java memory

When we specify the amount of memory using the Xms and Xmx parameters (or the ES_MIN_MEM and ES_MAX_MEM properties), we specify the minimum and maximum size of the JVM heap space. It is basically a reserved space of physical memory that can be used by the Java program, which in our case, is Elasticsearch. A Java process will never use more heap memory than what we've specified with the Xmx parameter (or the ES_MAX_MEM property). When a new object is created in a Java application, it is placed in the heap memory. After it is no longer used, the garbage collector will try to remove that object from the heap to free the memory space and for JVM to be able to reuse it in the future. You can imagine that if you don't have enough heap memory for your application to create new objects on the heap, then bad things will happen. JVM will throw an OutOfMemory exception, which is a sign that something is wrong with the memory—either we don't have enough of it, or we have some memory leak and we don't release the object that we don't use.

When running Elasticsearch on machines that are powerful and have a lot of free RAM memory, we may ask ourselves whether it is better to run a single large instance of Elasticsearch with plenty of RAM given to the JVM or a few instances with a smaller heap size. Before we answer this question, we need to remember that the more the heap memory is given to the JVM, the harder the work for the garbage collector itself gets. In addition to this, when setting the heap size to more than 31 GB, we don't benefit from the compressed operators, and JVM will need to use 64-bit pointers for the data, which means that we will use more memory to address the same amount of data. Given these facts, it is usually better to go for multiple smaller instances of Elasticsearch instead of one big instance.

The JVM memory (in Java 7) is divided into the following regions:

- **eden space**: This is the part of the heap memory where the JVM initially allocates most of the object types.

- **survivor space**: This is the part of the heap memory that stores objects that survived the garbage collection of the eden space heap. The survivor space is divided into survivor space 0 and survivor space 1.

- **tenured generation**: This is the part of the heap memory that holds objects that were living for some time in the survivor space heap part.

- **permanent generation**: This is the non-heap memory that stores all the data for the virtual machine itself, such as classes and methods for objects.

- **code cache**: This is the non-heap memory that is present in the HotSpot JVM that is used for the compilation and storage of native code.

The preceding classification can be simplified. The eden space and the survivor space is called the **young generation** heap space, and the tenured generation is often called **old generation**.

The life cycle of Java objects and garbage collections

In order to see how the garbage collector works, let's go through the life cycle of a sample Java object.

When a new object is created in a Java application, it is placed in the young generation heap space inside the eden space part. Then, when the next young generation garbage collection is run and the object survives that collection (basically, if it was not a one-time used object and the application still needs it), it will be moved to the survivor part of the young generation heap space (first to survivor 0 and then, after another young generation garbage collection, to survivor 1).

After living for sometime in the survivor 1 space, the object is moved to the tenured generation heap space, so it will now be a part of the old generation. From now on, the young generation garbage collector won't be able to move that object in the heap space. Now, this object will be live in the old generation until our application decides that it is not needed anymore. In such a case, when the next full garbage collection comes in, it will be removed from the heap space and will make place for new objects.

 There is one thing to remember: what you usually try to aim to do is smaller, but more garbage collections count rather than one but longer. This is because you want your application to be running at the same constant performance level and the garbage collector work to be transparent for Elasticsearch. When a big garbage collection happens, it can be a stop for the world garbage collection event, where Elasticsearch will be frozen for a short period of time, which will make your queries very slow and will stop your indexing process for some time.

Based on the preceding information, we can say (and it is actually true) that at least till now, Java used generational garbage collection; the more garbage collections our object survives, the further it gets promoted. Because of this, we can say that there are two types of garbage collectors working side by side: the young generation garbage collector (also called minor) and the old generation garbage collector (also called major).

> With the update 9 of Java 7, Oracle introduced a new garbage collector called G1. It is promised to be almost totally unaffected by stop the world events and should be working faster compared to other garbage collectors. To read more about G1, please refer to http://www.oracle.com/technetwork/tutorials/tutorials-1876574.html. Although Elasticsearch creators advise against using G1, numerous companies use it with success, and it allowed them to overcome problems with stop the world events when using Elasticsearch with large volumes of data and heavy queries.

Dealing with garbage collection problems

When dealing with garbage collection problems, the first thing you need to identify is the source of the problem. It is not straightforward work and usually requires some effort from the system administrator or the people responsible for handling the cluster. In this section, we will show you two methods of observing and identifying problems with the garbage collector; the first is to turn on logging for the garbage collector in Elasticsearch, and the second is to use the jstat command, which is present in most Java distributions.

In addition to the presented methods, please note that there are tools out there that can help you diagnose issues related to memory and the garbage collector. These tools are usually provided in the form of monitoring software solutions such as Sematext Group SPM (http://sematext.com/spm/index.html) or NewRelic (http://newrelic.com/). Such solutions provide sophisticated information not only related to garbage collection, but also the memory usage as a whole.

An example dashboard from the mentioned SPM application showing the garbage collector work looks as follows:

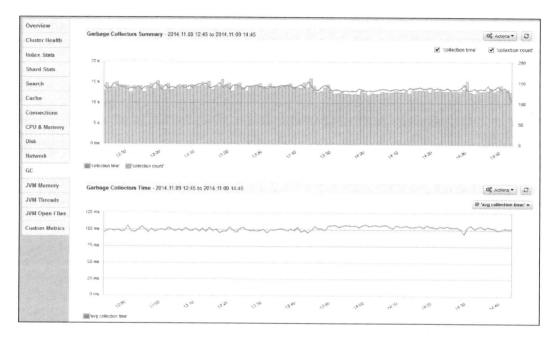

Turning on logging of garbage collection work

Elasticsearch allows us to observe periods when the garbage collector is working too long. In the default `elasticsearch.yml` configuration file, you can see the following entries, which are commented out by default:

```
monitor.jvm.gc.young.warn: 1000ms
monitor.jvm.gc.young.info: 700ms
monitor.jvm.gc.young.debug: 400ms
monitor.jvm.gc.old.warn: 10s
monitor.jvm.gc.old.info: 5s
monitor.jvm.gc.old.debug: 2s
```

As you can see, the configuration specifies three log levels and the thresholds for each of them. For example, for the `info` logging level, if the young generation collection takes 700 milliseconds or more, Elasticsearch will write the information to logs. In the case of the old generation, it will be written to logs if it will take more than five seconds.

Please note that in older Elasticsearch versions (before 1.0), the prefix to log information related to young generation garbage collection was monitor.jvm.gc.ParNew.*, while the prefix to log old garbage collection information was monitor.jvm.gc.ConcurrentMarkSweep.*.

What you'll see in the logs is something like this:

```
[2014-11-09 15:22:52,355][WARN ][monitor.jvm              ]
  [Lizard] [gc][old][964][1] duration [14.8s], collections
  [1]/[15.8s], total [14.8s]/[14.8s], memory [8.6gb]-
  >[3.4gb]/[11.9gb], all_pools {[Code Cache] [8.3mb]-
  >[8.3mb]/[48mb]}{[young] [13.3mb]->[3.2mb]/[266.2mb]}{[survivor]
  [29.5mb]->[0b]/[33.2mb]}{[old] [8.5gb]->[3.4gb]/[11.6gb]}
```

As you can see, the preceding line from the log file says that it is about the old garbage collector work. We can see that the total collection time took 14.8 seconds. Before the garbage collection operation, there was 8.6 GB of heap memory used (out of 11.9 GB). After the garbage collection work, the amount of heap memory used was reduced to 3.4 GB. After this, you can see information in more detailed statistics about which parts of the heap were taken into consideration by the garbage collector: the code cache, young generation space, survivor space, or old generation heap space.

When turning on the logging of the garbage collector work at a certain threshold, we can see when things don't run the way we would like by just looking at the logs. However, if you would like to see more, Java comes with a tool for that: jstat.

Using JStat

Running the jstat command to look at how our garbage collector works is as simple as running the following command:

jstat -gcutil 123456 2000 1000

The -gcutil switch tells the command to monitor the garbage collector work, 123456 is the virtual machine identifier on which Elasticsearch is running, 2000 is the interval in milliseconds between samples, and 1000 is the number of samples to be taken. So, in our case, the preceding command will run for a little more than 33 minutes (2000 * 1000 / 1000 / 60).

In most cases, the virtual machine identifier will be similar to your process ID or even the same but not always. In order to check which Java processes are running and what their virtual machines identifiers are, one can just run a `jps` command, which is provided with most JDK distributions. A sample command would be like this:

```
jps
```

The result would be as follows:

```
16232 Jps
11684 ElasticSearch
```

In the result of the `jps` command, we see that each line contains the JVM identifier, followed by the process name. If you want to learn more about the `jps` command, please refer to the Java documentation at `http://docs.oracle.com/javase/7/docs/technotes/tools/share/jps.html`.

> Please remember to run the `jstat` command from the same account that Elasticsearch is running, or if that is not possible, run `jstat` with administrator privileges (for example, using the `sudo` command on Linux systems). It is crucial to have access rights to the process running Elasticsearch, or the `jstat` command won't be able to connect to that process.

Now, let's look at a sample output of the `jstat` command:

S0	S1	E	O	P	YGC	YGCT	FGC	FGCT	GCT
12.44	0.00	27.20	9.49	96.70	78	0.176	5	0.495	0.672
12.44	0.00	62.16	9.49	96.70	78	0.176	5	0.495	0.672
12.44	0.00	83.97	9.49	96.70	78	0.176	5	0.495	0.672
0.00	7.74	0.00	9.51	96.70	79	0.177	5	0.495	0.673
0.00	7.74	23.37	9.51	96.70	79	0.177	5	0.495	0.673
0.00	7.74	43.82	9.51	96.70	79	0.177	5	0.495	0.673
0.00	7.74	58.11	9.51	96.71	79	0.177	5	0.495	0.673

The preceding example comes from the Java documentation and we decided to take it because it nicely shows us what `jstat` is all about. Let's start by saying what each of the columns mean:

- `S0`: This means that survivor space 0 utilization is a percentage of the space capacity

- `S1`: This means that survivor space 1 utilization is a percentage of the space capacity

- E: This means that the eden space utilization is a percentage of the space capacity
- O: This means that the old space utilization is a percentage of the space capacity
- YGC: This refers to the number of young garbage collection events
- YGCT: This is the time of young garbage collections in seconds
- FGC: This is the number of full garbage collections
- FGCT: This is the time of full garbage collections in seconds
- GCT: This is the total garbage collection time in seconds

Now, let's get back to our example. As you can see, there was a young garbage collection event after sample three and before sample four. We can see that the collection took 0.001 of a second (0.177 YGCT in the fourth sample minus 0.176 YGCT in the third sample). We also know that the collection promoted objects from the eden space (which is 0 percent in the fourth sample and was 83.97 percent in the third sample) to the old generation heap space (which was increased from 9.49 percent in the third sample to 9.51 percent in the fourth sample). This example shows you how you can analyze the output of jstat. Of course, it can be time consuming and requires some knowledge about how garbage collector works, and what is stored in the heap. However, sometimes, it is the only way to see why Elasticsearch is stuck at certain moments.

Remember that if you ever see Elasticsearch not working correctly—the S0, S1 or E columns at 100 percent and the garbage collector working and not being able to handle these heap spaces—then either your young is too small and you should increase it (of course, if you have sufficient physical memory available), or you have run into some memory problems. These problems can be related to memory leaks when some resources are not releasing the unused memory. On the other hand, when your old generation space is at 100 percent and the garbage collector is struggling with releasing it (frequent garbage collections) but it can't, then it probably means that you just don't have enough heap space for your Elasticsearch node to operate properly. In such cases, what you can do without changing your index architecture is to increase the heap space that is available for the JVM that is running Elasticsearch (for more information about JVM parameters, refer to http://www.oracle.com/technetwork/java/javase/tech/vmoptions-jsp-140102.html).

Creating memory dumps

One additional thing that we didn't mention till now is the ability to dump the heap memory to a file. Java allows us to get a snapshot of the memory for a given point in time, and we can use that snapshot to analyze what is stored in the memory and find problems. In order to dump the Java process memory, one can use the `jmap` (`http://docs.oracle.com/javase/7/docs/technotes/tools/share/jmap.html`) command, for example, like this:

```
jmap -dump:file=heap.dump 123456
```

The `123456` heap dump, in our case, is the identifier of the Java process we want to get the memory dump for, and `-dump:file=heap.dump` specifies that we want the dump to be stored in the file named `heap.dump`. Such a dump can be further analyzed by specialized software, such as `jhat` (`http://docs.oracle.com/javase/7/docs/technotes/tools/share/jhat.html`), but the usage of such programs are beyond the scope of this book.

More information on the garbage collector work

Tuning garbage collection is not a simple process. The default options set for us in Elasticsearch deployment are usually sufficient for most cases, and the only thing you'll need to do is adjust the amount of memory for your nodes. The topic of tuning the garbage collector work is beyond the scope of the book; it is very broad and is called black magic by some developers. However, if you would like to read more about garbage collector, what the options are, and how they affect your application, I can suggest a great article that can be found at `http://www.oracle.com/technetwork/java/javase/gc-tuning-6-140523.html`. Although the article in the link is concentrated on Java 6, most of the options, if not all, can be successfully used with deployments running on Java 7.

Adjusting the garbage collector work in Elasticsearch

We now know how the garbage collector works and how to diagnose problems with it, so it would be nice to know how we can change Elasticsearch start up parameters to change how garbage collector works. It depends on how you run Elasticsearch. We will look at the two most common ones: standard start up script provided with the Elasticsearch distribution package and when using the service wrapper.

Using a standard start up script

When using a standard start up script in order to add additional JVM parameters, we should include them in the JAVA_OPTS environment property. For example, if we would like to include -XX:+UseParNewGC -XX:+UseConcMarkSweepGC in our Elasticsearch start up parameters in Linux-like systems, we would do the following:

```
export JAVA_OPTS="-XX:+UseParNewGC -XX:+UseConcMarkSweepGC"
```

In order to check whether the property was properly considered, we can just run another command:

```
echo $JAVA_OPTS
```

The preceding command should result in the following output in our case:

```
-XX:+UseParNewGC -XX:+UseConcMarkSweepGC
```

Service wrapper

Elasticsearch allows the user to install it as a service using the Java service wrapper (https://github.com/elasticsearch/elasticsearch-servicewrapper). If you are using the service wrapper, setting up JVM parameters is different when compared to the method shown previously. What we need to do is modify the elasticsearch.conf file, which will probably be located in /opt/elasticsearch/bin/service/ (if your Elasticsearch was installed in /opt/elasticsearch). In the mentioned file, you will see properties such as:

```
set.default.ES_HEAP_SIZE=1024
```

You will see properties such as these as well:

```
wrapper.java.additional.1=-Delasticsearch-service
wrapper.java.additional.2=-Des.path.home=%ES_HOME%
wrapper.java.additional.3=-Xss256k
wrapper.java.additional.4=-XX:+UseParNewGC
wrapper.java.additional.5=-XX:+UseConcMarkSweepGC
wrapper.java.additional.6=-XX:CMSInitiatingOccupancyFraction=75
wrapper.java.additional.7=-XX:+UseCMSInitiatingOccupancyOnly
wrapper.java.additional.8=-XX:+HeapDumpOnOutOfMemoryError
wrapper.java.additional.9=-Djava.awt.headless=true
```

The first property is responsible for setting the heap memory size for Elasticsearch, while the rest are additional JVM parameters. If you would like to add another parameter, you can just add another `wrapper.java.additional` property, followed by a dot and the next available number, for example:

```
wrapper.java.additional.10=-server
```

 One thing to remember is that tuning the garbage collector work is not something that you do once and forget. It requires experimenting, as it is very dependent on your data, queries and all that combined. Don't fear making changes when something is wrong, but also observe them and look how Elasticsearch works after making changes.

Avoid swapping on Unix-like systems

Although this is not strict about garbage collection and heap memory usage, we think that it is crucial to see how to disable swap. Swapping is the process of writing memory pages to the disk (swap partition in Unix-based systems) when the amount of physical memory is not sufficient or the operating system decides that for some reason, it is better to have some part of the RAM memory written into the disk. If the swapped memory pages will be needed again, the operating system will load them from the swap partition and allow processes to use them. As you can imagine, such processes take time and resources.

When using Elasticsearch, we want to avoid its process memory being swapped. You can imagine that having parts of memory used by Elasticsearch written to the disk and then again read from it can hurt the performance of both searching and indexing. Because of this, Elasticsearch allows us to turn off swapping for it. In order to do that, one should set `bootstrap.mlockall` to `true` in the `elasticsearch.yml` file.

However, the preceding setting is only the beginning. You also need to ensure that the JVM won't resize the heap by setting the `Xmx` and `Xms` parameters to the same values (you can do that by specifying the same values for the `ES_MIN_MEM` and `ES_MAX_MEM` environment variables for Elasticsearch). Also remember that you need to have enough physical memory to handle the settings you've set.

Now if we run Elasticsearch, we can run into the following message in the logs:

```
[2013-06-11 19:19:00,858] [WARN ] [common.jna          ]
  Unknown mlockall error 0
```

This means that our memory locking is not working. So now, let's modify two files on our Linux operating system (this will require administration rights). We assume that the user who will run Elasticsearch is `elasticsearch`.

First, we modify `/etc/security/limits.conf` and add the following entries:

```
elasticsearch - nofile 64000
elasticsearch - memlock unlimited
```

The second thing is to modify the `/etc/pam.d/common-session` file and add the following:

```
session required pam_limits.so
```

After re-logging to the `elasticsearch` user account, you should be able to start Elasticsearch and not see the `mlockall` error message.

Benchmarking queries

There are a few important things when dealing with search or data analysis. We need the results to be precise, we need them to be relevant, and we need them to be returned as soon as possible. If you are a person responsible for designing queries that are run against Elasticsearch, sooner or later, you will find yourself in a position where you will need to improve the performance of your queries. The reasons can vary from hardware-based problems to bad data architecture to poor query design. When writing this book, the benchmark API was only available in the trunk of Elasticsearch, which means that it was not a part of official Elasticsearch distribution. For now we can either use tools like jMeter or ab (the Apache benchmark is `http://httpd.apache.org/docs/2.2/programs/ab.html`) or use trunk version of Elasticsearch. Please also note that the functionality we are describing can change with the final release, so keeping an eye on `http://www.elasticsearch.org/guide/en/elasticsearch/reference/master/search-benchmark.html` is a good idea if you want to use benchmarking functionality.

Preparing your cluster configuration for benchmarking

By default, the benchmarking functionality is disabled. Any attempt to use benchmarking on the Elasticsearch node that is not configured properly will lead to an error similar to the following one:

```
{
  "error" : "BenchmarkNodeMissingException[No available nodes for
  executing benchmark [benchmark_name]]",
  "status" : 503
}
```

This is okay; no one wants to take a risk of running potentially dangerous functionalities on production cluster. During performance testing and benchmarking, you will want to run many complicated and heavy queries, so running such benchmarks on the Elasticsearch cluster that is used by real users doesn't seem like a good idea. It will lead to the slowness of the cluster, and it could result in crashes and a bad user experience. To use benchmarking, you have to inform Elasticsearch which nodes can run the generated queries. Every instance we want to use for benchmarking should be run with the `--node.bench` option set to `true`. For example, we could run an Elasticsearch instance like this:

```
bin/elasticsearch --node.bench true
```

The other possibility is to add the `node.bench` property to the `elasticsearch.yml` file and, of course, set it to `true`. Whichever way we choose, we are now ready to run our first benchmark.

Running benchmarks

Elasticsearch provides the `_bench` REST endpoint, which allows you to define the task to run on benchmarking-enabled nodes in the cluster. Let's look at a simple example to learn how to do that. We will show you something practical; in the *Handling filters and why it matters* section in *Chapter 2, Power User Query DSL*, we talked about filtering. We tried to convince you that, in most cases, post filtering is bad. We can now check it ourselves and see whether the queries with post filtering are really slower. The command that allows us to test this looks as follows (we have used the Wikipedia database):

```
curl -XPUT 'localhost:9200/_bench/?pretty' -d '{
    "name": "firstTest",
    "competitors": [ {
        "name": "post_filter",
        "requests": [ {
            "post_filter": {
                "term": {
                    "link": "Toyota Corolla"
                }
            }
        }]
    },
    {
        "name": "filtered",
```

```
        "requests": [ {
          "query": {
            "filtered": {
              "query": {
                "match_all": {}
              },
              "filter": {
                "term": {
                  "link": "Toyota Corolla"
                }
              }
            }
          }
        }]
    }]
}'
```

The structure of a request to the _bench REST endpoint is pretty simple. It contains a list of competitors—queries or sets of queries (because each competitor can have more than a single query)—that will be compared to each other by the Elasticsearch benchmarking functionality. Each competitor has its name to allow easier results analysis. Now, let's finally look at the results returned by the preceding request:

```
{
    "status": "COMPLETE",
    "errors": [],
    "competitors": {
        "filtered": {
            "summary": {
                "nodes": [
                    "Free Spirit"
                ],
                "total_iterations": 5,
                "completed_iterations": 5,
                "total_queries": 5000,
                "concurrency": 5,
                "multiplier": 1000,
                "avg_warmup_time": 6,
                "statistics": {
                    "min": 1,
```

```
                "max": 5,
                "mean": 1.9590000000000019,
                "qps": 510.4645227156713,
                "std_dev": 0.6143244085137575,
                "millis_per_hit": 0.0009694501018329939,
                "percentile_10": 1,
                "percentile_25": 2,
                "percentile_50": 2,
                "percentile_75": 2,
                "percentile_90": 3,
                "percentile_99": 4
            }
        }
    },
    "post_filter": {
        "summary": {
            "nodes": [
                "Free Spirit"
            ],
            "total_iterations": 5,
            "completed_iterations": 5,
            "total_queries": 5000,
            "concurrency": 5,
            "multiplier": 1000,
            "avg_warmup_time": 74,
            "statistics": {
                "min": 66,
                "max": 217,
                "mean": 120.88000000000022,
                "qps": 8.272667107875579,
                "std_dev": 18.487886855778815,
                "millis_per_hit": 0.05085254582484725,
                "percentile_10": 98,
                "percentile_25": 109.26595744680851,
                "percentile_50": 120.32258064516128,
                "percentile_75": 131.3181818181818,
                "percentile_90": 143,
                "percentile_99": 171.01000000000022
            }
        }
    }
}
}
```

As you can see, the test was successful; Elasticsearch returned an empty `errors` table. For every test we've run with both `post_filter` and `filtered` queries, only a single node named `Free Spirit` was used for benchmarking. In both cases, the same number of queries was used (`5000`) with the same number of simultaneous requests (`5`). Comparing the warm-up time and statistics, you can easily draw conclusions about which query is better. We would like to choose the filtered query; what about you?

Our example was quite simple (actually it was very simple), but it shows you the usefulness of benchmarking. Of course, our initial request didn't use all the configuration options exposed by the Elasticsearch benchmarking API. To summarize all the options, we've prepared a list of the available global options for the `_bench` REST endpoint:

- `name`: This is the name of the benchmark, making it easy to distinguish multiple benchmarks (refer to the *Controlling currently run benchmarks* section).

- `competitors`: This is the definition of tests that Elasticsearch should perform. It is the array of objects describing each test.

- `num_executor_nodes`: This is the maximum number of Elasticsearch nodes that will be used during query tests as a source of queries. It defaults to `1`.

- `percentiles`: This is an array defining percentiles Elasticsearch should compute and return in results with the query execution time. The default value is `[10, 25, 50, 75, 90, 99]`.

- `iteration`: This defaults to `5` and defines the number of repetitions for each competitor that Elasticsearch should perform.

- `concurrency`: This is the concurrency for each iteration and it defaults to `5`, which means that five concurrent threads will be used by Elasticsearch.

- `multiplier`: This is the number of repetitions of each query in the given iteration. By default, the query is run `1000` times.

- `warmup`: This informs you that Elasticsearch should perform the warm-up of the query. By default, the warm-up is performed, which means that this value is set to `true`.

- clear_caches: By default, this is set to false, which means that before each iteration, Elasticsearch will not clean the caches. We can change this by setting the value to true. This parameter is connected with a series of parameters saying which cache should or should not be cleared. These additional parameters are clear_caches.filter (the filter cache), clear_caches.field_data (the field data cache), clear_caches.id (the ID cache), and clear_caches.recycler (the recycler cache). In addition, there are two parameters that can take an array of names: clear_caches.fields specifies the names of fields and which cache should be cleared and clear_caches.filter_keys specifies the names of filter keys to clear. For more information about caches, refer to the *Understanding Elasticsearch caching* section in *Chapter 6, Low-level Index Control*.

In addition to the global options, each competitor is an object that can contain the following parameters:

- name: Like its equivalent on the root level, this helps distinguish several competitors from each other.

- requests: This is a table of objects defining queries that should be run within given competitors. Each object is a standard Elasticsearch query that is defined using the query DSL.

- num_slowest: This is the number of the slowest queries tracked. It defaults to 1. If we want Elasticsearch to track and record more than one slow query, we should increase the value of that parameter.

- search_type: This indicates the type of searches that should be performed. Few of the options are query_then_fetch, dfs_query_then_fetch, and count. It defaults to query_then_fetch.

- indices: This is an array with indices names to which the queries should be limited.

- types: This is an array with type names to which the queries should be limited.

- iteration, concurrency, multiplier, warmup, clear_caches: These parameters override their version defined on the global level.

Controlling currently run benchmarks

Depending on the parameters we've used to execute our benchmark, a single benchmarking command containing several queries with thousands of repeats can run for several minutes or even hours. It is very handy to have a possibility to check how the tests run and estimate how long it will take for the benchmark command to end. As you can expect, Elasticsearch provides such information. To get this, the only thing we need to do is run the following command:

```
curl -XGET 'localhost:9200/_bench?pretty'
```

The output generated for the preceding command can look as follows (it was taken during the execution of our sample benchmark):

```
{
    "active_benchmarks" : {
        "firstTest" : {
            "status" : "RUNNING",
            "errors" : [ ],
            "competitors" : {
                "post_filter" : {
                    "summary" : {
                        "nodes" : [
                        "James Proudstar" ],
                        "total_iterations" : 5,
                        "completed_iterations" : 3,
                        "total_queries" : 3000,
                        "concurrency" : 5,
                        "multiplier" : 1000,
                        "avg_warmup_time" : 137.0,
                        "statistics" : {
                            "min" : 39,
                            "max" : 146,
                            "mean" : 78.95077720207264,
                            "qps" : 32.81378178835111,
                            "std_dev" : 17.42543552392229,
                            "millis_per_hit" : 0.031591310251188054,
                            "percentile_10" : 59.0,
                            "percentile_25" : 66.86363636363637,
                            "percentile_50" : 77.0,
                            "percentile_75" : 89.22727272727272,
                            "percentile_90" : 102.0,
                            "percentile_99" : 124.86000000000013
```

```
                }
              }
            }
          }
        }
      }
    }
```

Thanks to it, you can see the progress of tests and try to estimate how long you will have to wait for the benchmark to finish and return the results. If you would like to abort the currently running benchmark (for example, it takes too long and you already see that the tested query is not optimal), Elasticsearch has a solution. For example, to abort our benchmark called firstTest, we run a POST request to the _bench/abort REST endpoint, just like this:

```
curl -XPOST 'localhost:9200/_bench/abort/firstTest?pretty'
```

The response returned by Elasticsearch will show you a partial result of the test. It is almost the same as what we've seen in the preceding example, except that the status of the benchmark will be set to ABORTED.

Very hot threads

When you are in trouble and your cluster works slower than usual and uses large amounts of CPU power, you know you need to do something to make it work again. This is the case when the Hot Threads API can give you the information necessary to find the root cause of problems. A hot thread in this case is a Java thread that uses a high CPU volume and executes for longer periods of time. Such a thread doesn't mean that there is something wrong with Elasticsearch itself; it gives you information on what can be a possible hotspot and allows you to see which part of your deployment you need to look more deeply at, such as query execution or Lucene segments merging. The Hot Threads API returns information about which parts of the Elasticsearch code are hot spots from the CPU side or where Elasticsearch is stuck for some reason.

When using the Hot Threads API, you can examine all nodes, a selected few of them, or a particular node using the /_nodes/hot_threads or /_nodes/{node or nodes}/hot_threads endpoints. For example, to look at hot threads on all the nodes, we would run the following command:

```
curl 'localhost:9200/_nodes/hot_threads'
```

The API supports the following parameters:

- `threads` (the default: `3`): This is the number of threads that should be analyzed. Elasticsearch takes the specified number of the hottest threads by looking at the information determined by the `type` parameter.

- `interval` (the default: `500ms`): Elasticsearch checks threads twice to calculate the percentage of time spent in a particular thread on an operation defined by the `type` parameter. We can use the `interval` parameter to define the time between these checks.

- `type` (the default: `cpu`): This is the type of thread state to be examined. The API can check the CPU time taken by the given thread (`cpu`), the time in the blocked state (`block`), or the time in the waiting (`wait`) state. If you would like to know more about the thread states, refer to http://docs.oracle.com/javase/7/docs/api/java/lang/Thread.State.html.

- `snapshots` (the default: `10`): This is the number of stack traces (a nested sequence of method calls at a certain point of time) snapshots to take.

Using the Hot Threads API is very simple; for example, to look at hot threads on all the nodes that are in the waiting state with check intervals of one second, we would use the following command:

```
curl 'localhost:9200/_nodes/hot_threads?type=wait&interval=1s'
```

Usage clarification for the Hot Threads API

Unlike other Elasticsearch API responses where you can expect JSON to be returned, the Hot Threads API returns formatted text, which contains several sections. Before we discuss the response structure itself, we would like to tell you a bit about the logic that is responsible for generating this response. Elasticsearch takes all the running threads and collects various information about the CPU time spent in each thread, the number of times the particular thread was blocked or was in the waiting state, how long it was blocked or was in the waiting state, and so on. The next thing is to wait for a particular amount of time (specified by the `interval` parameter), and after that time passes, collect the same information again. After this is done, threads are sorted on the basis of time each particular thread was running. The sort is done in a descending order so that the threads running for the longest period of time are on top of the list. Of course, the mentioned time is measured for a given operation type specified by the `type` parameter. After this, the first N threads (where N is the number of threads specified by the `threads` parameter) are analyzed by Elasticsearch. What Elasticsearch does is that, at every few milliseconds, it takes a few snapshots (the number of snapshots is specified by the `snapshot` parameter) of stack traces of the threads that were selected in the previous step. The last thing that needs to be done is the grouping of stack traces in order to visualize changes in the thread state and return the response to the caller.

The Hot Threads API response

Now, let's go through the sections of the response returned by the Hot Threads API. For example, the following screenshot is a fragment of the Hot Threads API response generated for Elasticsearch that was just started:

```
> curl 'localhost:9200/_nodes/hot_threads'
::: [N'Gabthoth][aBb5552UQvyFCk1PNCaJnA][Banshee-3.local][inet[/10.0.1.3:9300]]

   1.4% (6.7ms out of 500ms) cpu usage by thread 'elasticsearch[N'Gabthoth][http_server_boss][T#1]{New I/O server boss #51}'
     10/10 snapshots sharing following 14 elements
       sun.nio.ch.KQueueArrayWrapper.kevent0(Native Method)
       sun.nio.ch.KQueueArrayWrapper.poll(KQueueArrayWrapper.java:200)
       sun.nio.ch.KQueueSelectorImpl.doSelect(KQueueSelectorImpl.java:103)
       sun.nio.ch.SelectorImpl.lockAndDoSelect(SelectorImpl.java:87)
       sun.nio.ch.SelectorImpl.select(SelectorImpl.java:98)
       sun.nio.ch.SelectorImpl.select(SelectorImpl.java:102)
       org.elasticsearch.common.netty.channel.socket.nio.NioServerBoss.select(NioServerBoss.java:163)
       org.elasticsearch.common.netty.channel.socket.nio.AbstractNioSelector.run(AbstractNioSelector.java:212)
       org.elasticsearch.common.netty.channel.socket.nio.NioServerBoss.run(NioServerBoss.java:42)
       org.elasticsearch.common.netty.util.ThreadRenamingRunnable.run(ThreadRenamingRunnable.java:108)
       org.elasticsearch.common.netty.util.internal.DeadLockProofWorker$1.run(DeadLockProofWorker.java:42)
       java.util.concurrent.ThreadPoolExecutor.runWorker(ThreadPoolExecutor.java:1145)
       java.util.concurrent.ThreadPoolExecutor$Worker.run(ThreadPoolExecutor.java:615)
       java.lang.Thread.run(Thread.java:744)

   0.7% (3.3ms out of 500ms) cpu usage by thread 'elasticsearch[N'Gabthoth][search][T#6]'
     10/10 snapshots sharing following 10 elements
       sun.misc.Unsafe.park(Native Method)
       java.util.concurrent.locks.LockSupport.park(LockSupport.java:186)
       java.util.concurrent.LinkedTransferQueue.awaitMatch(LinkedTransferQueue.java:735)
       java.util.concurrent.LinkedTransferQueue.xfer(LinkedTransferQueue.java:644)
       java.util.concurrent.LinkedTransferQueue.take(LinkedTransferQueue.java:1137)
       org.elasticsearch.common.util.concurrent.SizeBlockingQueue.take(SizeBlockingQueue.java:162)
       java.util.concurrent.ThreadPoolExecutor.getTask(ThreadPoolExecutor.java:1068)
       java.util.concurrent.ThreadPoolExecutor.runWorker(ThreadPoolExecutor.java:1130)
       java.util.concurrent.ThreadPoolExecutor$Worker.run(ThreadPoolExecutor.java:615)
       java.lang.Thread.run(Thread.java:744)

   0.5% (2.7ms out of 500ms) cpu usage by thread 'elasticsearch[N'Gabthoth][search][T#10]'
     10/10 snapshots sharing following 10 elements
       sun.misc.Unsafe.park(Native Method)
       java.util.concurrent.locks.LockSupport.park(LockSupport.java:186)
       java.util.concurrent.LinkedTransferQueue.awaitMatch(LinkedTransferQueue.java:735)
       java.util.concurrent.LinkedTransferQueue.xfer(LinkedTransferQueue.java:644)
       java.util.concurrent.LinkedTransferQueue.take(LinkedTransferQueue.java:1137)
       org.elasticsearch.common.util.concurrent.SizeBlockingQueue.take(SizeBlockingQueue.java:162)
       java.util.concurrent.ThreadPoolExecutor.getTask(ThreadPoolExecutor.java:1068)
       java.util.concurrent.ThreadPoolExecutor.runWorker(ThreadPoolExecutor.java:1130)
       java.util.concurrent.ThreadPoolExecutor$Worker.run(ThreadPoolExecutor.java:615)
       java.lang.Thread.run(Thread.java:744)
>
```

Now, let's discuss the sections of the response. To do that, we will use a slightly different response compared to the one shown previously. We do this to better visualize what is happening inside Elasticsearch. However, please remember that the general structure of the response will not change.

The first section of the Hot Threads API response shows us which node the thread is located on. For example, the first line of the response can look as follows:

```
::: [N'Gabthoth][aBb5552UQvyFCk1PNCaJnA][Banshee-
   3.local][inet[/10.0.1.3:9300]]
```

Thanks to it, we can see which node the Hot Threads API returns information about and which node is very handy when the Hot Threads API call goes to many nodes.

The next lines of the Hot Threads API response can be divided into several sections, each starting with a line similar to the following one:

```
0.5% (2.7ms out of 500ms) cpu usage by thread
  'elasticsearch[N'Gabthoth][search][T#10]'
```

In our case, we see a thread named `search`, which takes `0.5` percent of all the CPU time at the time when the measurement was done. The `cpu usage` part of the preceding line indicates that we are using `type` equal to `cpu` (other values you can expect here are `block usage` for threads in the blocked state and `wait usage` for threads in the waiting states). The thread name is very important here, because by looking at it, we can see which Elasticsearch functionality is the hot one. In our example, we see that this thread is all about searching (the `search` value). Other example values that you can expect to see are `recovery_stream` (for recovery module events), `cache` (for caching events), `merge` (for segments merging threads), `index` (for data indexing threads), and so on.

The next part of the Hot Threads API response is the section starting with the following information:

```
10/10 snapshots sharing following 10 elements
```

This information will be followed by a stack trace. In our case, `10/10` means that 10 snapshots have been taken for the same stack trace. In general, this means that all the examination time was spent in the same part of the Elasticsearch code.

Scaling Elasticsearch

As we already said multiple times both in this book and in *Elasticsearch Server Second Edition*, Elasticsearch is a highly scalable search and analytics platform. We can scale it both horizontally and vertically.

Vertical scaling

When we talk about **vertical scaling**, we often mean adding more resources to the server Elasticsearch is running on: we can add memory and we can switch to a machine with better CPU or faster disk storage. Of course, with better machines, we can expect increase in performance; depending on our deployment and its bottleneck, there can be smaller or higher improvement. However, there are limitations when it comes to vertical scaling. For example, one of such is the maximum amount of physical memory available for your servers or the total memory required by the JVM to operate. When you have large enough data and complicated queries, you can very soon run into memory issues, and adding new memory may not be helpful at all.

For example, you may not want to go beyond 31 GB of physical memory given to the JVM because of garbage collection and the inability to use compressed ops, which basically means that to address the same memory space, JVM will need to use twice the memory. Even though it seems like a very big issue, vertical scaling is not the only solution we have.

Horizontal scaling

The other solution available to us Elasticsearch users is **horizontal scaling**. To give you a comparison, vertical scaling is like building a sky scrapper, while horizontal scaling is like having many houses in a residential area. Instead of investing in hardware and having powerful machines, we choose to have multiple machines and our data split between them. Horizontal scaling gives us virtually unlimited scaling possibilities. Even with the most powerful hardware time, a single machine is not enough to handle the data, the queries, or both of them. If a single machine is not able to handle the amount of data, we have such cases where we divide our indices into multiple shards and spread them across the cluster, just like what is shown in the following figure:

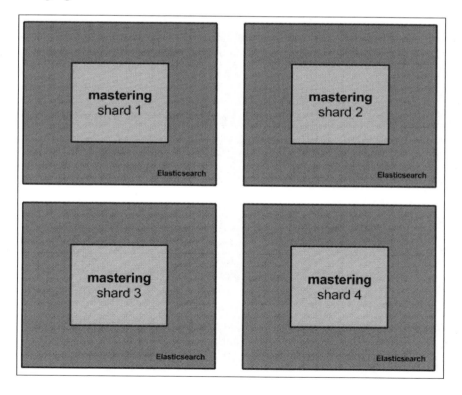

When we don't have enough processing power to handle queries, we can always create more replicas of the shards we have. We have our cluster: four Elasticsearch nodes with the `mastering` index created and running on it and built of four shards.

If we want to increase the querying capabilities of our cluster, we would just add additional nodes, for example, four of them. After adding new nodes to the cluster, we can either create new indices that will be built of more shards to spread the load more evenly, or add replicas to already existing shards. Both options are viable. We should go for more primary shards when our hardware is not enough to handle the amount of data it holds. In such cases, we usually run into out-of-memory situations, long shard query execution time, swapping, or high I/O waits. The second option — having replicas — is a way to go when our hardware is happily handling the data we have, but the traffic is so high that the nodes just can't keep up. The first option is simple, but let's look at the second case: having more replicas. So, with four additional nodes, our cluster would look as follows:

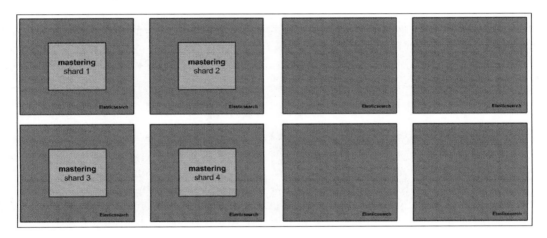

Now, let's run the following command to add a single replica:

```
curl -XPUT 'localhost:9200/mastering/_settings' -d '{
 "index" : {
  "number_of_replicas" : 1
 }
}'
```

Our cluster view would look more or less as follows:

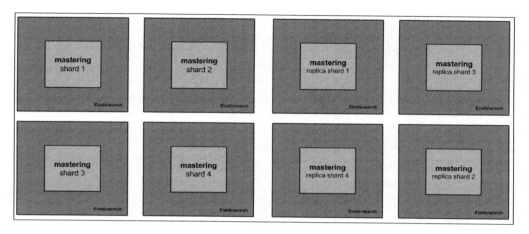

As you can see, each of the initial shards building the `mastering` index has a single replica stored on another node. Because of this, Elasticsearch is able to round robin the queries between the shard and its replicas so that the queries don't always hit one node. Because of this, we are able to handle almost double the query load compared to our initial deployment.

Automatically creating replicas

Elasticsearch allows us to automatically expand replicas when the cluster is big enough. You might wonder where such functionality can be useful. Imagine a situation where you have a small index that you would like to be present on every node so that your plugins don't have to run distributed queries just to get data from it. In addition to this, your cluster is dynamically changing; you add and remove nodes from it. The simplest way to achieve such a functionality is to allow Elasticsearch to automatically expand replicas. To do this, we would need to set `index.auto_expand_replicas` to `0-all`, which means that the index can have 0 replicas or be present on all the nodes. So if our small index is called `mastering_meta` and we would like Elasticsearch to automatically expand its replicas, we would use the following command to create the index:

```
curl -XPOST 'localhost:9200/mastering_meta/' -d '{
  "settings" : {
   "index" : {
    "auto_expand_replicas" : "0-all"
   }
  }
}'
```

We can also update the settings of that index if it is already created by running the following command:

```
curl -XPUT 'localhost:9200/mastering_meta/_settings' -d '{
  "index" : {
    "auto_expand_replicas" : "0-all"
  }
}'
```

Redundancy and high availability

The Elasticsearch replication mechanism not only gives us the ability to handle higher query throughput, but also gives us redundancy and high availability. Imagine an Elasticsearch cluster hosting a single index called mastering that is built of 2 shards and 0 replicas. Such a cluster could look as follows:

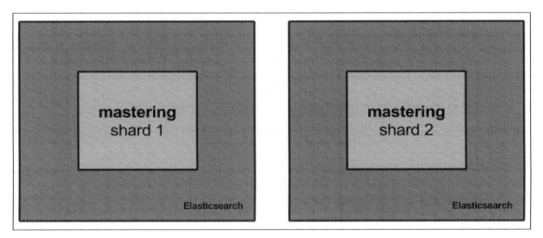

Now, what would happen when one of the nodes fails? The simplest answer is that we lose about 50 percent of the data, and if the failure is fatal, we lose that data forever. Even when having backups, we would need to spin up another node and restore the backup; this takes time. If your business relies on Elasticsearch, downtime means money loss.

Now let's look at the same cluster but with one replica:

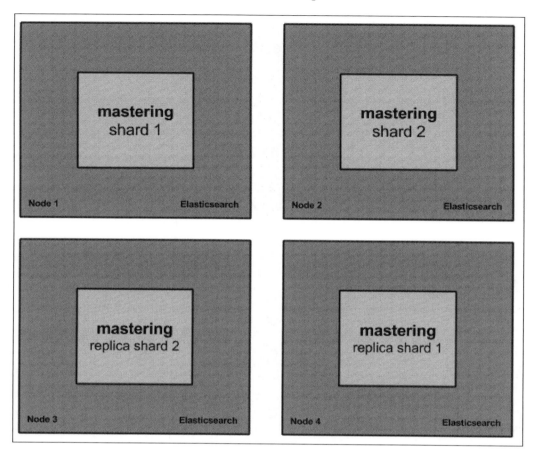

Now, losing a single Elasticsearch node means that we still have the whole data available and we can work on restoring the full cluster structure without downtime. What's more, with such deployment, we can live with two nodes failing at the same time in some cases, for example, Node 1 and Node 3 or Node 2 and Node 4. In both the mentioned cases, we would still be able to access all the data. Of course, this will lower performance because of less nodes in the cluster, but this is still better than not handling queries at all.

Because of this, when designing your architecture and deciding on the number of nodes, how many nodes indices will have, and the number of shards for each of them, you should take into consideration how many nodes' failure you want to live with. Of course, you can't forget about the performance part of the equation, but redundancy and high availability should be one of the factors of the scaling equation.

Cost and performance flexibility

The default distributed nature of Elasticsearch and its ability to scale horizontally allow us to be flexible when it comes to performance and costs that we have when running our environment. First of all, high-end servers with highly performant disks, numerous CPU cores, and a lot of RAM are expensive. In addition to this, cloud computing is getting more and more popular and it not only allows us to run our deployment on rented machines, but it also allows us to scale on demand. We just need to add more machines, which is a few clicks away or can even be automated with some degree of work.

Getting this all together, we can say that having a horizontally scalable solution, such as Elasticsearch, allows us to bring down the costs of running our clusters and solutions. What's more, we can easily sacrifice performance if costs are the most crucial factor in our business plan. Of course, we can also go the other way. If we can afford large clusters, we can push Elasticsearch to hundreds of terabytes of data stored in the indices and still get decent performance (of course, with proper hardware and property distributed).

Continuous upgrades

High availability, cost, performance flexibility, and virtually endless growth are not the only things worth saying when discussing the scalability side of Elasticsearch. At some point in time, you will want to have your Elasticsearch cluster to be upgraded to a new version. It can be because of bug fixes, performance improvements, new features, or anything that you can think of. The thing is that when having a single instance of each shard, an upgrade without replicas means the unavailability of Elasticsearch (or at least its parts), and that may mean downtime of the applications that use Elasticsearch. This is another point why horizontal scaling is so important; you can perform upgrades, at least to the point where software such as Elasticsearch is supported. For example, you could take Elasticsearch 1.0 and upgrade it to Elasticsearch 1.4 with only rolling restarts, thus having all the data still available for searching and indexing happening at the same time.

Multiple Elasticsearch instances on a single physical machine

Although we previously said that you shouldn't go for the most powerful machines for different reasons (such as RAM consumption after going above 31 GB JVM heap), we sometimes don't have much choice. This is out of the scope of the book, but because we are talking about scaling, we thought it may be a good thing to mention what can be done in such cases.

In cases such as the ones we are discussing, when we have high-end hardware with a lot of RAM memory, a lot of high speed disk, numerous CPU cores, among others, we should think about diving the physical server into multiple virtual machines and running a single Elasticsearch server on each of the virtual machines.

> There is also a possibility of running multiple Elasticsearch servers on a single physical machine without running multiple virtual machines. Which road to take—virtual machines or multiple instances—is really your choice; however, we like to keep things separate and, because of that, we are usually going to divide any large server into multiple virtual machines. When dividing a large server into multiple smaller virtual machines, remember that the I/O subsystem will be shared across these smaller virtual machines. Because of this, it may be good to wisely divide the disks between virtual machines.

To illustrate such a deployment, please look at the following provided figure. It shows how you could run Elasticsearch on three large servers, each divided into four separate virtual machines. Each virtual machine would be responsible for running a single instance of Elasticsearch.

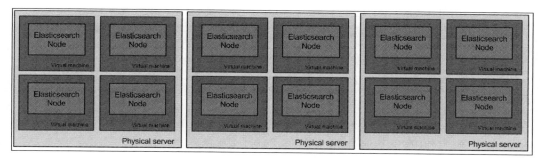

Preventing the shard and its replicas from being on the same node

There is one additional thing worth mentioning. When having multiple physical servers divided into virtual machines, it is crucial to ensure that the shard and its replica won't end up on the same physical machine. This would be tragic if a server crashes or is restarted. We can tell Elasticsearch to separate shards and replicas using cluster allocation awareness. In our preceding case, we have three physical servers; let's call them `server1`, `server2`, and `server3`.

Now for each Elasticsearch on a physical server, we define the `node.server_name` property and we set it to the identifier of the server. So, for the example of all Elasticsearch nodes on the first physical server, we would set the following property in the `elasticsearch.yml` configuration file:

```
node.server_name: server1
```

In addition to this, each Elasticsearch node (no matter on which physical server) needs to have the following property added to the `elasticsearch.yml` configuration file:

```
cluster.routing.allocation.awareness.attributes: server_name
```

It tells Elasticsearch not to put the primary shard and its replicas on the nodes with the same value in the `node.server_name` property. This is enough for us, and Elasticsearch will take care of the rest.

Designated nodes' roles for larger clusters

There is one more thing that we wanted to tell you; actually, we already mentioned that both in the book you are holding in your hands and in *Elasticsearch Server Second Edition, Packt Publishing*. To have a fully fault-tolerant and highly available cluster, we should divide the nodes and give each node a designated role. The roles we can assign to each Elasticsearch node are as follows:

* The master eligible node
* The data node
* The query aggregator node

By default, each Elasticsearch node is master eligible (it can serve as a master node), can hold data, and can work as a query aggregator node, which means that it can send partial queries to other nodes, gather and merge the results, and respond to the client sending the query. You may wonder why this is needed. Let's give you a simple example: if the master node is under a lot of stress, it may not be able to handle the cluster state-related command fast enough and the cluster can become unstable. This is only a single, simple example, and you can think of numerous others.

Because of this, most Elasticsearch clusters that are larger than a few nodes usually look like the one presented in the following figure:

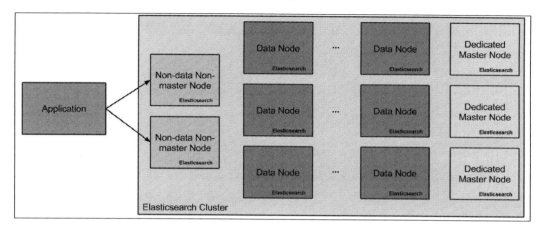

As you can see, our hypothetical cluster contains two aggregator nodes (because we know that there will not be too many queries, but we want redundancy), a dozen of data nodes because the amount of data will be large, and at least three master eligible nodes that shouldn't be doing anything else. Why three master nodes when Elasticsearch will only use a single one at any given time? Again, this is because of redundancy and to be able to prevent split brain situations by setting the discovery.zen.minimum_master_nodes to 2, which would allow us to easily handle the failure of a single master eligible node in the cluster.

Let's now give you snippets of the configuration for each type of node in our cluster. We already talked about this in the *Discovery and recovery modules* section in *Chapter 7, Elasticsearch Administration*, but we would like to mention it once again.

Query aggregator nodes

The query aggregator nodes' configuration is quite simple. To configure them, we just need to tell Elasticsearch that we don't want these nodes to be master eligible and hold data. This corresponds to the following configuration in the elasticsearch.yml file:

```
node.master: false
node.data: false
```

Data nodes

Data nodes are also very simple to configure; we just need to say that they should not be master eligible. However, we are not big fans of default configurations (because they tend to change) and, thus, our Elasticsearch data nodes' configuration looks as follows:

```
node.master: false
node.data: true
```

Master eligible nodes

We've left the master eligible nodes for the end of the general scaling section. Of course, such Elasticsearch nodes shouldn't be allowed to hold data, but in addition to that, it is good practice to disable the HTTP protocol on such nodes. This is done in order to avoid accidentally querying these nodes. Master eligible nodes can be smaller in resources compared to data and query aggregator nodes, and because of that, we should ensure that they are only used for master-related purposes. So, our configuration for master eligible nodes looks more or less as follows:

```
node.master: true
node.data: false
http.enabled: false
```

Using Elasticsearch for high load scenarios

Now that we know the theory (and some examples of Elasticsearch scaling), we are ready to discuss the different aspects of Elasticsearch preparation for high load. We decided to split this part of the chapter into three sections: one dedicated to preparing Elasticsearch for a high indexing load, one dedicated for the preparation of Elasticsearch for a high query load, and one that can be taken into consideration in both cases. This should give you an idea of what to think about when preparing your cluster for your use case.

Please consider that performance testing should be done after preparing the cluster for production use. Don't just take the values from the book and go for them; try them with your data and your queries and try altering them, and see the differences. Remember that giving general advices that works for everyone is not possible, so treat the next two sections as general advices instead of ready for use recipes.

General Elasticsearch-tuning advices

In this section, we will look at the general advices related to tuning Elasticsearch. They are not connected to indexing performance only or querying performance only but to both of them.

Choosing the right store

One of the crucial aspects of this is that we should choose the right store implementation. This is mostly important when running an Elasticsearch version older than 1.3.0. In general, if you are running a 64-bit operating system, you should again go for mmapfs. If you are not running a 64-bit operating system, choose the niofs store for Unix-based systems and simplefs for Windows-based ones. If you can allow yourself to have a volatile store, but a very fast one, you can look at the memory store: it will give you the best index access performance but requires enough memory to handle not only all the index files, but also to handle indexing and querying.

With the release of Elasticsearch 1.3.0, we've got a new store type called default, which is the new default store type. As Elasticsearch developers said, it is a hybrid store type. It uses memory-mapped files to read term dictionaries and doc values, while the rest of the files are accessed using the NIOFSDirectory implementation. In most cases, when using Elasticsearch 1.3.0 or higher, the default store type should be used.

The index refresh rate

The second thing we should pay attention to is the index refresh rate. We know that the refresh rate specifies how fast documents will be visible for search operations. The equation is quite simple: the faster the refresh rate, the slower the queries will be and the lower the indexing throughput. If we can allow ourselves to have a slower refresh rate, such as 10s or 30s, it may be a good thing to set it. This puts less pressure on Elasticsearch, as the internal objects will have to be reopened at a slower pace and, thus, more resources will be available both for indexing and querying. Remember that, by default, the refresh rate is set to 1s, which basically means that the index searcher object is reopened every second.

To give you a bit of an insight into what performance gains we are talking about, we did some performance tests, including Elasticsearch and a different refresh rate. With a refresh rate of 1s, we were able to index about 1.000 documents per second using a single Elasticsearch node. Increasing the refresh rate to 5s gave us an increase in the indexing throughput of more than 25 percent, and we were able to index about 1280 documents per second. Setting the refresh rate to 25s gave us about 70 percent of throughput more compared to a 1s refresh rate, which was about 1700 documents per second on the same infrastructure. It is also worth remembering that increasing the time indefinitely doesn't make much sense, because after a certain point (depending on your data load and the amount of data you have), the increase in performance is negligible.

Thread pools tuning

This is one of the things that is very dependent on your deployment. By default, Elasticsearch comes with a very good default when it comes to all thread pools' configuration. However, there are times when these defaults are not enough. You should remember that tuning the default thread pools' configuration should be done only when you really see that your nodes are filling up the queues and they still have processing power left that could be designated to the processing of the waiting operations.

For example, if you did your performance tests and you see your Elasticsearch instances not being saturated 100 percent, but on the other hand, you've experienced rejected execution errors, then this is a point where you should start adjusting the thread pools. You can either increase the amount of threads that are allowed to be executed at the same time, or you can increase the queue. Of course, you should also remember that increasing the number of concurrently running threads to very high numbers will lead to many CPU context switches (http://en.wikipedia.org/wiki/Context_switch), which will result in a drop in performance. Of course, having massive queues is also not a good idea; it is usually better to fail fast rather than overwhelm Elasticsearch with several thousands of requests waiting in the queue. However, this all depends on your particular deployment and use case. We would really like to give you a precise number, but in this case, giving general advice is rarely possible.

Adjusting the merge process

Lucene segments' merging adjustments is another thing that is highly dependent on your use case and several factors related to it, such as how much data you add, how often you do that, and so on. There are two things to remember when it comes to Lucene segments and merging. Queries run against an index with multiple segments are slower than the ones with a smaller number of segments. Performance tests show that queries run against an index built of several segments are about 10 to 15 percent slower than the ones run against an index built of only a single segment. On the other hand, though, merging is not free and the fewer segments we want to have in our index, the more aggressive a merge policy should be configured.

Generally, if you want your queries to be faster, aim for fewer segments for your indices. For example, for `log_byte_size` or `log_doc` merge policies, setting the `index.merge.policy.merge_factor` property to a value lower than the default of `10` will result in less segments, lower RAM consumption, faster queries, and slower indexing. Setting the `index.merge.policy.merge_factor` property to a value higher than `10` will result in more segments building the index, higher RAM consumption, slower queries, and faster indexing.

There is one more thing: throttling. By default, Elasticsearch will throttle merging to `20mb/s`. Elasticsearch uses throttling so that your merging process doesn't affect searching too much. What's more, if merging is not fast enough, Elasticsearch will throttle the indexing to be single threaded so that the merging could actually finish and not have an extensive number of segments. However, if you are running SSD drives, the default `20mb/s` throttling is probably too much and you can set it to 5 to 10 times more (at least). To adjust throttling, we need to set the `indices.store.throttle.max_bytes_per_sec` property in `elasticsearch.yml` (or using the Cluster Settings API) to the desired value, such as `200mb/s`.

In general, if you want indexing to be faster, go for more segments for indices. If you want your queries to be faster, your I/O can handle more work because of merging, and you can live with Elasticsearch consuming a bit more RAM memory, go for more aggressive merge policy settings. If you want Elasticsearch to index more documents, go for a less aggressive merge policy, but remember that this will affect your queries' performance. If you want both of these things, you need to find a golden spot between them so that the merging is not too often but also doesn't result in an extensive number of segments.

Data distribution

As we know, each index in the Elasticsearch world can be divided into multiple shards, and each shard can have multiple replicas. In cases where you have multiple Elasticsearch nodes and indices divided into shards, proper data distribution may be crucial to even the load the cluster and not have some nodes doing more work than the other ones.

Let's take the following example—imagine that we have a cluster that is built of four nodes, and it has a single index built of three shards and one replica allocated. Such deployment could look as follows:

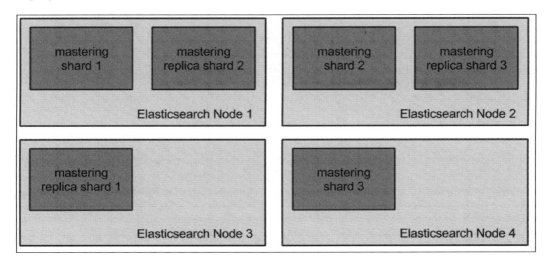

As you can see, the first two nodes have two physical shards allocated to them, while the last two nodes have one shard each. So the actual data allocation is not even. When sending the queries and indexing data, we will have the first two nodes do more work than the other two; this is what we want to avoid. We could make the `mastering` index have two shards and one replica so that it would look like this:

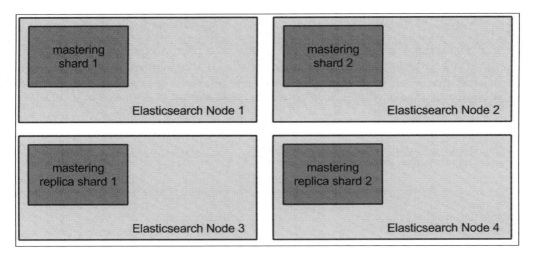

Or, we could have the mastering index divided into four shards and have one replica.

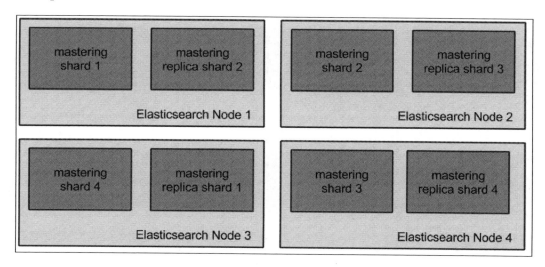

In both cases, we will end up with an even distribution of shards and replicas, with Elasticsearch doing a similar amount of work on all the nodes. Of course, with more indices (such as having daily indices), it may be trickier to get the data evenly distributed, and it may not be possible to have evenly distributed shards, but we should try to get to such a point.

One more thing to remember when it comes to data distribution, shards, and replicas is that when designing your index architecture, you should remember what you want to achieve. If you are going for a very high indexing use case, you may want to spread the index into multiple shards to lower the pressure that is put on the CPU and the I/O subsystem of the server. This is also true in order to run expensive queries, because with more shards, you can lower the load on a single server. However, with queries, there is one more thing: if your nodes can't keep up with the load caused by queries, you can add more Elasticsearch nodes and increase the number of replicas so that physical copies of the primary shards are placed on these nodes. This will make the indexing a bit slower but will give you the capacity to handle more queries at the same time.

Advices for high query rate scenarios

One of the great features of Elasticsearch is its ability to search and analyze the data that was indexed. However, sometimes, the user is needed to adjust Elasticsearch, and our queries to not only get the results of the query, but also get them fast (or in a reasonable amount of time). In this section, we will not only look at the possibilities but also prepare Elasticsearch for high query throughput use cases. We will also look at general performance tips when it comes to querying.

Filter caches and shard query caches

The first cache that can help with query performance is the filter cache (if our queries use filters, and if not, they should probably use filters). We talked about filters in the *Handling filters and why it matters* section in *Chapter 2, Power User Query DSL*. What we didn't talk about is the cache that is responsible for storing results of the filters: the filter cache. By default, Elasticsearch uses the filter cache implementation that is shared among all the indices on a single node, and we can control its size using the `indices.cache.filter.size` property. It defaults to `10` percent by default and specifies the total amount of memory that can be used by the filter cache on a given node. In general, if your queries are already using filters, you should monitor the size of the cache and evictions. If you see that you have many evictions, then you probably have a cache that's too small, and you should consider having a larger one. Having a cache that's too small may impact the query performance in a bad way.

The second cache that has been introduced in Elasticsearch is the shard query cache. It was added to Elasticsearch in Version 1.4.0, and its purpose is to cache aggregations, suggester results, and the number of hits (it will not cache the returned documents and, thus, it only works with `search_type=count`). When your queries are using aggregations or suggestions, it may be a good idea to enable this cache (it is disabled by default) so that Elasticsearch can reuse the data stored there. The best thing about the cache is that it promises the same near real-time search as search that is not cached.

To enable the shard query cache, we need to set the `index.cache.query.enable` property to `true`. For example, to enable the cache for our mastering index, we could issue the following command:

```
curl -XPUT 'localhost:9200/mastering/_settings' -d '{
 "index.cache.query.enable": true
}'
```

Please remember that using the shard query cache doesn't make sense if we don't use aggregations or suggesters.

One more thing to remember is that, by default, the shard query cache is allowed to take no more than 1 percent of the JVM heap given to the Elasticsearch node. To change the default value, we can use the `indices.cache.query.size` property. By using the `indices.cache.query.expire` property, we can specify the expiration date of the cache, but it is not needed, and in most cases, results stored in the cache are invalidated with every index refresh operation.

Think about the queries

This is the most general advice we can actually give: you should always think about optimal query structure, filter usage, and so on. We talked about it extensively in the *Handling filters and why it matters* section in *Chapter 2, Power User Query DSL*, but we would like to mention that once again, because we think it is very important. For example, let's look at the following query:

```
{
  "query" : {
   "bool" : {
    "must" : [
      {
       "query_string" : {
        "query" : "name:mastering AND department:it AND
        category:book"
       }
      },
      {
       "term" : {
        "tag" : "popular"
       }
      },
      {
       "term" : {
        "tag" : "2014"
       }
      }
     ]
    }
   }
}
```

It returns the book name that matches a few conditions. However, there are a few things we can improve in the preceding query. For example, we could move a few things to filtering so that the next time we use some parts of the query, we save CPU cycles and reuse the information stored in the cache. For example, this is what the optimized query could look like:

```
{
  "query" : {
    "filtered" : {
      "query" : {
        "match" : {
          "name" : "mastering"
        }
      },
      "filter" : {
        "bool" : {
          "must" : [
            {
              "term" : {
                "department" : "it"
              }
            },
            {
              "term" : {
                "category" : "book"
              }
            },
            {
              "terms" : {
                "tag" : [ "popular", "2014" ]
              }
            }
          ]
        }
      }
    }
  }
}
```

As you can see, there are a few things that we did. First of all, we used the `filtered` query to introduce filters and we moved most of the static, non-analyzed fields to filters. This allows us to easily reuse the filters in the next queries that we execute. Because of such query restructuring, we were able to simplify the main query, so we changed `query_string_query` to the `match` query, because it is enough for our use case. This is exactly what you should be doing when optimizing your queries or designing them — have optimization and performance in mind and try to keep them as optimal as they can be. This will result in faster query execution, lower resource consumption, and better health of the whole Elasticsearch cluster.

However, performance is not the only difference when it comes to the outcome of queries. As you know, filters don't affect the score of the documents returned and are not taken into consideration when calculating the score. Because of this, if you compare the scores returned by the preceding queries for the same documents, you would notice that they are different. This is worth remembering.

Using routing

If your data allows routing, you should consider using it. The data with the same routing value will always end up in the same shard. Because of this, we can save ourselves the need to query all the shards when asking for certain data. For example, if we store the data of our clients, we may use a client identifier as the routing value. This will allow us to store the data of a single client inside a single shard. This means that during querying, Elasticsearch needs to fetch data from only a single shard, as shown in the following figure:

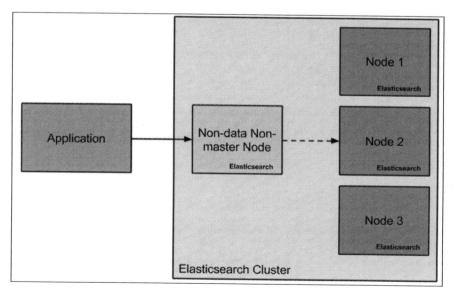

If we assume that the data lives in a shard allocated to Node 2, we can see that Elasticsearch only needed to run the query against that one particular node to get all the data for the client. If we don't use routing, the simplified query execution could look as follows:

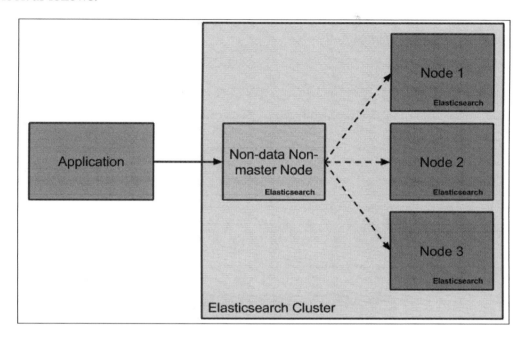

In the case of nonrouting, Elasticsearch first needs to query all the index shards. If your index contains dozen of shards, the performance improvement will be significant as long as a single Elasticsearch instance can handle the shard size.

Please remember that not every use case is eligible to use routing. To be able to use it, your data needs to be virtually divided so that it is spread across the shards. For example, it usually doesn't make sense to have dozens of very small shards and one massive one, because for the massive one, performance may not be decent.

Parallelize your queries

One thing that is usually forgotten is the need to parallelize queries. Imagine that you have a dozen nodes in your cluster, but your index is built of a single shard. If the index is large, your queries will perform worse than you would expect. Of course, you can increase the number of replicas, but that won't help; a single query will still go to a single shard in that index, because replicas are not more than the copies of the primary shard, and they contain the same data (or at least they should).

One thing that will actually help is dividing your index into multiple shards—the number of shards depends on the hardware and deployment. In general, it is advised to have the data evenly divided so that nodes are equally loaded. For example, if you have four Elasticsearch nodes and two indices, you may want to have four shards for each index, just like what is shown in the following figure:

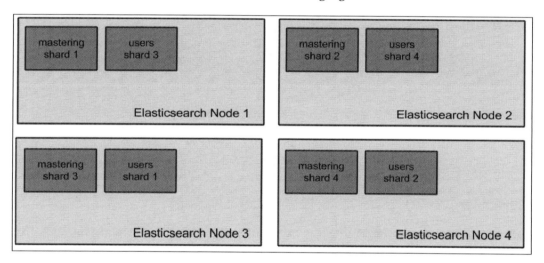

Field data cache and breaking the circuit

By default, the field data cache in Elasticsearch is unbounded. This can be very dangerous, especially when you are using faceting and sorting on many fields. If these fields are high cardinality ones, then you can run into even more trouble. By trouble, we mean running out of memory.

We have two different factors we can tune to be sure that we won't run into out-of-memory errors. First of all, we can limit the size of the field data cache. The second thing is the circuit breaker, which we can easily configure to just throw an exception instead of loading too much data. Combining these two things will ensure that we don't run into memory issues.

However, we should also remember that Elasticsearch will evict data from the field data cache if its size is not enough to handle faceting request or sorting. This will affect the query performance, because loading field data information is not very efficient. However, we think that it is better to have our queries slower rather than having our cluster blown up because of out-of-memory errors.

Finally, if your queries are using field data cache extensively (such as aggregations or sorting) and you are running into memory-related issues (such as `OutOfMemory` exceptions or GC pauses), consider using doc values that we already talked about. Doc values should give you performance that's similar to field data cache, and support for doc values is getting better and better with each Elasticsearch release (improvements to doc values are made in Lucene itself).

Keeping size and shard_size under control

When dealing with queries that use aggregations, for some of them, we have the possibility of using two properties: `size` and `shard_size`. The `size` parameter defines how many buckets should be returned by the final aggregation results; the node that aggregates the final results will get the top buckets from each shard that returns the result and will only return the top size of them to the client. The `shard_size` parameter tells Elasticsearch about the same but on the shard level. Increasing the value of the `shard_size` parameter will lead to more accurate aggregations (such as in the case of significant terms' aggregation) at the cost of network traffic and memory usage. Lowering this parameter will cause aggregation results to be less precise, but we will benefit from lower memory consumption and lower network traffic. If we see that the memory usage is too large, we can lower the `size` and `shard_size` properties of problematic queries and see whether the quality of the results is still acceptable.

High indexing throughput scenarios and Elasticsearch

In this section, we will discuss some optimizations that will allow us to concentrate on the indexing throughput and speed. Some use cases are highly dependent on the amount of data you can push to Elasticsearch every second, and the next few topics should cover some information regarding indexing.

Bulk indexing

This is very obvious advice, but you would be surprised by how many Elasticsearch users forget about indexing data in bulk instead of sending the documents one by one. The thing to remember, though, is to not overload Elasticsearch with too many bulk requests. Remember about the bulk thread pool and its size (equal to the number of CPU cores in the system by default with a queue of 50 requests), and try to adjust your indexers so that they don't to go beyond it. Or, you will first start to queue their requests and if Elasticsearch is not able to process them, you will quickly start seeing rejected execution exceptions, and your data won't be indexed. On the other hand, remember that your bulk requests can't be too large, or Elasticsearch will need a lot of memory to process them.

Just as an example, I would like to show you two types of indexing happening. In the first figure, we have indexing throughput when running the indexation one document by one. In the second figure, we do the same, but instead of indexing documents one by one, we index them in batches of 10 documents.

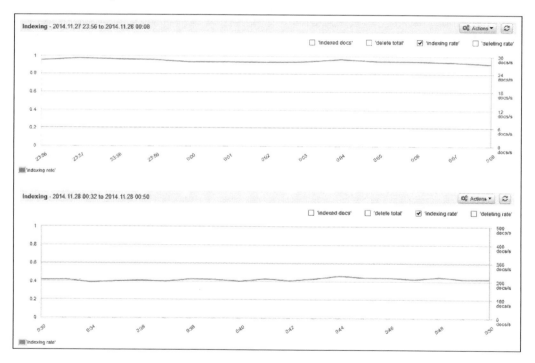

As you can see, when indexing documents one by one, we were able to index about 30 documents per second and it was stable. The situation changed with bulk indexing and batches of 10 documents. We were able to index slightly more than 200 documents per second, so the difference can be clearly seen.

Of course, this is a very basic comparison of indexing speed, and in order to show you the real difference, we should use dozens of threads and push Elasticsearch to its limits. However, the preceding comparison should give you a basic view of the indexing throughput gains when using bulk indexing.

Doc values versus indexing speed

When talking about indexing speed, we have to talk about doc values. As we already said a few times in the book, doc values allows us to fight gigantic JVM heap requirements when Elasticsearch needs to uninvert fields for functionalities such as sorting, aggregations, or faceting. However, writing doc values requires some additional work during the indexation. If we are all about the highest indexing speed and the most indexing throughput, you should consider not going for doc values. On the other hand, if you have a lot of data—and you probably have when you are indexing fast—using doc values may be the only way that will allow using aggregations or sorting on field values without running into memory-related problems.

Keep your document fields under control

The amount of data you index makes the difference, which is understandable. However, this is not the only factor; the size of the documents and their analysis matters as well. With larger documents, you can expect not only your index to grow, but also make the indexation slightly slower. This is why you may sometimes want to look at all the fields you are indexing and storing. Keep your stored fields to a minimum or don't use them at all; the only stored field you need in most cases is the _source field.

There is one more thing — apart from the `_source` field, Elasticsearch indexes the `_all` field by default. Let's remind you: the `_all` field is used by Elasticsearch to gather data from all the other textual fields. In some cases, this field is not used at all and because of that, it is nice to turn it off. Turning it off is simple and the only thing to do is add the following entry to the type mappings:

```
"_all" : {"enabled" : false}
```

We can do this during the index creation, for example, like this:

```
curl -XPOST 'localhost:9200/disabling_all' -d '{
  "mappings" : {
   "test_type" : {
    "_all" : { "enabled" : false },
    "properties" : {
     "name" : { "type" : "string" },
     "tag" : { "type" : "string", "index" : "not_analyzed" }
    }
   }
  }
}'
```

The indexing should be slightly faster depending on the size of your documents and the number of textual fields in it.

There is an additional thing, which is good practice when disabling the `_all` field: setting a new default search field. We can do this by setting the `index.query.default_field` property. For example, in our case, we can set it in the `elasticsearch.yml` file and set it to the `name` field from our preceding mappings:

```
index.query.default_field: name
```

The index architecture and replication

When designing the index architecture, one of the things you need to think about is the number of shards and replicas that the index is built of. During that time, we also need to we think about data distribution among Elasticsearch nodes, optimal performance, high availability, reliability, and so on. First of all, distributing primary shards of the index across all nodes we have will parallelize indexing operations and will make them faster.

The second thing is data replication. What we have to remember is that too many replicas will cause the indexation speed to drop. This is because of several reasons. First of all, you need to transfer the data between primary shards and replicas. The second thing is that, usually, replicas and primary shards may live on the same nodes (not primary shards and its replicas, of course, but replicas of other primaries). For example, take a look at what is shown in the following figure:

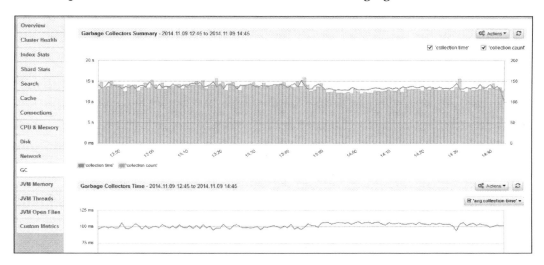

Because of this, Elasticsearch will need the data for both primary shards and replicas and, thus, it will use the disk. Depending on the cluster setup, the indexing throughput may drop in such cases (depends on the disks, number of documents indexed at the same time, and so on).

Tuning write-ahead log

We already talked about transaction logs in the *Data flushing, index refresh and transaction log handling* section of *Chapter 6, Low-level Index Control*. Elasticsearch has an internal module called translog (http://www.elasticsearch.org/guide/en/elasticsearch/reference/current/index-modules-translog.html). It is a per-shard structure that serves the purpose of write-ahead logging (http://en.wikipedia.org/wiki/Write-ahead_logging). Basically, it allows Elasticsearch to expose the newest updates for GET operations, ensure data durability, and optimize writing to Lucene indices.

By default, Elasticsearch keeps a maximum of 5000 operations in the transaction log with a maximum size of 200 MB. However, if we can pay the price of data not being available for search operations for longer periods of time but we want more indexing throughput, we can increase these defaults. By specifying the index.translog. flush_threshold_ops and index.translog.flush_threshold_size properties (both are set per index and can be updated in real time using the Elasticsearch API), we can set the maximum number of operations allowed to be stored in the transaction log and its maximum size. We've seen deployments having this property values set to 10 times the default values.

One thing to remember is that in case of failure, shard initialization will be slower — of course on the ones that had large transaction logs. This is because Elasticsearch needs to process all the information from the transaction log before the shard is ready for use.

Think about storage

One of the crucial things when it comes to high indexing use cases is the storage type and its configuration. If your organization can afford SSD disks (solid state drives), go for them. They are superior in terms of speed compared to the traditional spinning disks, but of course, that comes at the cost of price. If you can't afford SSD drives, configure your spinning disks to work in RAID 0 (http://en.wikipedia. org/wiki/RAID) or point Elasticsearch to use multiple data paths.

What's more, don't use shared or remote filesystems for Elasticsearch indices; use local storage instead. Remote and shared filesystems are usually slower compared to local disk drives and will cause Elasticsearch to wait for read and write, and thus result in a general slowdown.

RAM buffer for indexing

Remember that the more the available RAM for the indexing buffer (the indices. memory.index_buffer_size property), the more documents Elasticsearch can hold in the memory, but of course, we don't want to occupy 100 percent of the available memory only to Elasticsearch. By default, this is set to 10 percent, but if you really need a high indexing rate, you can increase it. It is advisable to have approximately 512 MB of RAM for each active shard that takes part in the indexing process, but remember that the indices.memory.index_buffer_size property is per node and not per shard. So, if you have 20 GB of heap given to the Elasticsearch node and 10 shards active on the node, Elasticsearch will give each shard about 200 MB of RAM for indexing buffering (10 percent of 20 GB / 10 shards) by default.

Summary

In this chapter, we were focused on the performance and scaling of Elasticsearch. We looked at how doc values can help us with improving the query performance, how garbage collector works, and what to look at when changing its configuration. We benchmarked our queries and we saw what the Hot Threads API is. Finally, we discussed how to scale Elasticsearch and how to prepare it for high querying and indexing use cases.

In the next chapter, we will write some code. We will create the Apache Maven project used to write Elasticsearch plugins. We will write a custom REST action to extend the Elasticsearch functionality. In addition to this, we will learn what needs to be done in order to introduce new analysis plugins for Elasticsearch, and we will create such plugins.

9
Developing Elasticsearch Plugins

In the previous chapter, we were focused on the performance and scaling of our Elasticsearch clusters. We looked at how doc values can help us improve query performance and lower the memory for queries, which deals with field data cache at the cost of slightly slower indexing. We looked at how garbage collector works and what to look at when changing its configuration. We've benchmarked our queries, and we've seen what Hot Threads API gives us. Finally, we discussed how to scale Elasticsearch. By the end of this chapter, you will have learned:

- How to set up the Apache Maven project for Elasticsearch plugins' development
- How to develop a custom REST action plugin
- How to develop a custom analysis plugin extending Elasticsearch analysis capabilities

Creating the Apache Maven project structure

Before we start with showing you how to develop a custom Elasticsearch plugin, we would like to discuss a way to package it so that it can be installed by Elasticsearch using the `plugin` command. In order to do that, we will use Apache Maven (`http://maven.apache.org/`), which is designed to simplify software projects' management. It aims to make your build process easier, provide a unifying build system, manage dependencies, and so on.

> Please note that the chapter you are currently reading was written and tested using Elasticsearch 1.4.1.

Also remember that the book you are holding in your hands is not about Maven but Elasticsearch, and we will keep Maven-related information to the required minimum.

> Installing Apache Maven is a straightforward task; we assume that you already have it installed. However, if you have problems with it, please consult `http://maven.apache.org/` for more information.

Understanding the basics

The result of a Maven build process is an artifact. Each artifact is defined by its identifier, its group, and its version. This is crucial when working with Maven, because every dependency you'll use will need to be identified by these three mentioned properties.

The structure of the Maven Java project

The idea behind Maven is quite simple—you create a project structure that looks something like this:

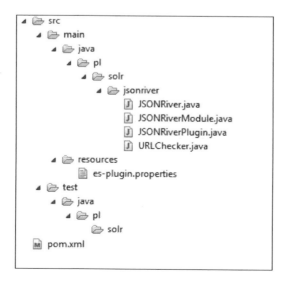

You can see that the code is placed in the `src` folder—the code is in the `main` folder and the unit tests are located in the `test` folder. Although you can change the default layout, Maven tends to work best with the default layout.

The idea of POM

In addition to the code, you can see a file named `pom.xml` that is located in the root directory in the previous image. This is a project object model file that describes the project, its properties, and its dependencies. That's right—you don't need to manually download dependencies if they are present in one of the available Maven repositories—during its work, Maven will download them, put them in your local repository on your hard disk, and use it when needed. All you need to care about is writing an appropriate `pom.xml` section that will inform Maven which dependencies should be used.

For example, this is an example Maven `pom.xml` file:

```
<project xmlns="http://maven.apache.org/POM/4.0.0" xmlns:xsi="http://
www.w3.org/2001/XMLSchema-instance"
    xsi:schemaLocation="http://maven.apache.org/POM/4.0.0 http://
maven.apache.org/xsd/maven-4.0.0.xsd">
    <modelVersion>4.0.0</modelVersion>

    <groupId>pl.solr</groupId>
    <artifactId>analyzer</artifactId>
    <version>1.0-SNAPSHOT</version>
    <packaging>jar</packaging>

    <name>analyzer</name>
    <url>http://solr.pl</url>

    <properties>
        <elasticsearch.version>1.4.1</elasticsearch.version>
        <project.build.sourceEncoding>UTF-8</project.build.
sourceEncoding>
    </properties>

    <dependencies>
        <dependency>
            <groupId>org.elasticsearch</groupId>
            <artifactId>elasticsearch</artifactId>
            <version>${elasticsearch.version}</version>
        </dependency>
```

```
    </dependencies>
  </project>
```

This is a simplified version of a `pom.xml` file that we will extend in the rest of the chapter. You can see that it starts with the root `project` tag and then defines the group identifier, the artifact identifier, the version, and the packaging method (in our case, the standard build command will create a jar file). In addition to this, we've specified a single dependency — the Elasticsearch library Version 1.4.1.

Running the build process

In order to run the build process, what we need to do is simply run the following command in the directory where the `pom.xml` file is present:

```
mvn clean package
```

It will result in running Maven. It will clean all the generated content in the working directory, compile and package our code. Of course, if we have unit tests, they will have to pass in order for the package to be built. The built package will be written into the `target` directory created by Maven.

> If you want to learn more about the Maven life cycle, please refer to http://maven.apache.org/guides/introduction/introduction-to-the-lifecycle.html.

Introducing the assembly Maven plugin

In order to build the ZIP file that will contain our plugin code, we need to package it. By default, Maven doesn't support pure ZIP files' packaging, so in order to make it all work, we will use the Maven Assembly plugin (you can find more about the plugin at http://maven.apache.org/plugins/maven-assembly-plugin/). In general, the described plugin allows us to aggregate the project output along with its dependencies, documentations, and configuration files into a single archive.

In order for the plugin to work, we need to add the `build` section to our `pom.xml` file that will contain information about the assembly plugin, the jar plugin (which is responsible for creating the proper jar), and the compiler plugin, because we want to be sure that the code will be readable by Java 7. In addition to this, let's assume that we want our archive to be put into the `target/release` directory of our project. The relevant section of the `pom.xml` file should look as follows:

```
<build>
 <plugins>
   <plugin>
```

```
        <groupId>org.apache.maven.plugins</groupId>
        <artifactId>maven-jar-plugin</artifactId>
        <version>2.3</version>
        <configuration>
            <finalName>elasticsearch-${project.name}-
${elasticsearch.version}</finalName>
        </configuration>
    </plugin>

    <plugin>
        <groupId>org.apache.maven.plugins</groupId>
        <artifactId>maven-assembly-plugin</artifactId>
        <version>2.2.1</version>
        <configuration>
        <finalName>elasticsearch-${project.name}-
${elasticsearch.version}</finalName>
            <appendAssemblyId>false</appendAssemblyId>
                <outputDirectory>${project.build.directory}/release/</
outputDirectory>
            <descriptors>
              <descriptor>assembly/release.xml</descriptor>
            </descriptors>
        </configuration>
        <executions>
         <execution>
         <id>generate-release-plugin</id>
          <phase>package</phase>
          <goals>
           <goal>single</goal>
          </goals>
         </execution>
        </executions>
    </plugin>

    <plugin>
     <artifactId>maven-compiler-plugin</artifactId>
     <configuration>
      <source>1.7</source>
      <target>1.7</target>
    </configuration>
     </plugin>
  </plugins>
</build>
```

If you look closely at the assembly plugin configuration, you'll notice that we specify the assembly descriptor called `release.xml` in the `assembly` directory. This file is responsible for specifying what kind of archive we want to have as the output. Let's put the following `release.xml` file in the `assembly` directory of our project:

```xml
<?xml version="1.0"?>
<assembly>
 <id>bin</id>
 <formats>
  <format>zip</format>
 </formats>
 <includeBaseDirectory>false</includeBaseDirectory>
 <dependencySets>
  <dependencySet>
   <unpack>false</unpack>
   <outputDirectory>/</outputDirectory>
   <useProjectArtifact>false</useProjectArtifact>
   <useTransitiveFiltering>true</useTransitiveFiltering>
   <excludes>
    <exclude>org.elasticsearch:elasticsearch</exclude>
   </excludes>
  </dependencySet>
 </dependencySets>
 <fileSets>
  <fileSet>
   <directory>${project.build.directory}/</directory>
   <outputDirectory>/</outputDirectory>
   <includes>
    <include>elasticsearch-${project.name}-
${elasticsearch.version}.jar</include>
   </includes>
  </fileSet>
 </fileSets>
</assembly>
```

Again, we don't need to know all the details; however, it is nice to understand what is going on, even on the general level. The preceding code file tells the Maven Assembly plugin that we want our archive to be packed with ZIP (`<format>zip</format>`), and we want Elasticsearch libraries to be excluded (the `exclude` section), because they will already be present in Elasticsearch, where we will install the plugin. In addition to this, we've specified that we want our project jar to be included (the `includes` section).

If you want to see the full project structure with the full pom.xml file and all the needed files, please look at the code provided with the book for *Chapter 9, Developing Elasticsearch Plugins*.

Creating custom REST action

Let's start the journey of extending Elasticsearch by creating a custom REST action. We've chosen this as the first extension, because we wanted to take the simplest approach as the introduction to extending Elasticsearch.

 We assume that you already have a Java project created and that you are using Maven, just like we did in the *Creating the Apache Maven project structure* section in the beginning of this chapter. If you would like to use an already created and working example and start from there, please look at the code for *Chapter 9, Developing Elasticsearch Plugins* that is available with the book.

The assumptions

In order to illustrate how to develop a custom REST action, we need to have an idea of how it should work. Our REST action will be really simple—it should return names of all the nodes or names of the nodes that start with the given prefix if the prefix parameter is passed to it. In addition to that, it should only be available when using the HTTP GET method, so POST requests, for example, shouldn't be allowed.

Implementation details

We will need to develop two Java classes:

- A class that extends the BaseRestHandler Elasticsearch abstract class from the org.elasticsearch.rest package that will be responsible for handling the REST action code—we will call it a CustomRestAction.
- A class that will be used by Elasticsearch to load the plugin—this class needs to extend the Elasticsearch AbstractPlugin class from the org.elasticsearch.plugin package—we will call it CustomRestActionPlugin.

In addition to the preceding two, we will need a simple text file that we will discuss after implementing the two mentioned Java classes.

Using the REST action class

The most interesting class is the one that will be used to handle the user's requests—we will call it CustomRestAction. In order to work, it needs to extend the BaseRestHandler class from the org.elasticsearch.rest package—the base class for REST actions in Elasticsearch. In order to extend this class, we need to implement the handleRequest method in which we will process the user request and a three argument constructor that will be used to initialize the base class and register the appropriate handler under which our REST action will be visible.

The whole code for the CustomRestAction class looks as follows:

```java
public class CustomRestAction extends BaseRestHandler {
  @Inject
  public CustomRestAction(Settings settings, RestController
  controller, Client client) {
    super(settings, controller, client);
    controller.registerHandler(Method.GET, "/_mastering/nodes", this);
  }
  @Override
  public void handleRequest(RestRequest request, RestChannel
  channel, Client client) {
    final String prefix = request.param("prefix", "");
    client.admin().cluster().prepareNodesInfo().all().execute(new
    RestBuilderListener<NodesInfoResponse>(channel) {
      @Override
      public RestResponse buildResponse(
      NodesInfoResponse response, XContentBuilder builder)
      throws Exception {
        List<String> nodes = new ArrayList<String>();
        for (NodeInfo nodeInfo : response.getNodes()) {
          String nodeName = nodeInfo.getNode().getName();
          if (prefix.isEmpty()) {
            nodes.add(nodeName);
          } else if (nodeName.startsWith(prefix)) {
            nodes.add(nodeName);
          }
        }
        builder.startObject()
        .field("nodes", nodes)
```

```
      .endObject();
      return new BytesRestResponse(RestStatus.OK, builder);
      }
    });
  }
}
```

The constructor

For each custom REST class, Elasticsearch will pass three arguments when creating an object of such type: the Settings type object, which holds the settings; the RestController type object that we will use to bind our REST action to the REST endpoint; and the Client type object, which is an Elasticsearch client and entry point for cooperation with it. All of these arguments are also required by the super class, so we invoke the base class constructor and pass them.

There is one more thing: the @Inject annotation. It allows us to inform Elasticsearch that it should put the objects in the constructor during the object creation. For more information about it, please refer to the Javadoc of the mentioned annotation, which is available at https://github.com/elasticsearch/elasticsearch/blob/master/src/main/java/org/elasticsearch/common/inject/Inject.java.

Now, let's focus on the following code line:

```
controller.registerHandler(Method.GET, "/_mastering/nodes", this);
```

What it does is that it registers our custom REST action implementation and binds it to the endpoint of our choice. The first argument is the HTTP method type, the REST action will be able to work with. As we said earlier, we only want to respond to GET requests. If we would like to respond to multiple types of HTTP methods, we should just include multiple registerHandler method invocations with each HTTP method. The second argument specifies the actual REST endpoint our custom action will be available at; in our case, it will available under the /_mastering/nodes endpoint. The third argument tells Elasticsearch which class should be responsible for handling the defined endpoint; in our case, this is the class we are developing, thus we are passing this.

Handling requests

Although the `handleRequest` method is the longest one in our code, it is not complicated. We start by reading the request parameter with the following line of code:

```
String prefix = request.param("prefix", "");
```

We store the prefix request parameter in the variable called `prefix`. By default, we want an empty `String` object to be assigned to the `prefix` variable if there is no prefix parameter passed to the request (the default value is defined by the second parameter of the `param` method of the `request` object).

Next, we retrieve the `NodesInfoResponse` object using the Elasticsearch client object and its abilities to run administrative commands. In this case, we have used the possibility of sending queries to Elasticsearch in an asynchronous way. Instead of the call `execute().actionGet()` part, which waits for a response and returns it, we have used the `execute()` call, which takes a future object that will be informed when the query finishes. So, the rest of the method is in the `buildResponse()` callback of the `RestBuilderListener` object. The `NodesInfoResponse` object will contain an array of `NodeInfo` objects, which we will use to get node names. What we need to do is return all the node names that start with a given prefix or all if the `prefix` parameter was not present in the request. In order to do this, we create a new array:

```
List<String> nodes = new ArrayList<String>();
```

We iterate over the available nodes using the following `for` loop:

```
for (NodeInfo nodeInfo : response.getNodes())
```

We get the node name using the `getName` method of the `DiscoveryNode` object, which is returned after invoking the `getNode` method of `NodeInfo`:

```
String nodeName = nodeInfo.getNode().getName();
```

If `prefix` is empty or if it starts with the given prefix, we add the name of the node to the array we've created. After we iterate through all the `NodeInfo` objects, we call the are starting build the response and sent it through the HTTP.

Writing response

The last thing regarding our `CustomRestAction` class is the response handling, which is the responsibility of the last part of the `buildResponse()` method that we created. It is simple because an appropriate response builder is already provided by Elasticsearch under the `builder` argument. It takes into consideration the `format` parameter used by the client in the call, so by default, we send the response in a proper JSON format just like Elasticsearch does and also take the YAML (http://en.wikipedia.org/wiki/YAML) format for free.

Now, we use the `builder` object we got to start the response object (using the `startObject` method) and start a `nodes` field (because the value of the field is a collection, it will automatically be formatted as an array). The `nodes` field is created inside the initial object, and we will use it to return matching nodes names. Finally, we close the object using the `endObject` method.

After we have our object ready to be sent as a response, we return the `BytesRestResponse` object. We do this in the following line:

```
return new BytesRestResponse(RestStatus.OK, builder);
```

As you can see, to create the object, we need to pass two parameters: `RestStatus` and the `XContentBuilder`, which holds our response. The `RestStatus` class allows us to specify the response code, which is `RestStatus.OK` in our case, because everything went smoothly.

The plugin class

The `CustomRestActionPlugin` class will hold the code that is used by Elasticsearch to initialize the plugin itself. It extends the `AbstractPlugin` class from the `org.elasticsearch.plugin` package. Because we are creating an extension, we are obliged to implement the following code parts:

- constructor: This is a standard constructor that will take a single argument; in our case, it will be empty
- The `onModule` method: This is the method that includes the code that will add our custom REST action so that Elasticsearch will know about it
- The `name` method: This is the name of our plugin
- The `description` method: This is a short description of our plugin

The code of the whole class looks as follows:

```
public class CustomRestActionPlugin extends AbstractPlugin {
  @Inject
  public CustomRestActionPlugin(Settings settings) {
  }

  public void onModule(RestModule module) {
    module.addRestAction(CustomRestAction.class);
  }

  @Override
  public String name() {
    return "CustomRestActionPlugin";
  }

  @Override
  public String description() {
    return "Custom REST action";
  }
}
```

The constructor, name, and description methods are very simple, and we will just skip discussing them, and we will focus on the onModule method. This method takes a single argument: the RestModule class object, which is the class that allows us to register our custom REST action. Elasticsearch will call the onModule method for all the modules that are available and eligible (all REST actions). What we do is just a simple call to the RestModule addRestAction method, passing in our CustomRestAction class as an argument. That's all when it comes to Java development.

Informing Elasticsearch about our REST action

We have our code ready, but we need one additional thing; we need to let Elasticsearch know what the class registering our plugin is — the one we've called CustomRestActionPlugin. In order to do this, we create an es-plugin.properties file in the src/main/resources directory with the following content:

```
plugin=pl.solr.rest.CustomRestActionPlugin
```

We just specify the plugin property there, which should have a value of the class we use to register our plugins (the one that extends the Elasticsearch AbstractPlugin class). This file will be included in the jar file that will be created during the build process and will be used by Elasticsearch during the plugin load process.

Time for testing

Of course, we could leave it now and say that we are done, but we won't. We would like to show you how to build each of the plugins, install it, and finally, test it to see whether it actually works. Let's start with building our plugin.

Building the REST action plugin

We start with the easiest part—building our plugin. In order to do this, we run a simple command:

```
mvn compile package
```

We tell Maven that we want the code to be compiled and packaged. After the command finishes, we can find the archive with the plugin in the `target/release` directory (assuming you are using a project setup similar to the one we've described at the beginning of the chapter).

Installing the REST action plugin

In order to install the plugin, we will use the `plugin` command that is located in the `bin` directory of the Elasticsearch distributable package. Assuming that we have our plugin archive stored in the `/home/install/es/plugins` directory, we will run the following command (we run it from the Elasticsearch home directory):

```
bin/plugin --install rest --url
file:/home/install/es/plugins/elasticsearch-rest-1.4.1.zip
```

We need to install the plugin on all the nodes in our cluster, because we want to be able to run our custom REST action on each Elasticsearch instance.

 In order to learn more about installing Elasticsearch plugins, please refer to our previous book, *Elasticsearch Server Second Edition*, or check out the official Elasticsearch documentation at http://www.elasticsearch.org/guide/reference/modules/plugins/.

After we have the plugin installed, we need to restart our Elasticsearch instance we were making the installation on. After the restart, we should see something like this in the logs:

```
[2014-12-12 21:04:48,348][INFO ][plugins                         ]
[Archer] loaded [CustomRestActionPlugin], sites []
```

As you can see, Elasticsearch informed us that the plugin named `CustomRestActionPlugin` was loaded.

Checking whether the REST action plugin works

We can finally check whether the plugin works. In order to do that, we will run the following command:

```
curl -XGET 'localhost:9200/_mastering/nodes?pretty'
```

As a result, we should get all the nodes in the cluster, because we didn't provide the `prefix` parameter and this is exactly what we've got from Elasticsearch:

```
{
  "nodes" : [ "Archer" ]
}
```

Because we only had one node in our Elasticsearch cluster, we've got the `nodes` array with only a `single` entry.

Now, let's test what will happen if we add the `prefix=Are` parameter to our request. The exact command we've used was as follows:

```
curl -XGET 'localhost:9200/_mastering/nodes?prefix=Are&pretty'
```

The response from Elasticsearch was as follows:

```
{
  "nodes" : [ ]
}
```

As you can see, the `nodes` array is empty, because we don't have any node in the cluster that would start with the `Are` prefix. At the end, let's check another format of response:

```
curl -XGET 'localhost:9200/_mastering/nodes?pretty&format=yaml'
```

Now the response is not in a JSON format. Look at the example output for a cluster consisting of two nodes:

```
---
nodes:
- "Atalon"
- "Slapstick"
```

As we can see, our REST plugin is not so complicated but already has several features.

Creating the custom analysis plugin

The last thing we want to discuss when it comes to custom Elasticsearch plugins is the analysis process extension. We've chosen to show how to develop a custom analysis plugin because this is sometimes very useful, for example, when you want to have the custom analysis process that you use in your company introduced, or when you want to use the Lucene analyzer or filter that is not present in Elasticsearch itself or as a plugin for it. Because creating an analysis extension is more complicated compared to what we've seen when developing a custom REST action, we decided to leave it until the end of the chapter.

Implementation details

Because developing a custom analysis plugin is the most complicated, at least from the Elasticsearch point of view and the number of classes we need to develop, we will have more things to do compared to previous examples. We will need to develop the following things:

- The `TokenFilter` class extension (from the `org.apache.lucene.analysis` package) implementation that will be responsible for handling token reversing; we will call it `CustomFilter`

- The `AbstractTokenFilterFactory` extension (from the `org.elasticsearch.index.analysis` package) that will be responsible for providing our `CustomFilter` instance to Elasticsearch; we will call it `CustomFilterFactory`

- The custom analyzer, which will extend the `org.apache.lucene.analysis.Analyzer` class and provide the Lucene analyzer functionality; we will call it `CustomAnalyzer`

- The analyzer provider, which we will call `CustomAnalyzerProvider`, which extends `AbstractIndexAnalyzerProvider` from the `org.elasticsearch.index.analysis` package, and which will be responsible for providing the analzyer instance to Elasticsearch

- An extension of `AnalysisModule.AnalysisBinderProcessor` from the `org.elasticsearch.index.analysis` package, which will have information about the names under which our analyzer and token filter will be available in Elasticsearch; we will call it `CustomAnalysisBinderProcessor`

- An extension of the `AbstractComponent` class from the `org.elasticsearch.common.component` package, which will inform Elasticsearch which factories should be used for our custom analyzer and token filter; we will call it `CustomAnalyzerIndicesComponent`

- The AbstractModule extension (from the org.elasticsearch.
  common.inject package) that will inform Elasticsearch that our
  CustomAnalyzerIndicesComponent module should be a singleton; we will
  call it CustomAnalyzerModule

- Finally, the usual AbstractPlugin extension (from the org.
  elasticsearch.plugins package) that will register our plugin; we will call
  it CustomAnalyzerPlugin

So let's start discussing the code.

Implementing TokenFilter

The funniest thing about the currently discussed plugin is that the whole analysis
work is actually done on a Lucene level, and what we need to do is write the
org.apache.lucene.analysis.TokenFilter extension, which we will call
CustomFilter. In order to do this, we need to initialize the super class and override
the incrementToken method. Our class will be responsible for reversing the tokens,
so that's the logic we want our analyzer and filter to have. The whole implementation
of our CustomFilter class looks as follows:

```
public class CustomFilter extends TokenFilter {
  private final CharTermAttribute termAttr =
addAttribute(CharTermAttribute.class);

  protected CustomFilter(TokenStream input) {
    super(input);
  }

  @Override
  public boolean incrementToken() throws IOException {
    if (input.incrementToken()) {
      char[] originalTerm = termAttr.buffer();
      if (originalTerm.length > 0) {
        StringBuilder builder = new StringBuilder(new
String(originalTerm).trim()).reverse();
        termAttr.setEmpty();
        termAttr.append(builder.toString());
      }
      return true;
    } else {
      return false;
    }
  }
}
```

The first thing we see in the implementation is the following line:

```
private final CharTermAttribute termAttr =
addAttribute(CharTermAttribute.class);
```

It allows us to retrieve the text of the token we are currently processing. In order to get access to the other token information, we need to use other attributes. The list of attributes can be found by looking at the classes implementing Lucene's `org.apache.lucene.util.Attribute` interface (`http://lucene.apache.org/core/4_10_0/core/org/apache/lucene/util/Attribute.html`). What you need to know now is that by using the static `addAttribute` method, we can bind different attributes and use them during token processing.

Then, we have the constructor, which is only used for super class initialization, so we can skip discussing it.

Finally, there is the `incrementToken` method, which returns `true` when there is a token in the token stream left to be processed, and `false` if there is no token left to be processed. So, what we do first is we check whether there is a token to be processed by calling the `incrementToken` method of input, which is the `TokenStream` instance stored in the super class. Then, we get the term text by calling the `buffer` method of the attribute we bind in the first line of our class. If there is text in the term (its length is higher than zero), we use a `StringBuilder` object to reverse the text, we clear the term buffer (by calling `setEmpty` on the attribute), and we append the reversed text to the already emptied term buffer (by calling the `append` method of the attribute). After this, we return `true`, because our token is ready to be processed further—on a token filter level, we don't know whether the token will be processed further or not, so we need to be sure we return the correct information, just in case.

Implementing the TokenFilter factory

The factory for our token filter implementation is one of the simplest classes in the case of the discussed plugins. What we need to do is create an `AbstractTokenFilterFactory` (from the `org.elasticsearch.index.analysis` package) extension that overrides a single `create` method in which we create our token filter. The code of this class looks as follows:

```
public class CustomFilterFactory extends
AbstractTokenFilterFactory {
  @Inject
  public CustomFilterFactory(Index index, @IndexSettings Settings
indexSettings, @Assisted String name, @Assisted Settings settings)
{
    super(index, indexSettings, name, settings);
  }
```

```
@Override
public TokenStream create(TokenStream tokenStream) {
  return new CustomFilter(tokenStream);
}
}
```

As you can see, the class is very simple. We start with the constructor, which is needed, because we need to initialize the parent class. In addition to this, we have the create method, in which we create our CustomFilter class with the provided TokenStream object.

Before we go on, we would like to mention two more things: the @IndexSettings and @Assisted annotations. The first one will result in index settings being injected as the Settings class object to the constructor; of course, this is done automatically. The @Assisted keyword results in the annotated parameter value to be injected from the argument of the factory method.

Implementing the class custom analyzer

We wanted to keep the example implementation as simple as possible and, because of that, we've decided not to complicate the analyzer implementation. To implement our analyzer, we need to extend an abstract Analyzer class from Lucene's org. apache.lucene.analysis package, and we did that. The whole code of our CustomAnalyzer class looks as follows:

```
public class CustomAnalyzer extends Analyzer {
  public CustomAnalyzer() {
  }

  @Override
  protected TokenStreamComponents createComponents(String field,
Reader reader) {
    final Tokenizer src = new WhitespaceTokenizer(reader);
    return new TokenStreamComponents(src, new CustomFilter(src));
  }
}
```

If you want to see more complicated analyzer implementations, please look at the source code of Apache Lucene, Apache Solr, and Elasticsearch.

The `createComponent` method is the one we need to implement, and it should return a `TokenStreamComponents` object (from the `org.apache.lucene.analysis` package) for a given field name (the `String` type object—the first argument of the method) and data (the `Reader` type object—the second method argument). What we do is create a `Tokenizer` object using the `WhitespaceTokenizer` class available in Lucene. This will result in the input data to be tokenized on whitespace characters. Then, we create a Lucene `TokenStreamComponents` object, to which we give the source of tokens (our previously created `Tokenizer` object) and our `CustomFilter` object. This will result in our `CustomFilter` object to be used by `CustomAnalyzer`.

Implementing the analyzer provider

Let's talk about another provider implementation in addition to the token filter factory we've created earlier. This time, we need to extend `AbstractIndexAnalyzerProvider` from the `org.elasticsearch.index.analysis` package in order for Elasticsearch to be able to create our analyzer. The implementation is very simple, as we only need to implement the `get` method in which we should return our analyzer. The `CustomAnalyzerProvider` class code looks as follows:

```
public class CustomAnalyzerProvider extends
AbstractIndexAnalyzerProvider<CustomAnalyzer> {
  private final CustomAnalyzer analyzer;

  @Inject
  public CustomAnalyzerProvider(Index index, @IndexSettings
Settings indexSettings, Environment env, @Assisted String name,
@Assisted Settings settings) {
     super(index, indexSettings, name, settings);
     analyzer = new CustomAnalyzer();
  }

  @Override
  public CustomAnalyzer get() {
     return this.analyzer;
  }
}
```

As you can see, we've implemented the constructor in order to be able to initialize the super class. In addition to that, we are creating a single instance of our analyzer, which we will return when Elasticsearch requests it. We do this because we don't want to create an analyzer every time Elasticsearch requests it; this is not efficient. We don't need to worry about multithreading because our analyzer is thread-safe and, thus, a single instance can be reused. In the `get` method, we are just returning our analyzer.

Implementing the analysis binder

The binder is a part of our custom code that informs Elasticsearch about the names under which our analyzer and token filter will be available. Our `CustomAnalysisBinderProcessor` class extends `AnalysisModule.AnalysisBinderProcessor` from `org.elasticsearch.index.analysis`, and we override two methods of this class: `processAnalyzers` in which we will register our analyzer and `processTokenFilters` in which we will register our token filter. If we had only an analyzer or only a token filter, we would only override a single method. The code of `CustomAnalysisBinderProcessor` looks as follows:

```
public class CustomAnalysisBinderProcessor extends
AnalysisModule.AnalysisBinderProcessor {
  @Override
  public void processAnalyzers(AnalyzersBindings
analyzersBindings) {
    analyzersBindings.processAnalyzer("mastering_analyzer",
CustomAnalyzerProvider.class);
  }

  @Override
  public void processTokenFilters(TokenFiltersBindings
tokenFiltersBindings) {
    tokenFiltersBindings.processTokenFilter("mastering_filter",
CustomFilterFactory.class);
  }
}
```

The first method—`processAnalyzers`—takes a single `AnalysisBinding` object type, which we can use to register our analyzer under a given name. We do this by calling the `processAnalyzer` method of the `AnalysisBinding` object and pass in the name under which our analyzer will be available and the implementation of `AbstractIndexAnalyzerProvider`, which is responsible for creating our analyzer, which in our case, is the `CustomAnalyzerProvider` class.

The second method—`procesTokenFilters`—again takes a single `TokenFiltersBindings` class, which enables us to register our token filter. We do this by calling the `processTokenFilter` method and passing the name under which our token filter will be available and the token filter factory class, which in our case, is `CustomFilterFactory`.

Implementing the analyzer indices component

Now, we need to implement a node level component that will allow our analyzer and token filter to be reused. However, we will tell Elasticsearch that our analyzer should be reusable only on the indices level and not globally (just to show you how to do it). What we need to do is extend the `AbstractComponent` class from the `org.elasticsearch.common.component` package. In fact, we only need to develop a constructor for the class we called `CustomAnalyzerIndicesComponent`. The whole code for the mentioned class looks as follows:

```
public class CustomAnalyzerIndicesComponent extends
AbstractComponent {
  @Inject
  public CustomAnalyzerIndicesComponent(Settings settings,
IndicesAnalysisService indicesAnalysisService) {
    super(settings);
    indicesAnalysisService.analyzerProviderFactories().put(
        "mastering_analyzer",
        new PreBuiltAnalyzerProviderFactory("mastering_analyzer",
AnalyzerScope.INDICES, new CustomAnalyzer()));

    indicesAnalysisService.tokenFilterFactories().put("mastering_filte
r",
        new PreBuiltTokenFilterFactoryFactory(new
TokenFilterFactory() {
          @Override
          public String name() {
            return "mastering_filter";
          }

          @Override
          public TokenStream create(TokenStream tokenStream) {
            return new CustomFilter(tokenStream);
          }
        }));
  }
}
```

First of all, we pass the constructor arguments to the super class in order to initialize it. After that, we create a new analyzer, which is our `CustomAnalyzer` class, by using the following code snippet:

```
indicesAnalysisService.analyzerProviderFactories().put(
        "mastering_analyzer",
        new PreBuiltAnalyzerProviderFactory("mastering_analyzer",
AnalyzerScope.INDICES, new CustomAnalyzer()));
```

As you can see, we've used the `IndicesAnalysisService` object and its `analyzerProviderFactories` method to get the map of `PreBuiltAnalyzerProviderFactory` (as a value and the name as a key in the map), and we've put a newly created `PreBuiltAnalyzerProviderFactory` object with the name of `mastering_analyzer`. In order to create the `PreBuiltAnalyzerProviderFactory` we've used our `CustomAnalyzer` and `AnalyzerScope.INDICES` enum values (from the `org.elasticsearch.index.analysis` package). The other values of `AnalyzerScope` enum are `GLOBAL` and `INDEX`. If you would like the analyzer to be globally shared, you should use `AnalyzerScope.GLOBAL` and `AnalyzerScope.INDEX`, both of which should be created for each index separately.

In a similar way, we add our token filter, but this time, we use the `tokenFilterFactories` method of the `IndicesAnalysisService` object, which returns a `Map` of `PreBuiltTokenFilterFactoryFactory` as a value and a name (a `String` object) as a key. We put a newly created `TokenFilterFactory` object with the name of `mastering_filter`.

Implementing the analyzer module

A simple class called `CustomAnalyzerModule` extends `AbstractModule` from the `org.elasticsearch.common.inject` package. It is used to tell Elasticsearch that our `CustomAnalyzerIndicesComponent` class should be used as a singleton; we do this because it's enough to have a single instance of that class. Its code looks as follows:

```
public class CustomAnalyzerModule extends AbstractModule {
  @Override
  protected void configure() {
    bind(CustomAnalyzerIndicesComponent.class).asEagerSingleton();
  }
}
```

As you can see, we implement a single configure method, which tells you to bind the `CustomAnalyzerIndicesComponent` class as a singleton.

Implementing the analyzer plugin

Finally, we need to implement the plugin class so that Elasticsearch knows that
there is a plugin to be loaded. It should extend the `AbstractPlugin` class from the
`org.elasticsearch.plugins` package and thus implement at least the `name` and
`descriptions` methods. However, we want our plugin to be registered, and that's
why we implement two additional methods, which we can see in the following
code snippet:

```
public class CustomAnalyzerPlugin extends AbstractPlugin {
  @Override
  public Collection<Class<? extends Module>> modules() {
      return ImmutableList.<Class<? extends
Module>>of(CustomAnalyzerModule.class);
  }

  public void onModule(AnalysisModule module) {
      module.addProcessor(new CustomAnalysisBinderProcessor());
  }

  @Override
  public String name() {
    return "AnalyzerPlugin";
  }

  @Override
  public String description() {
    return "Custom analyzer plugin";
  }
}
```

The `name` and `description` methods are quite obvious, as they are returning
the name of the plugin and its description. The `onModule` method adds our
`CustomAnalysisBinderProcessor` object to the `AnalysisModule` object
provided to it.

The last method is the one we are not yet familiar with: the `modules` method:

```
public Collection<Class<? extends Module>> modules() {
  return ImmutableList.<Class<? extends
Module>>of(CustomAnalyzerModule.class);
}
```

We override this method from the super class in order to return a collection of modules that our plugin is registering. In this case, we are registering a single module class — CustomAnalyzerModule — and we are returning a list with a single entry.

Informing Elasticsearch about our custom analyzer

Once we have our code ready, we need to add one additional thing: we need to let Elasticsearch know what the class registering our plugin is — the one we've called CustomAnalyzerPlugin. In order to do that, we create an es-plugin.properties file in the src/main/resources directory with the following content:

```
plugin=pl.solr.analyzer.CustomAnalyzerPlugin
```

We just specify the plugin property there, which should have a value of the class we use to register our plugins (the one that extends the Elasticsearch AbstractPlugin class). This file will be included in the JAR file that will be created during the build process and will be used by Elasticsearch during the plugin load process.

Testing our custom analysis plugin

Now, we want to test our custom analysis plugin just to be sure that everything works. In order to do that, we need to build our plugin, install it on all nodes in our cluster, and finally, use the Admin Indices Analyze API to see how our analyzer works. Let's do that.

Building our custom analysis plugin

We start with the easiest part: building our plugin. In order to do that, we run a simple command:

```
mvn compile package
```

We tell Maven that we want the code to be compiled and packaged. After the command finishes, we can find the archive with the plugin in the target/release directory (assuming you are using a project setup similar to the one we've described at the beginning of the chapter).

Installing the custom analysis plugin

To install the plugin, we will use the plugin command, just like we did previously. Assuming that we have our plugin archive stored in the /home/install/es/ plugins directory, would run the following command (we run it from the Elasticsearch home directory):

```
bin/plugin --install analyzer --url
file:/home/install/es/plugins/elasticsearch-analyzer-1.4.1.zip
```

We need to install the plugin on all the nodes in our cluster, because we want Elasticsearch to be able to find our analyzer and filter no matter on which node the analysis process is done. If we don't install the plugin on all nodes, we can be certain that we will run into issues.

 In order to learn more about installing Elasticsearch plugins, please refer to our previous book, *Elasticsearch Server Section Edition*, by *Packt Publishing* or refer to the official Elasticsearch documentation.

After we have the plugin installed, we need to restart our Elasticsearch instance we were creating the installation on. After the restart, we should see something like this in the logs:

```
[2014-12-03 22:39:11,231][INFO ][plugins                     ]
[Tattletale] loaded [AnalyzerPlugin], sites []
```

With the preceding log line, Elasticsearch informs us that the plugin named AnalyzerPlugin was successfully loaded.

Checking whether our analysis plugin works

We can finally check whether our custom analysis plugin works as it should. In order to do that, we start with creating an empty index called analyzetest (the index name doesn't matter). We do this by running the following command:

```
curl -XPOST 'localhost:9200/analyzetest/'
```

After this we use the Admin Indices Analyze API (http://www.elasticsearch. org/guide/en/elasticsearch/reference/current/indices-analyze.html) to see how our analyzer works. We do that by running the following command:

```
curl -XGET 'localhost:9200/analyzetest/_analyze?analyzer=mastering_
analyzer&pretty' -d 'mastering elasticsearch'
```

So, what we should see in response is two tokens: one that should be reversed —
mastering — gniretsam and another one that should also be reversed —
elasticsearch — hcraescitsale. The response Elasticsearch returns looks as follows:

```
{
  "tokens" : [ {
    "token" : "gniretsam",
    "start_offset" : 0,
    "end_offset" : 9,
    "type" : "word",
    "position" : 1
  }, {
    "token" : "hcraescitsale",
    "start_offset" : 10,
    "end_offset" : 23,
    "type" : "word",
    "position" : 2
  } ]
}
```

As you can see, we've got exactly what we expected, so it seems that our custom
analysis plugin works as intended.

Summary

In this chapter, we were focused on developing custom plugins for Elasticsearch.
We learned how to properly set up your Maven project to be able to automatically
build your Elasticsearch plugins. You saw how to develop a custom REST action
plugin, and we extended Elasticsearch analysis capabilities by creating a plugin that
included a custom token filter and new analyzer.

We've reached the end of the book, and we wanted to write a small summary and
say a few words to the brave reader who managed to get to the end. We decided to
write the second edition of *Mastering Elasticsearch* after writing *Elasticsearch Server
Second Edition*. We thought that we had left a number of topics uncovered, and we
wanted to write them in this book. We went from introducing Apache Lucene and
Elasticsearch to querying and data handling — both on the Lucene index and the
Elasticsearch level. We hope that, by now, you know how Lucene works and how
Elasticsearch uses it, and you will find this knowledge worthy in your journey with
this great search engine. We talked about some topics that can be useful when things
are hot, such as I/O throttling, Hot Threads API, and how to speed up your queries.
We also concentrated on things such as choosing the right query for the use case and
Elasticsearch scaling.

Finally, we dedicated one chapter to discussing Java development on how to extend Elasticsearch with your own plugins. In the first version of the book, we also described the Java API briefly, but we decided it doesn't make sense. The API would require its own book and showing only some things regarding them just feels wrong. Hopefully, you'll be able to write your own plugins and even though we didn't write about all the possibilities, we hope that you'll be able to find the things we didn't write about.

Thank you for reading the book; we hope that you like it and that it brought you some knowledge that you were seeking, and that you'll be able to use it whether you use Elasticsearch professionally or just as a hobby.

Finally, please stop by at `http://elasticsearchserverbook.com/` from time to time. In addition to the usual posts we make, we will publish the book fragments that didn't make it to the book or were cut down because the book would be too broad.

Index

data field caches
  issues 314, 315
data node
  about 17, 349
  configuring 280
data-only nodes
  configuring 280
default shard allocation behaviour
  allocation awareness 219, 220
  altering 218
  filtering 221
  runtime allocation, updating 222
  total shards allowed per node, defining 224
  total shards allowed per physical server,
    defining 224
default similarity model
  selecting 237, 238
default store type
  about 243
  for Elasticsearch 1.3.0 243
  for Elasticsearch versions older
    than 1.3.0 243
desired merge scheduler
  setting 255
DFR similarity
  configuring 238
direct generators
  about 171
  configuring 172-175
discovery module
  about 277
  configuration 278
  Zen discovery configuration 278, 279
divergence from randomness similarity
  model 234
document
  about 16
  relations 120
documents grouping
  about 114
  additional parameters 118-120
  example 115-118
  top hits aggregation 114
document types 16

doc values
  about 11
  example, of usage 315-318
  used, for optimizing queries 314

E

EC2 discovery configuration options
  cloud.aws.ec2.endpoint 284
  cloud.aws.protocol 284
  cloud.aws.proxy_host 285
  cloud.aws.proxy_port 285
  cloud.aws.region 284
  discovery.ec2.ping_timeout 285
EC2 nodes scanning configuration
  discovery.ec2.any_group 285
  discovery.ec2.availability_zones 285
  discovery.ec2.groups 285
  discovery.ec2.host_type 285
  discovery.ec2.tag 286
EC2 plugin's generic configuration
  cluster.aws.access_key 284
  cluster.aws.secret_key 284
Elasticsearch
  about 15
  basic concepts 16
  communicating with 21
  failure detection 20
  filters 49
  informing, about custom analyzer 392
  informing, about REST action 380
  key concepts 18
  query rewrite 34
  scaling 339
  startup process 19, 20
  workings 19
Elasticsearch Azure plugin, settings
  base_path 304
  chunk_size 304
  container 304
Elasticsearch caching
  about 259
  all caches, clearing 274
  caches, clearing 274
  circuit breakers, using 273

AbstractPlugin extension 384
AbstractTokenFilterFactory extension 383
AnalysisModule.AnalysisBinder
    Processor 383
analyzer provider 383
custom analyzer 383
TokenFilter class extension 383
implementation, custom REST action
    about 375
    Elasticsearch, informing 380
    plugin class 379, 380
    REST action class, using 376
include parameter 222
index
    about 16
    changes, committing 245
    default refresh time, changing 246
    transaction log 246, 247
    updating 245
index distribution architecture
    about 203
    example, overallocation 206
    multiple shards, versus multiple
        indices 206
    overallocation 204, 205
    replicas 206, 207
    right amount of shards and replicas,
        selecting 204
    sharding 204, 205
indexing
    altering 244
index-level filter cache configuration
    about 261
    index.cache.filter.expire 261
    index.cache.filter.max_size 261
    index.cache.filter.type 261
index-level recovery settings
    about 291
    full 291
    full-1 291
    integer value 292
    quorum 291
    quorum-1 291
indices conflicts
    handling 310, 311
indices recovery API 292, 295
inverted index 8, 9

I/O throttling
    about 256
    controlling 256
I/O throttling configuration
    about 256
    example 258, 259
    maximum throughput per second 257
    node throttling defaults 257
    performance considerations 257
    throttling type, configuring 257

J

Java memory
    about 319
    code cache 320
    eden space 319
    permanent generation 320
    survivor space 319
    tenured generation 320
Java objects
    life cycle 320
Java service wrapper
    URL 327
Java Virtual Machine (JVM) 21
JSON document
    URL 21

L

Laplace smoothing model 171
Least Recently Used cache type (LRU) 260
limitations, significant terms aggregation
    about 113
    approximated counts 113
    avoiding, as top level aggregation 113
    floating point fields, avoiding 113
    memory consumption 113
linear interpolation smoothing model 171
LM Dirichlet similarity
    configuring 239
LM Jelinek Mercer similarity
    configuring 239
log byte size merge policy
    about 251
    configuration options 253

log doc merge policy
about 251
configuration options 254
lowercase filter 11
low-level recovery configuration
about 290
cluster-level recovery configuration 290
index-level recovery settings 291
Lucene. *See* **Apache Lucene**
Lucene analyzer 11
Lucene expressions
about 146
basics 146
example 146-149
Lucene index
about 10
doc values 11
norm 10
posting formats 10
term vectors 10
Lucene query language
about 12
basics 12
Boolean operators 12
fields, querying 13, 14
special characters, handling 15
term modifiers 14, 15

M

mapping 16
master election
about 280
configuration 281, 282
Zen discovery configuration 282
Zen discovery fault detection 282
master eligible nodes 349
master node
about 17, 280
Amazon EC2 discovery 283
configuring 280
discovery implementations 286
master-only nodes
configuring 281
Maven Assembly plugin
about 372

URL 372
using 372-374
memory store
about 242
properties 242
merge policy
log byte size merge policy 251
log doc merge policy 251
selecting 250
tiered merge policy 251
merge schedulers
about 254
concurrent merge scheduler 255
desired merge scheduler, selecting 255
serial merge scheduler 255
MMap filesystem store 241
most fields matching 97, 98
multicast Zen discovery configuration
about 279
discovery.zen.ping.multicast.address 279
discovery.zen.ping.multicast.
buffer_size 279
discovery.zen.ping.multicast.enabled 279
discovery.zen.ping.multicast.group 279
discovery.zen.ping.multicast.port 279
discovery.zen.ping.multicast.ttl 279
discovery.zen.ping.unicats.concurrent_
connects 280
multimatch
best fields matching 92-95
controlling 91
cross fields matching 95-97
most fields matching 97, 98
phrase matching 98
phrase with prefixes matching 99, 100
types 92
multi_match query 91
multiple Elasticsearch instances, on single physical machine
about 345, 346
shard and replicas, preventing from being on same node 346, 347
multiple language stemming filters 11
multiple shards
versus multiple indices 206

_primary_first property 229
_primary property 229
_shards:0,1 property 230
about 229
custom, string value property 230

Q

query aggregator nodes 348
Query API 23
query categorization
about 59
basic queries 59, 60
compound queries 59, 61
full text search queries 59, 62
not analyzed queries 59
pattern queries 60, 63
position aware queries 60, 64
score altering queries 60, 63
similarity supporting queries 60, 63
structure aware queries 60, 64
Query DSL 27, 59
query execution preference
about 228, 229
preference parameter 229
query processing-only nodes
configuring 281
query relevance improvment
about 181
data 181-185
faceting 196-200
garbage, removing 190-192
misspelling-proof search, making 194-196
multi match query 186, 187
phrase queries, boosting 193
phrases 187-190
quest 185
standard query 185, 186
query rescoring
about 85, 86
example query 86
rescore parameters 89, 90
scoring mode, selecting 90
structure, rescore query 86-89
query rewrite
about 34
Apache Lucene 37-39

prefix query example 35-37
properties 39-42
working 34
query templates
about 42-44
conditional expressions 46
default values 47
loops 46
Mustache template engine 45
providing, as string value 45
storing, in files 48

R

real-time GET operation 248
recovery module 278
relations, between documents
about 120
alternatives 129
nested documents 125, 126
object type 121-125
parent-child relationship 126
replica 18, 206, 207
repository 301
request circuit breaker 273
require parameter 222
rescore parameters
query_weight 90
rescore_query_weight 90
window_size 89
REST action class
constructor 377
requests, handling 378
response, writing 379
using 376
REST action plugin
building 381
checking 382
installing 381
rewrite property
about 39
constant_score_boolean 40
constant_score_filter 40
scoring_boolean 39
top_terms_boost_N 40
top_terms_N 40

master-level read operations 308, 309
master-level write operations 309, 310
unicast discovery, using 306, 307

U

unicast Zen discovery configuration
  about 280
  discovery.zen.ping.unicats.hosts 280
use cases, queries
  about 64
  basic queries use cases 66
  compound queries use cases 67
  example data 65
  full text search queries use cases 73
  not analyzed queries use cases 71
  pattern queries use cases 74, 79
  score altering queries use cases 77
  similarity supporting queries use cases 75
  structure aware queries use cases 81
user spelling mistakes, correcting
  about 152
  data, testing 152, 153
  technical details 153

V

vertical scaling 339, 340

W

write operations
  blocking 311

Y

YAML
  URL 379
young generation heap space 320

Z

Zen discovery
  about 278
  multicast Zen discovery configuration 279
  unicast Zen discovery configuration 280

Thank you for buying
Mastering ElasticSearch
Second Edition

About Packt Publishing

Packt, pronounced 'packed', published its first book, *Mastering phpMyAdmin for Effective MySQL Management*, in April 2004, and subsequently continued to specialize in publishing highly focused books on specific technologies and solutions.

Our books and publications share the experiences of your fellow IT professionals in adapting and customizing today's systems, applications, and frameworks. Our solution-based books give you the knowledge and power to customize the software and technologies you're using to get the job done. Packt books are more specific and less general than the IT books you have seen in the past. Our unique business model allows us to bring you more focused information, giving you more of what you need to know, and less of what you don't.

Packt is a modern yet unique publishing company that focuses on producing quality, cutting-edge books for communities of developers, administrators, and newbies alike. For more information, please visit our website at www.packtpub.com.

About Packt Open Source

In 2010, Packt launched two new brands, Packt Open Source and Packt Enterprise, in order to continue its focus on specialization. This book is part of the Packt Open Source brand, home to books published on software built around open source licenses, and offering information to anybody from advanced developers to budding web designers. The Open Source brand also runs Packt's Open Source Royalty Scheme, by which Packt gives a royalty to each open source project about whose software a book is sold.

Writing for Packt

We welcome all inquiries from people who are interested in authoring. Book proposals should be sent to author@packtpub.com. If your book idea is still at an early stage and you would like to discuss it first before writing a formal book proposal, then please contact us; one of our commissioning editors will get in touch with you.

We're not just looking for published authors; if you have strong technical skills but no writing experience, our experienced editors can help you develop a writing career, or simply get some additional reward for your expertise.

ElasticSearch Cookbook

ISBN: 978-1-78216-662-7   Paperback: 422 pages

Over 120 advanced recipes to search, analyze, deploy, manage, and monitor data effectively with ElasticSearch

1. Write native plugins to extend the capabilities of ElasticSearch to boost your business.

2. Integrate the power of ElasticSearch in your Java applications using the native API or Python applications, with the ElasticSearch community client.

3. Step-by step-instructions to help you easily understand ElasticSearch's capabilities, that act as a good reference for everyday activities.

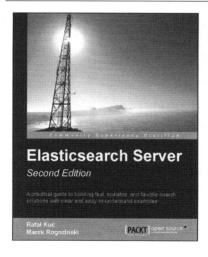

Elasticsearch Server
Second Edition

ISBN: 978-1-78398-052-9   Paperback: 428 pages

A practical guide to building fast, scalable, and flexible search solutions with clear and easy-to-understand examples

1. Learn about the fascinating functionalities of ElasticSearch like data indexing, data analysis, and dynamic mapping.

2. Fine-tune ElasticSearch and understand its metrics using its API and available tools, and see how it behaves in complex searches.

3. A hands-on tutorial that walks you through all the features of ElasticSearch in an easy-to-understand way, with examples that will help you become an expert in no time.

Please check **www.PacktPub.com** for information on our titles

Practical Data Science Cookbook

ISBN: 978-1-78398-024-6   Paperback: 396 pages

89 hands-on recipes to help you complete real-world data science projects in R and Python

1. Learn about the data science pipeline and use it to acquire, clean, analyze, and visualize data.

2. Understand critical concepts in data science in the context of multiple projects.

3. Expand your numerical programming skills through step-by-step code examples and learn more about the robust features of R and Python.

Practical Data Analysis

ISBN: 978-1-78328-099-5   Paperback: 360 pages

Transform, model, and visualize your data through hands-on projects, developed in open source tools

1. Explore how to analyze your data in various innovative ways and turn them into insight.

2. Learn to use the D3.js visualization tool for exploratory data analysis.

3. Understand how to work with graphs and social data analysis.

4. Discover how to perform advanced query techniques and run MapReduce on MongoDB.

Please check **www.PacktPub.com** for information on our titles